KERRY McSWEENEY

Tennyson and Swinburne as Romantic Naturalists

UNIVERSITY OF TORONTO PRESS
Toronto Buffalo London

© University of Toronto Press 1981
Toronto Buffalo London
Printed in Canada
ISBN 0-8020-2381-9

Canadian Cataloguing in Publication Data

McSweeney, Kerry, 1941–
    Tennyson and Swinburne as romantic naturalists

    Includes index.
    ISBN 0-8020-2381-9
    1. Tennyson, Alfred Tennyson, Baron, 1809–1892–
    Criticism and interpretation. 2. Swinburne,
    Algernon Charles, 1837–1909 – Criticism and
    interpretation. 3. English poetry – 19th century –
    History and criticism. 4. Romanticism – England.
    I. Title.
    PR5581.M37   821'.809145   c81-094066-3

31,145

To the Memory of my Mother
Lucy Kingen McSweeney

Contents

Preface

In the Preface to *The Renaissance* (1873), Walter Pater described the principal function of what he called 'the aesthetic critic':

Few artists ... work quite cleanly, casting off all *débris*, and leaving us only what the heat of their imagination has wholly fused and transformed. Take, for instance, the writings of Wordsworth. The heat of his genius, entering into the substance of his work, has crystallised a part, but only a part, of it; and in that great mass of verse there is much which might well be forgotten. But scattered up and down it ... we trace the action of his unique, incommunicable faculty, that strange, mystical sense of a life in natural things, and of man's life as a part of nature, drawing strength and colour and character from local influences, from the hills and streams, and from natural sights and sounds. Well! that is the *virtue*, the active principle in Wordsworth's poetry; and then the function of the critic of Wordsworth is to follow up that active principle, to disengage it, to mark the degree in which it penetrates his verse.[1]

Pater outlines a dual, mutually reinforcing, critical activity: the making of qualitative distinctions and the simultaneous tracing out of Wordsworth's naturalistic vision, 'that strange, mystical sense of a life in natural things, and of man's life as a part of nature.'

In the present study I have attempted to trace the same active principle in two of the most gifted and copious of Wordsworth's nineteenth-century poetic successors. And for similar reasons: to make qualitative distinctions, which I hope will contribute to a significant revaluation of the achievement of Tennyson and Swinburne; and at the same time to call attention to the central importance of naturalistic vision in the poetry of each. In Tennyson, this Romantic principle, greatly under-noticed by previous commentators, is often at odds with another, more characteristically Victorian principle. But in Swinburne,

Romantic naturalism is nothing less than the heat crystallizing most of that portion of the great mass of his verse which should not be forgotten.

With regard to the poetry of Tennyson and Swinburne, it seems to me there is an unquestionable need for qualitative discriminations. The poetry of the latter has long suffered critical neglect. As late as 1971, Cecil Lang could say in the introduction to a special Swinburne double issue of *Victorian Poetry* that 'serious evaluation of Swinburne's poetry' was only beginning.[2] And there is still only a handful of items – Jerome McGann's *Swinburne: An Experiment in Criticism* and John Rosenberg's introduction to a selection of the poet's verse are two of them – that can be recommended with confidence to students. Of course almost everyone has read at least a few Swinburne poems, usually a chorus or two of *Atalanta in Calydon* (1865), plus a few of the following year's first series of *Poems and Ballads*, and 'Hertha' and another one or two of the 1871 *Songs before Sunrise*; and almost everyone has an opinion about Swinburne's poetry. But these opinions, even those of some Victorian literature specialists, tend to be based only on the few poems mentioned above and on a few stale dicta, principally T.S. Eliot's.

Tennyson, on the other hand, can hardly be said to suffer any longer from critical neglect. But while the post-war trickle of critical writing on Victoria's Laureate has become a flood, there is nevertheless no real agreement among professional critics of English literature on Tennyson's achievement and stature. Particularly striking is the gap between the claims made for his work by the Victorian specialists who have written on him during the past fifteen years or so, and his much less exalted reputation among non-specialists. In the case of most major English poets, Donne, Keats, or Yeats, say, there is little difference between the judgments of seventeenth-century, Romantic, or Modern specialists and those of non-specialists. But with Tennyson the gap is wide. This state of affairs, which should be a source of embarrassment to Victorian poetry scholars, was acutely diagnosed in 1970 by the late Kenneth Allott:

It disturbs me that we have failed so signally in the universities to meet the radical attack on the limitations of Victorian poetry made by an earlier generation of critics from T.S. Eliot and F.R. Leavis downwards ... It strikes me that most of the trouble arises from our failure to recognize sharply enough – to use [Christopher] Ricks's words ... that 'verbal achievement is an essential issue *whenever* a poem is quoted,' which is another way of saying with Mallarmé: 'Ce n'est point avec des idées, mon cher Degas, qu'on fait des Vers. C'est avec des mots.' It is by forgetting or paying no more than lip-service to this golden axiom that some critics of Victorian poetry in the 1960s have been able to delude themselves that Tennyson's *Idylls of the King* deserve to be taken as seriously as *In Memoriam*, Browning's collections of verse in the 1870s and 1880s as seriously as *Men and Women* ... If we insist that 'verbal achievement is an essential issue *whenever* a poem is quoted,' we are inoculated against supposing ... that any poetic work that allows us to develop an ingenious critical argument is necessarily poetically valuable. In cultivating our Victorian garden no amount of agreement among ourselves as professional gardeners will persuade the onlookers that the cabbages are really roses.[3]

A major reason why cabbages can come to look like roses is the employment of a history-of-ideas approach to Victorian poetry, which analyses poetic works in the context of the moral, intellectual, and religious preoccupations of the age. There is of course much to be gained from such an approach; but there are dangers as well, particularly the tendency to confuse high seriousness with imaginative achievement, or moral concern and spiritual struggle with vital poetry. The approach to the poetry of Tennyson and Swinburne in what follows is rather different and, I believe, more conducive to the making of qualitative distinctions.

This approach has been influenced by one of the major critical reorientations of the past twenty years in English studies: the recognition of the essential continuity and the essentially Romantic basis of British and American poetry from the beginning of the nineteenth century to the present. This recognition has come from a number of different quarters. In 1968, for example, Donald Davie announced his belated recognition that 'the historical developments which we label "Romanticism" were not a series of aberrations which we can and should disown, but rather a sort of landslide which permanently transformed the mental landscape which in the 20th century we inhabit, however reluctantly.'[4] Two seminal studies which helped create this reorientation appeared as early as 1957. In *Romantic Image*, Frank Kermode located the continuity of much nineteenth- and twentieth-century literature in two 'thoroughly Romantic' beliefs – 'in the Image as a radiant truth out of space and time, and in the necessary isolation or estrangement of men who can perceive it.'[5] Different continuities were studied by Robert Langbaum in *The Poetry of Experience: The Dramatic Monologue in Modern Literary Tradition*, which argued that 'the essential idea of romanticism [is] the doctrine that the imaginative apprehension gained through immediate experience is primary and certain, whereas the analytic reflection that follows is secondary and problematical.'[6]

Other more recent studies have taken a more synoptic view of the Romantic tradition. M.H. Abrams' *Natural Supernaturalism: Tradition and Revolution in Romantic Literature* (1971) set out to show that 'Romantic thought and literature represented a decisive turn in Western culture ... This fact has been obvious to most of the important writers from the mid nineteenth century to the present time, and many of these writers have defined their own literary enterprise by either a positive or negative reference to the forms and inherent ethos of the Romantic achievement.'[7] In *A Study of English Romanticism* (1968) Northrop Frye argued a similar case in archetypal terms. He showed how Romanticism involved a major change in nothing less than the mythological structure of Western culture. Early nineteenth-century Romanticism was 'the first major phase in an imaginative revolution which has carried on until our own day ... This means that everything that has followed Romanticism, including the anti-Romantic movements in France and England of fifty to sixty years ago, is best understood as post-Romantic.'[8] And in a proliferating number of increasingly difficult and controversial studies, beginning with *The Ringers in the Tower: Studies in Romantic Tradition* (1971) and *The Anxiety of Influence: A Theory of Poetry* (1973), Harold Bloom has charted a number of the darker ramifications of post-Romantic Romanticism in England and America.

General studies like those of Abrams, Frye, and Bloom have led to more narrowly focused studies of Romantic continuities and mutations. Two examples are George Bornstein's *Transformations of Romanticism in Yeats, Eliot and Stevens* (1976), which makes an excellent case for the view that modern poetry continues and develops Romantic tradition much more than it rejects or breaks with it, and Ross C. Murfin's *Swinburne, Hardy, Lawrence, and the Burden of Belief* (1978), which studies the ways in which its three subjects responded to the philosophic and poetic vision of their Romantic forbears. (Murfin's study arrived too late for me to make use of it in my chapters on Swinburne.)

Romanticism is of course a many-splendoured thing, and I should perhaps briefly summarize those features of it which figure most importantly in what follows. Like all major nineteenth-century poets from Wordsworth on, Tennyson and Swinburne live in a post-Enlightenment world characterized by 'the disappearance of God.'[9] Traditional religious beliefs in a God-created universe and a God-created soul or self have been undermined, together with supernatural moral and social sanctions and with the Christian assurance of a life after death. Man feels increasingly homeless and isolated in the world and seeks to reorient himself in the universe, discover new grounds for identity and new religious beliefs. As Abrams puts it: 'Much of what distinguishes the writers I call "Romantic" derives from the fact that they undertook, whatever their religious creed or lack of creed, to save traditional concepts, schemes, and values which had been based on the relation of the Creator to his creature and creation, but to reformulate them within the prevailing two-term system of subject and object, ego and non-ego, the human mind or consciousness and its transactions with nature.'[10]

For the Romantics, the active imagination becomes the chief mental power and the poet's prime responsibility is to his own vision. Through imaginative vision man can come to reorient himself in the world by seeing into the life of things (Wordsworth's phrase) and feeling the deep pulsations of the world (Tennyson's phrase). For those with imaginative insight, natural facts can become symbols of spiritual facts. The imagination can also go beyond penetration of the visible and create images of desire, gardens or cities of art and apocalyptic prefigurations of a renovated world. Poets, those in whom the imagination is most intense, tend to become the priests of the religion of what Carlyle called 'natural supernaturalism' or the hierophants of visionary transformation. But poetic vocation also tends to estrange the poet from the world of ordinary humanity. As the nineteenth century progresses, isolation, instability, and irremediable affliction seem ever more dominant features of what Swinburne oxymoronically calls 'this gift, this doom' of poetic vocation.

Poets in the Romantic tradition have been usefully divided into two major groups: on the one hand anti-naturalists like Blake, Shelley, and Yeats, for whom the natural world is ultimately a limitation and an impediment to vision; on the other hand, those who, in Pater's phrase, see 'man's life as a part of nature.' Wordsworth, Keats, Thoreau, Hardy, Frost are Romantic naturalists; so are Tennyson (albeit complexly and imperfectly) and Swinburne. Romantic naturalists regard man's intimate sympathy with the natural world and its patterns of cyclic change as wholesome and liberating, not as confining and destructive. Romantic naturalists see man as most creatively alive and most rooted when in vital reciprocal contact with the world around him, and as most isolated and anguished when the bond between self and nature, inner and outer, is broken. Self-consciousness, like abstract thought, is a danger and can become a disease, for it intensifies awareness of the otherness of nature and of man's separateness, even as it sharpens the desire for union.

But the natural world is not simply a benignly maternal presence; in Romantic nature poetry there is often found an awareness, even a secret fear, of nature's destructiveness and latent savagery. This was felt even by Keats in the pre-evolutionary decades of the nineteenth century:

> but I saw
> Too far into the sea; where every maw
> The greater on the less feeds evermore: –
> But I saw too distinct into the core
> Of an eternal fierce destruction,
> And so from Happiness I far was gone.
> Still am I sick of it: and though to day

I've gathered young spring-leaves, and flowers gay
Of Periwinkle and wild strawberry,
Still do I that most fierce destruction see,
The Shark at savage prey – the Hawk at pounce,
The gentle Robin, like a pard or ounce,
Ravening a worm.[11]

Natural process is not only potentially destructive; it is also amoral and its regenerative rhythms know nothing of the idealizings of Christian love or Romantic passion. Sexuality, then, as in Thoreau's *Walden* and certain poems of Tennyson, may be seen both as natural and attractive, and as destructive and feral, by the Romantic artist.

A final point: the inevitability of death and the burden of mortality are major poetic concerns for most poets in the Romantic tradition, both the anti-naturalists and the naturalists. For the latter the question arises: can a naturalistic vision of man's life as a part of nature reconcile man to his mortality and lighten the burden (unknown to the world of nature) of self-consciousness, of being in Tennyson's phrase 'half-dead to know that I shall die'? Some Romantic poets search the limits of the visible world for intimations or symbols of a transcendent realm beyond; others are borne back into the past, re-contacting through memory and intimate sympathy with natural settings their childhood sense of immortality and of oneness with the visible world. Still others desire to burn always with a hard gemlike flame and endeavour to live fully in the here and now of the present. Through the naturalistic grace of the good moments of union with the visible world, Romantic poets can gain a sense of experiential immortality in which the boundaries of space and time seem transcended.

In the above paragraphs, most of the emphasis has fallen on Romantic positives, but as the nineteenth century progresses the dark side of the Romantic moon becomes more and more dominant. Tennyson belongs to the first generation of post-Romantic Romantic artists, as do Carlyle, Browning, and Arnold. All these writers begin as thoroughgoing Romantics but swerve away from their predecessors in not dissimilar ways. Some of the underlying causes of this mutation from Romantic into Victorian are discussed in the first part of my second chapter. Together with Pater, Rossetti, Hopkins, and Hardy, Swinburne belongs to the second generation of post-Romantic Romantics. All these writers swerve away from their immediate predecessors, the high Victorians; but while their vision is more purely Romantic, it is also more attenuated, dark, and tragic than that of their early nineteenth-century forbears.

Since Swinburne's naturalistic vision is more clear cut and more of a piece than Tennyson's, my chapters on his poetry do not involve any of the de-idealizing operations I have found it necessary to perform on some of the latter's works. It is also true to say that where understanding is central to my reading of Swinburne's works, evaluation is central to my reading of Tennyson's, a difference in emphasis made inevitable and necessary by the great differences in the quantity and quality of critical commentary on the two poets during the past thirty years. But it would be wrong to infer that my approach to Tennyson is essentially negative. I believe there is a good deal more debris (to use Pater's phrase) in his canon than do most other Tennyson critics; but there is also much that has been magnificently transformed by the heat of his genius. Similarly, while my chapters on Swinburne's poetry take his characteristic weaknesses for granted and concentrate attention on his insufficiently recognized strengths, it would also be wrong to infer that I regard his achievement to be at all the equal of Tennyson's. Alfred Tennyson is the great exemplary poet of the Victorian period, and Swinburne himself asserted that he was the greatest of the poets born in the early decades of the nineteenth century. Indeed, one indication of Tennyson's greater achievement is that he is a poet of real accomplishment in several areas of which my study makes no mention, but which have been well studied by other commentators.

While the following chapters employ different critical stances, all are concerned with tracing naturalistic vision through the work of both poets, thereby locating and providing a context for analysing much of their finest poetry. The first chapter, 'Swinburne's Tennyson,' is literary historical; it examines the former's critical and creative response to the latter over a period of thirty years, the central thread of which was Swinburne's perception of what Tennyson's suppression of naturalistic vision, and consequent overemphasis on morality and metaphysical speculation, had done to his poetry. Tennyson's reponse to Swinburne is also examined. The opening chapter, then, offers an initial comparison of the two poets, as seen through each other's eyes, in order to provide a context for a fresh examination of the major works of each. The first part of the second chapter, 'Tennyson's Poetry 1830 to 1842,' is also literary historical; it is concerned with the literary climate of the 1820s and 1830s, an unpropitious time for poets concerned with self-expression, vision, a life of immediate sympathy with the natural world, and the apprehension and creation of beauty. This background is necessary for an understanding of the central feature of Tennyson's artistic development: the complex mutation during these years which transformed him from a wholly Romantic into a largely Victorian poet. The second and longer part of the chapter offers close examinations of ten of Tennyson's best known and most frequently analysed poems: 'Mariana,' 'Mariana in the South,' 'The Lady of Shalott,' 'The Hesperides,' 'The Palace of Art,' 'Supposed Confessions of a Second-Rate Sensitive Mind,' 'The Two

Voices,' 'The Vision of Sin,' 'Tithonus,' and 'The Lotos Eaters.' Chapters 3 and 4 are non-formalist in that they disengage parts of *In Memoriam* and *Idylls of the King* from their larger contexts and argue that these parts can be better understood and appreciated when placed in different contexts. The third chapter studies one of the two informing principles of *In Memoriam*: recompense for loss through memory and through sympathy with the natural world; the fourth locates the imaginative achievement of *Idylls of the King* in the two clusters of idylls in which moral concerns are not dominant: the Tristram group (*Balin and Balan, Pelleas and Ettarre*, and *The Last Tournament*), in which psychological and naturalistic themes are central; and the Holy Grail group (*The Coming of Arthur, The Holy Grail*, and *The Passing of Arthur*) in which the informing theme is vision, its loss and possible recovery.

The fifth chapter, the first of two devoted to Swinburne, offers a thematic overview of his poetic canon. George Meredith said that he could not find an 'internal centre' in Swinburne's work and Gerard Manley Hopkins complained that Swinburne's genius did not have 'adequate matter' to work on. But I argue that there is an active principle, a sense of man's life as a part of nature, in Swinburne's poetry. A number of poems are closely examined, including 'Itylus,' 'Hymn to Proserpine,' 'Anactoria,' 'Laus Veneris,' 'Neap-Tide,' 'The Sundew,' 'The Last Oracle,' 'Ave atque Vale,' and 'A Vision of Spring in Winter.' The method of chapter 6 might be described as formalist: it attempts to show through close readings how finely put together and cumulative in effect are four of the most important poems of the second half of Swinburne's career: 'By the North Sea,' *Tristram of Lyonesse*, 'A Nympholept,' and 'The Lake of Gaube.' The concluding chapter, 'Tennyson and Swinburne,' brings together again the two subjects of my study.

All quotations from Tennyson's poetry are from *The Poems of Tennyson*, edited by Christopher Ricks (London: Longmans 1968). Unless otherwise noted, all quotations from Swinburne's poetry are from the two-volume *Collected Poetical Works* (London: Heinemann 1924). 'Swinburne's Tennyson, the first chapter, was originally published in *Victorian Studies*. My sixth chapter has its roots in three articles which were published in the *Modern Language Review, Queen's Quarterly*, and *Victorian Poetry*. Parts of the third and fourth chapter incorporate in revised form material first published in *Victorian Poetry*.

This book has been published with the help of a grant from the Canadian Federation for the Humanities, using funds provided by the Social Sciences and Humanities Research Council of Canada.

I am grateful to Professor Malcolm Ross, formerly of the University of Toronto, now of Dalhousie University, and Professor F.E.L. Priestley of the

University of Toronto for their advice and encouragement; to Professor F.S. Colwell of Queen's University, who was good enough to read and comment on portions of my text; to Professors A.C. Hamilton and George Whalley of Queen's University; to the Canada Council for the award of a leave fellowship during 1975–6; and to Professor C.J. Rawson of the University of Warwick, who offered me the hospitality of his university, where a first draft of this work was completed. I am grateful most of all to my wife Susanne for her assistance and good humour over sixteen years.

Kerry McSweeney
Queen's University
January 1980

TENNYSON AND SWINBURNE AS
ROMANTIC NATURALISTS

1

Swinburne's Tennyson

Despite basic temperamental, aesthetic, and philosophical differences, Swinburne, throughout his long career as a poet and critic, never denied either the pre-eminence of Tennyson among Victorian poets or the extent of his influence on himself and his contemporaries. Tennyson was 'the greatest of those writers who were born in the infancy or in the adolescence of the nineteenth century'; his best lyrical work remained 'unimitated, being in the main inimitable'; 'the singular and splendid persistence of [his] genius' into the later decades of his life was remarkable; all the poets of Swinburne's time were 'born and baptized' into the church of Tennyson, and grew up and took delight 'in the sunshine of [his] noble genius.' Finally, in a letter to Tennyson in 1891 Swinburne spoke of 'a debt which has been accumulating ever since I was twelve years old.'[1]

Swinburne's assessment of Tennyson, however, is remarkably free of the panegyrical excesses that sometimes mar his critical writing on Victor Hugo and others. He once remarked: 'I allow no one to laugh at Tennyson except myself,'[2] and did so most memorably in his two excellent parodies of Tennyson poems. On several other occasions over a thirty-year period from the late 1860s to the late 1890s he gave voice to serious reservations about individual works of Tennyson and about Tennyson's conception of the role of the artist and the function of poetry. Considering the stature of both poets and the fact that Swinburne is a major critic as well as a major poet, it is surprising that these reservations have never been carefully examined. To do so can provide a suggestive perspective from which to view *In Memoriam* and *Idylls of the King*, illuminate important aspects of Tennyson's poetic thought and practice, and stimulate a reassessment of his artistic achievement. Such a survey will at the same time bring into focus important aspects of Swinburne's own poetic theory and practice, and enhance understanding of certain poems by both poets.

Finally, this examination should help to point up the interaction of the poets with each other, a reciprocal example, I would suggest, of what has been called 'the anxiety of influence.'[3]

Anxiety is most immediately apparent in Tennyson's reaction to the appearance of Swinburne on the English poetic scene in the 1860s, and before beginning to detail the younger man's views on the elder it will be useful to sketch in something of the powerful impact of Swinburne's early work on the Laureate, then in his late fifties and at the height of his fame and influence. It is well known that after reading *Atalanta in Calydon* (1865) Tennyson, impressed by the 'fine metrical invention which I envy you,' nevertheless wondered if it was '*fair* for a Greek chorus to abuse the Deity something in the *style* of the Hebrew prophets,' and that he later said of Swinburne: 'He is a reed through which all things blow into music.'[4] It is less well known that after reading Swinburne's play *Chastelard* in 1865, his objections to its sensuality and materialism were profound.[5] In the next year, after the publication of the first *Poems and Ballads*, D.G. Rossetti wrote to Tennyson, assuring him that the 'qualities which displease you in Swinburne's poetry' were in no way 'owing to his intimacy with me.'[6] (Rossetti was never as good a friend to Swinburne as Swinburne was to him.) A short while later the Laureate's loathing of recent tendencies in French art – 'The frightful corruption of their literature makes one feel that they are going straight to Hell' – was exacerbated by his learning that Swinburne had written in praise of Gautier's *Mademoiselle de Maupin*.[7]

Tennyson was, of course, hardly alone in these opinions. The condemnation of Swinburne's early work for its immorality, flaunted sexuality, and espousal of poisonous art-for-art's-sake doctrines was every bit as widespread as Swinburne himself could have wished. There are two reasons, however, why Tennyson would have been peculiarly sensitive to the rise of Swinburne's star. The first was the threat to his pre-eminence among Victorian poets. In 1868 Robert Browning suggested that the growing popularity of Swinburne's poetry was the reason why sales of Tennyson's books were beginning to fall off.[8] The second reason is pinpointed by Leonard M. Findlay in the fullest discussion to date of the influence of Swinburne on Tennyson: 'In condemning some of Swinburne's proclivities, Tennyson would be condemning himself: in condemning others he would be reminded of the unflattering circumstances behind his abandoning similar themes.'[9]

These two pressures, one external, the other internal, are both strongly felt in 'Lucretius' (first published in *Macmillan's Magazine* in May 1868). Findlay has shown how centrally present in the poem the Swinburne of the first *Poems and Ballads* is, and Charles Tennyson's suggestion that the Laureate's choice of subject was influenced by the desire to show how, in contrast to the first *Poems and Ballads*, erotic subject matter could be handled without offence seems confirmed by Oscar Browning's report that in the middle of a reading of his poem Tennyson stopped to exclaim: 'What a mess little Swinburne would have made of this!'[10]

What makes 'Lucretius' such a powerful poem, however, and gives it a central place in Tennyson's canon, is not Tennyson's quarrel with Swinburne but his quarrel with himself. The longing to withdraw from active involvement in life; the impulse to suicide coloured by longings for the peaceful oblivion of a natural paradise; apocalyptic previsions of the destruction of the physical world; the attractiveness of a purely naturalistic vision of human existence (so beautifully conveyed in Tennyson's poem through his Englishing of passages from *De Rerum Natura*); the debilitating impact of strange sexual passions: all of these subjects, the topoi of 'Lucretius,' also figure importantly in the poetry of Swinburne. But they figure just as importantly in the earlier poetry of Tennyson (much of it written before Swinburne was born), and though the younger poet's stimulus doubtless quickened in Tennyson conflicts which had become increasingly dormant, they are present in 'Lucretius' because they are deeply rooted in Tennyson's psyche.

The one comment Swinburne is known to have made on 'Lucretius' may be taken to adumbrate the central differences within the shared themes and subject matter of the two poets. After reading the poem in *Macmillan's*, Swinburne remarked at the end of a letter to W.M. Rossetti: 'How very fine Tennyson's "Lucretius" is – all but the last lines. I read it last evening with quite surprised admiration.'[11] In the last lines, Tennyson has Lucretius stab himself. He dies bitterly saying 'Thy duty? What is duty? Fare thee well!' to his remorseful wife Lucilia, who at the beginning of the poem had given her husband the love philtre that was to destroy him. One reason Swinburne did not care for the poem's closing lines must have been that the love philtre and its consequences are an outrageous libel on the historical Lucretius. This legend is, as George Santayana says, 'too edifying an end to an atheist and Epicurean not to be suspected.'[12] The legend was promulgated by Saint Jerome for sectarian reasons and utilized by Tennyson because, no matter how drawn towards it he may sometimes have been, he could not for long countenance a naturalistic vision of human existence like Lucretius', which insisted that death meant extinction and that the beginning of wisdom was to recognize that man is mortal and his joys and loves ephemeral. Tennyson often stated that such a view led only to a crudely hedonistic existence or to self-destruction.[13] Since there is no hint in *De Rerum Natura* of either overtaking its stoic, ascetic author, the Tennysonian logic necessitates Jerome's nemesis of the philtre and its consequences.

Swinburne's deepest beliefs are precisely the opposite of Tennyson's. The principal themes of some of the finest and most characteristic of his post-1866 poems, themes already adumbrated in a number of the first *Poems and Ballads*, are that a purely naturalistic vision of human existence can sustain and fulfil man despite the iron limitations placed on human desires; that human love, though doomed to extinction and sometimes twisted into dark, feral shapes, can be enough; and that the acceptance of death as the final end is a necessary step on the path to self-realization and freedom. It was Tennyson's distrust of Swinburne's reading of human life, and of his own strong inclination towards naturalism, that led him again and again in his later years – in 'Lucretius,' in two epigrams dating from the late 1860s or early 1970s,[14] in 'Despair' and 'Demeter and Persephone,' in 'Happy: the Leper's Bride,' and in 'Saint Telemachus' – directly or indirectly to answer poems of the young Swinburne. And it was Swinburne's apprehension of what Tennyson's suppression of naturalistic vision within himself, and his consequent over-emphasis on morality and vague metaphysical speculation, had done to his poetry that was to be the central thread running through his critical animadversions on the Laureate and his work.

Swinburne's earliest critical remarks on Tennyson occur in an 1865 letter to Lord Houghton. He is discussing Walter Savage Landor:

Apart from their executive perfection, all those Greek poems of his always fitted on to my own way of feeling and thought infinitely more than even Tennyson's modern versions: and now I am more than ever sure that the 'Hamadryad' [in Landor's *Hellenics* (1847)] is a purer and better piece of work, from the highest point of view that art can take, than such magnificent hashes and stews of old and new with a sharp sauce of personality as 'Oenone' and 'Ulysses.' Not that I am disloyal to Tennyson, into whose church we were all in my time born and baptized as far back as we can remember at all; but he is not a Greek nor a heathen; and I imagine does not want to be; and I greatly fear believes it possible to be something better: an absurdity which should be left to the Brownings and other blatant creatures begotten on the slime of the modern chaos.[15]

It would be wrong to make too much of this passage; Swinburne was seldom at his most judicious when writing to Houghton, as the empty hyperbole of his last phrase attests, and few will agree that the prosy narrative of 'Hamadryad' is 'a better piece of work' than Tennyson's superbly evocative poems. The comments are nonetheless suggestive. The criticism is twofold: the first point concerns decorum; the second extends consideration of decorum into the area of philosophic or religious disagreement. Late in life Tennyson explained to his son Hallam that when he wrote a poem on an 'antique' (or classical) subject he had to supply 'something modern … It is no use giving a mere réchauffé of old legends.'[16] It is precisely this mixing of ancient and modern that Swinburne finds objectionable in 'Oenone' and 'Ulysses.' In the former poem his objection surely refers to the obtrusive sermon of Pallas Athene on 'Self-reverence, self-knowledge, self-control,' which is delivered in Miltonic cadences jarringly different from the blank verse of the rest of the poem. As Douglas Bush has said, her speech 'is so very Victorian that we become embarrassingly aware that she is undressed, apart from a spear.'[17] The objection to 'Ulysses' is less clear. It presumably refers to the fact that the speaker is not Homer's Ulysses but Dante's, with the admixture of a Tennysonian lassitude all his own. It is hard to see how the quality or the purity of this particular 'piece of work' is adulterated by the fact that Tennyson has given us his Ulysses rather than someone else's; one might just as well complain that in 'Anactoria,' a poem Swinburne wrote about this time, the speaker is Swinburne's Sappho, not someone else's. Swinburne's objection suggests that while raising a point of decorum he has another point in mind: that Tennyson is not content to be a Greek or a heathen but wishes to be 'something better,' presumably a Christian (as the allusion to churches and baptism suggests), certainly a Victorian moralist (the Pallas Athene speech), and that consequently he ought not to write poems on classical (pagan) subjects. There is also the implication that matters of moral improvement and religious uplift should be left to less gifted poets.

Clearly Swinburne is stating a personal preference ('my own way of feeling and thought') and were it not for the telling affinities between him and Tennyson one might be tempted to dismiss his remarks as quirky value judgments. If one does not, however, it can be seen that Swinburne's preference raises a suggestive question for the critic of Tennyson concerning the possible misuse of the instruments of his art when the chosen vehicle (the literary form and the subject matter) is made to convey a tenor of moral concern and theological implication to which it is ill adapted. Swinburne subsequently brought up these matters again, in connection with Tennyson's greatest work. But he again did so in a tangential manner which necessitates extrapolation and inference.

Swinburne published a long complimentary essay on 'Matthew Arnold's New Poems' in 1867. Between then and 1875 (when the article was reprinted in *Essays and Studies*) he added a long passage in French, put into the mouth of an imaginary 'French critic.' The latest editor of Swinburne's essay thinks that this dazzling pastiche implies 'a criticism of Browning's point of view,' but the major part of the interpolation clearly refers to *In Memoriam*.[18] The passage comes just after Swinburne's praise of *Empedocles on Etna*, especially of Empedocles' long speech near the end of the first act, for its delineation of the inexorable limitations placed on human existence and the stark prescription of endurance and resignation as the only antidote to a world in which 'To tunes we did not call our being must keep chime.' The tough-minded gravity of *Empedocles* is then contrasted with what Swinburne regards as a characteristic malaise of mid-nineteenth-century English poetry: the making of declamations of doubt and baffled quests for religious certainty the subject matter of poetry: 'Nothing in verse or out of verse is more wearisome than the delivery of reluctant doubt, of half-hearted hope and half-incredulous faith. A man who suffers from the strong desire either to believe or disbelieve something he cannot may be worthy of sympathy, is certainly worthy of pity, until he begins to speak; and if he tries to speak in verse, he misuses the implement of an artist.'[19] Then comes the interpolation, which opens with the French critic noting that the English 'always want to reconcile things irreconcilable,' and goes on, after a glance at Browning, to give this description of *In Memoriam*:

Here is a beautiful poet's soul who weeps, who searches, who envisions death, nothing-ness, the infinite; who wishes to weigh facts, sort out beliefs, sift faith; and here is his last word: Let us believe, in order to suffer less; let us endeavour at least to make ourselves believe that we believe in something consoling. It is sad not to believe that we are to live once more sometime, see again our dead friends, fulfil new destinies. Let us affirm, then, that this is true, that it has to be; that it is absolutely necessary to believe in it, or at least to pretend to ourselves to believe in it ... Life without a future is impossible. No more reasonings of the unbeliever. The heart starts up like a man incensed and answers: I have felt! You lack faith, you say, you lack proofs, but it is enough that you have had feelings. This being true, it is well worth the trouble to set the poetic car rolling on the rails of philosophy, to mire the wheels in the muddy ruts of theology. ... Death, grief, oblivion, distress – these are undoubtedly painful things that one would wish to avoid. Clearly, we would all do our best to escape them. Does that prove that these things do not exist?

The French critic goes on to say that there is nothing wrong with the mixture of religious emotions and poetry as long as the emotions are full-throated, unlike 'the half-way faith that weeps sceptical tears,' and as long as no one kind of religious emotion is regarded as poetically superior to any other, for – and here I detect a reference to Tennyson's classical poem – 'Lucretius has his place as well as Moses, Omar as well as Job.'[20]

Because this sparkling passage is a satiric and ironic tour de force, the critical reservations which lie behind it have to be inferred. This can be done with confidence, however, particularly if the passage is considered in conjunction with the comments on *In Memoriam* that Swinburne made in his own voice in his 1881 essay 'Tennyson and Musset.' Swinburne's central point is that – in the phrase T.S. Eliot would use a half-century later – the faith of *In Memoriam* 'is a poor thing,'[21] largely founded on the substitution of the wish for the deed. Like some other Victorian writers (Browning, for example) Tennyson forces his work to culminate in a version of Carlyle's 'Everlasting Yea,' the foundations of which cannot withstand close scrutiny. *In Memoriam* attempts to go beyond the stoic wisdom of Empedocles' 'Nor does being weary prove that [man] has where to rest,' or of Swinburne's own insistence in 'Ave atque Vale' (which, if one is careful to respect the differences of scale, can be read as a palinode to *In Memoriam*):

> There is no help for these things; none to mend
> And none to mar; not all our songs, O friend,
> Will make death clear or make life durable.

Tennyson's hankering after faith necessitates a machinery of reasoning that Yeats would later call 'the scientific and moral discursiveness of *In Memoriam*'[22] and that Swinburne calls 'pretentiously unpretentious philosophy.' Since *In Memoriam* is an elegy, the poetry that is overshadowed by philosophy is the lament, the expression of personal loss, and the eventual consolation brought by the passage of time and the revivification of memory. It is in its emotional authenticities, not in its philosophy, that the greatness of *In Memoriam* lies: 'the possession of a book so wholly noble and so profoundly beautiful in itself is more precious than the most coherent essay towards the solution of any less insoluble problem.'[23]

It may be thought permissible to round off this examination of Swinburne on Tennyson's classical poems and on *In Memoriam* by bringing forward a poem on which Swinburne has unfortunately left no comment. 'Demeter and Persephone,' first published in 1889, is perhaps the finest poem (short lyrics aside) Tennyson wrote during the second half of his career. In the poem Demeter tells the story of her daughter's abduction by Dis, recalls the stages of her sorrow, and celebrates Persephone's eventual seasonal return to the world of the living. In conclusion she longs for the intimation of a more than seasonal dispensation which will again allow her to enjoy her daughter's presence the year round. It was with reference to this poem that Tennyson observed that 'antique' stories need 'something modern' added to their retelling. Everyone agrees that the something modern in this poem is the concluding intimation of the Christian revelation. And, as Curtis Dahl has argued, a second modern something is its optimistic answer to Swinburne's fatalistic 'Hymn to Proserpine' (1866).[24]

But the extent to which 'Demeter and Persephone' may be regarded as a rewriting of *In Memoriam* has not been generally recognized. Demeter's sudden loss of her daughter parallels Tennyson's loss of Hallam; and in recapitulating the stages of her grief she outlines in condensed form stages of Tennyson's grief in the Hallam elegy. The numbed sense of catastrophic loss in the early poems of *In Memoriam* parallels Demeter's initial desolation, which sends her searching wildly through the world screaming 'Where?' Both grievers are troubled by the ambiguous presentiments of dreams and both have horrific visions of a world dominated by random violence inimical to man. The 'Nature, red in tooth and claw / With ravine' of *In Memoriam* becomes the equally nightmarish description of

> The jungle rooted in [man's] shattered hearth,
> The serpent coiled about his broken shaft
> The scorpion crawling over naked skulls.

And Demeter, 'lost in utter grief,' failing to send her life 'through olive-yard and vine / And golden grain,' followed by her once more blessing the farmer's field after her daughter has been returned to her, repeats the *In Memoriam* pattern of estrangement from the natural world being followed by celebrations of natural process and of identity with it after the apparition of Hallam in section xcv.

There is, however, a major difference between the two poems, one which it is tempting to consider as influenced by Swinburne's strictures on *In Memoriam*. In 'Demeter and Persephone,' the more than naturalistic consolation of Love (which bestows immortality) remains wholly implicit; the wish to be permanently and not just seasonally (or naturalistically) united to the dead beloved is not mistaken for the deed and consequently does not need to be supported by the machinery of reasoning. In the poem's final lines the longing to have her daughter 'see no more' what she in fact must continue to see remains a wish, and the poem ends with a grim picture of the lower world to which Persephone must still seasonally return. 'Demeter and Persephone,' then, not only answers Swinburne's 'Hymn to Proserpine'; it also may be said to answer his strictures about *In Memoriam*, and, in its success at alluding to a 'modern' subject – the Christian revelation of a God of Love – without making itself into a hash of old and new, to answer his reservations about 'Oenone' and 'Ulysses.'

The 'Greek' or 'heathen' point of view from which Swinburne criticized Tennyson's attempts to reach 'something better' may also be called a 'Romantic' one, a designation which Swinburne would certainly have accepted. In many places in his prose and poetry Swinburne restates the high Romantic doctrines that the imagination is autonomous, that the poet's responsibility is only to his own vision, his task being to convey (in the words of Wallace Stevens) 'not the revelations of belief, but the precious portents of our own powers,'[25] and that joy and fulfilment must be sought within the self or in the self's relation to the human and natural worlds out there, not to any supernatural realm up there. These Romantic doctrines were of course the imaginative inheritance of Tennyson as well as of Swinburne. In assessing Tennyson and his work from a Romantic point of view, therefore, Swinburne is not only evaluating Tennyson by germane criteria, but also calculating the effects on his poetry of his transformation from a Romantic into a largely Victorian poet.

Swinburne's most savage criticism of this transformation is contained in the poem called 'Prelude,' which prefaced *Songs before Sunrise*, his 1871 collection of Republican and revolutionary poems. In the 'Prelude,' an autobiographical poem of the type of Milton's 'How soon hath time' sonnet, Keats' 'Sleep and Poetry,' and Stevens' 'Farewell to Florida,' Swinburne reassesses his early poems, dedicates himself to the power of which and through which he sings, and presages the more mature poetry he hopes to go on to write. Since its subject is the imaginative growth of a nineteenth-century poet and its theme that there are no supernatural interventions in human existence and that the naturalistic given must and will suffice, it is not surprising that Tennyson figures in the poem as a negative exemplum. In its opening stanzas, after a period of 'Delight whose germ grew never grain' and of 'passion dyed in its own pain' (it is the world of the 1866 *Poems and Ballads*), the Youth, Swinburne's name for himself, puts behind him his poetic childhood and the fears, desires, and dreams which have kept him in that state. Stanza 4 begins the centre of the poem, a visionary chant of poetic incarnation, independence, and naturalistic acceptance:

For what has he whose will sees clear
To do with doubt and faith and fear,
   Swift hopes and slow despondencies?
   ...
... his soul communes and takes cheer
   With the actual earth's equalities,
Air, light, and night, hills, winds, and streams,
And seeks not strength from strengthless dreams.

His soul is even with the sun
Whose spirit and whose eye are one,
   Who seeks not stars by day, nor light
   And heavy heat of day by night.
   ...

To him the lights of even and morn
Speak no vain things of love or scorn,
   Fancies and passions miscreate
   By man in things dispassionate.

In reading these lines it is possible, but difficult, not to think of Tennyson. Doubt and faith and fear (together with love) are the subjects of *In Memoriam*; the alternation of 'swift hopes and slow despondencies' is an excellent description of the basic movement of the first three-fifths of the poem; and in no English poet's canon (except perhaps that of Swinburne himself) do 'the lights of even and morn' play a more important role than in Tennyson's.

It is patent that the next two stanzas refer principally to Tennyson:

He builds not half of doubts and half
Of dreams his own soul's cenotaph,
   Whence hopes and fears with helpless eyes,
   Wrapt loose in cast-off cerecloths, rise
   ...
And drain his soul of faith and strength
It might have lived on a life's length.

He hath given himself and hath not sold
To God for heaven or man for gold,
   Or grief for comfort that it gives,
   Or joy for grief's restoratives.
He hath given himself to time, whose fold
   Shuts in the mortal flock that lives
On its plain pasture's heat and cold
   And the equal year's alternatives.

Certainly the first of these stanzas gives an extremely partial account of *In Memoriam* (to say the least), concentrating exclusively on those moods in which the poem's speaker was 'half dead to know that I shall die.' Swinburne's accusation in the second stanza is equally extreme: Tennyson is charged with not having given himself to time, relativity, mortality, and a naturalistic acceptance of 'the equal year's alternatives' (charges to which of course the later Tennyson would have readily admitted). The reasons for this refusal are said to be – I am extrapolating from the first four lines of the second stanza – the cosy promise of immortality that belief in God makes possible, the emoluments showered on the public poet who has become, in T.S. Eliot's phrase, 'the surface flatterer of his own time,'[26] and the comforts of indulging grief rather than replacing it with the stoic acceptance of human limitations and of transience, the 'little time we gain from time / To set our seasons in some chime' of which Swinburne speaks later in his poem.

There is no need to underline the unfairness and animus of the picture of Tennyson given in the 'Prelude.' But the degree of over-reaction, the unqualified rejection, unmitigated by humour or irony, does call for at least a tentative explanation. In the 'Prelude,' Swinburne is not speaking as a literary critic but as a Romantic poet passionately chanting his most deeply held convictions. He is concerned not with refinement of taste or accuracy of judgment but with the need to identify, and separate himself from, a kind of poetry which would deny him the freedom, dignity, and the possible sublimities of trusting in no power higher than himself or other than the natural processes with which he identifies himself. In *The Anxiety of Influence* and the studies which followed it, Harold Bloom has thrown much light on the complex apprehensions with which poets regard their precursors, conditions that can lead to the deliberate misinterpretation or ruthless rejection of an older poet's message as a way of a younger poet's clearing imaginative space for himself – as a necessary condition of fresh poetic utterance. There are perhaps traces of such anxiety in Swinburne's more dispassionate reflections on Tennyson; but in the 'Prelude,' a poem about Swinburne's fate as a poet, the anxiety becomes dominant and full-throated because the very survival of Swinburne's imaginative powers seems at stake. As Keats said of Milton: 'Life to him would be death to me.'[27]

When Swinburne returned to the subject of the Laureate's work the year after the publication of the 'Prelude' to *Songs before Sunrise*, he returned to a more judicious prose discourse (which nevertheless did not preclude hyperbolic and tongue-in-cheek effects). Near the middle of his extended critical sally, *Under the Microscope* (1872), Swinburne contrived an opportunity 'to intercalate a few words' on the most ambitious of Tennyson's poems, the *Idylls of the King* – the 'Morte d'Albert' as Swinburne habitually called it. Swinburne had himself been creatively interested in the Arthurian legends at least since his under-graduate years at Oxford in the late 1850s. When he began a long poem on the Tristram and Iseult story in 1869 it was partially because of the competitive desire to 'lick the Morte d'Albert.'[28] And it may have been advance information about the imminent publication of *The Last Tournament* (in which Tennyson gives his version of the Tristram story) that led Swinburne to publish his 'Prelude to an Unfinished Poem' (that is, to what became *Tristram of Lyonesse*) at the end of 1871.[29] One cannot therefore discount the possibility that professional rivalry, if not creative anxiety, coloured his reading of the *Idylls*. But this need not keep one from seeing that Swinburne's intercalation (taken in conjunction with his comments on the *Idylls* in the 1881 'Tennyson and Musset') offers a fundamentally suggestive criticism of a work which has always had its distinguished detractors, Carlyle, Hopkins, and Yeats among them.

Swinburne best summarizes his views at the beginning of his remarks on the *Idylls* in 'Tennyson and Musset': 'Towards the Morte d'Albert, or Idylls of the Prince Consort, I should almost equally regret to seem desirous of playing the aforesaid part of devil's advocate ... [No one can] pretend or profess a more cordial and thankful admiration than I have always felt for the exquisite magnificence of style, the splendid flashes of episodical illumination, with which those poems are vivified or adorned. But when they are presented to us as a great moral and poetic whole, the flower at once of all epics and all ethics – "Cette promotion me laisse un peu rêveur".'[30] Had Swinburne chosen to instance the stylistic brilliance or the 'splendid flashes of episodical illumination' he would of course have had numerous examples to choose from. He does elaborate on the poem's failings as a moral or poetic whole. With regard to the latter point, the 'radical flaw' in the poem's structure is said to result 'from the incongruity of materials which are radically incapable of combination or coherence.' Tennyson attempted to meld together 'the various Arthurs of different national legends' (not to mention Prince Albert, whom Tennyson himself identified as his Arthur's contemporary counterpart), but not even 'the utmost ingenuity of eclecticism' could keep his poem from resembling 'the Horatian ideal of artistic monstrosity.' It is as if an author attempted to combine 'in one typic figure' the Achilles of the *Iliad* with the Achilles of Shakespeare's *Troilus and Cressida*.[31] Furthermore, because Tennyson wished to make Arthur 'the noble and perfect symbol of an ideal man,' he removed 'not merely the excuse but the explanation of the fatal and tragic loves of Launcelot and Guenevere.' For 'the hinge of the whole legend of the Round Table' is Arthur's coupling with his half-sister, from which union Modred is born. Only the 'calamitous fate' which grows from the seed of Arthur's incest can confer on the story of the Round Table 'the proper significance and the necessary dignity.'[32]

At first glance Swinburne's stricture might be thought para-critical cavil. Every artist working in a non-reportorial medium may be granted the right to do what he likes with his sources and to have his work assessed on the basis of internal coherence. Swinburne knows this perfectly well. Indeed, he praises Malory for melding various sources together into his Arthurian work which, although incongruous in its earlier parts, becomes 'so nobly consistent, so profoundly harmonious in its close.'[33] Swinburne's accusation of lack of unity within the *Idylls* has to do not with incompatibility of source materials per se but with the relation of parts of the *Idylls* to each other and to the whole, and with considerations of decorum and propriety – the matching of theme to subject matter, of tenor to vehicle.

Swinburne gives one striking example of incompatibility of parts. The tone of *The Passing of Arthur*, the earliest written of the *Idylls* as Swinburne points out (it had been published in the *Poems* of 1842 as the 'Morte d'Arthur'), especially its presentation of the broken, 'faulty' King, has been 'incongruously incorporated' with later-written material which presents a quite different Arthur, 'the blameless King' in Tennyson's phrase, 'the Albertine ideal of later days' in Swinburne's.[34] The point is important enough to warrant a concrete illustration which Swinburne does not pause to provide. In *The Passing of Arthur* the King speaks as a defeated, dying man in tones of confusion, uncertainty, and near-despair:

> for on my heart hath fallen
> Confusion, till I know not what I am,
> Nor whence I am, nor whether I be King.
> Behold, I seem but King among the dead.

But in the notorious lines of *Guinevere*, a passage of such contemporary renown that it was quoted by William Acton in the 1870 edition of his book on *Prostitution*, Arthur speaks in the tones of Dickens' Mr Podsnap:

> I hold that man the worst of public foes
> Who either for his own or children's sake,
> To save his blood from scandal, lets his wife
> Whom he knows false, abide and rule the house:
> For being through his cowardice allowed
> Her station, taken everywhere for pure,
> She like a new disease, unknown to men,
> Creeps, no precaution used, among the crowd,
> Makes wicked lightnings of her eyes, and saps
> The fealty of friends, and stirs the pulse
> With devil's leaps, and poisons half the young.[35]

The Passing of Arthur may be said to belong to a group of poems within the *Idylls* (*The Coming of Arthur* and *The Holy Grail* are the others) in which epistemological and spiritual themes are dominant. Another group, consisting of six idylls (*Gareth and Lynette* and those first published in 1859, including *Guinevere*) may be said to present 'the Albertine ideal.' In these idylls moral considerations, principally relating to sexual purity and marital fidelity, are dominant. It is with reference to this group, with their distinctively Victorian preoccupations, that Swinburne in *Under the Microscope* concentrates his assault on the *Idylls'* failings in decorum and propriety. For Swinburne, 'the moral tone of the Arthurian story had been on the whole lowered and degraded by Mr. Tennyson's mode of treatment.'[36] By removing the 'hinge' of the story Tennyson transformed his medieval subject matter into a Victorian moral parable in fancy dress – '*Charades from the Middle Ages*,' in Hopkins' phrase.[37] 'Treated as he has treated it,' Swinburne says, 'the story is rather a case for the divorce court than for poetry.' Arthur has been reduced to 'the level of a wittol, Guenevere to the level of a woman of intrigue and Launcelot to the level of a "co-respondent".' From this follows the similar degradation of the other figures in the legend, especially Vivien, whose 'utterly ignoble quality' makes her 'unspeakably repulsive and unfit for artistic treatment.' The loathsome dialogue of Merlin and Vivien in their idyll, which depicts 'the erotic fluctuations and vacillations of a dotard under the moral and physical manipulation of a prostitute,' is a more salacious piece of immorality than anything in Gautier or Baudelaire.[38]

Certainly Swinburne's dislike of conventional morality, and his desire to turn the tables on those who proclaimed the *Idylls* 'an epic poem of profound and exalted morality'[39] while excoriating the sensuality and immorality of the first *Poems and Ballads, Les Fleurs du mal,* and *Mademoiselle de Maupin,* colours his attack on *Idylls of the King.* But this should not keep us from recognizing that he has identified perhaps the most difficult artistic problem that Tennyson had with his work: the characterization of Arthur as 'the blameless King' of immaculate purity. Swinburne insists that by removing from Arthur any hint of moral blemish, 'Mr. Tennyson has blemished the whole story: by the very exaltation of his hero as something more than man he has left him in the end something less.'[40] To use an analogy different from Swinburne's comparison with Achilles: in his presentation of King Arthur, Tennyson attempted to combine in one 'typic' figure Milton's Adam, whose predicament before the creation of Eve is that of Arthur before his marriage, and Milton's God the Father, whom Arthur sometimes resembles in speech, as in the places that have led critics to call him priggish and George Meredith to say he talks like a curate.

Since 1967 five full-length critical studies of *Idylls of the King* have been published. The authors of at least two of them have been aware of the shadow that the characterization of Arthur casts on their claims for the greatness of the poem. They have consequently attempted to present a less than immaculate King and to draw a distinction between Arthur's character and his creator's moral ideals. J. Philip Eggers sees Arthur as a Quixotic figure whose tragic flaw is his excessive idealism.[41] John D. Rosenberg says that the King is 'never more blind' to the multiple causes of his kingdom's destruction 'than when he concludes his denunciation of Guinevere, "And all through thee!" Under the particular circumstances the charge is cruel; under any circumstances it is simplistic.'[42] It seemed clear to Swinburne, however, that Tennyson meant what he said when he described Arthur as 'ideal manhood closed in real man,'[43] and that he was speaking in earnest when he dedicated the *Idylls* to the memory of the Prince Consort. But even if the question of whether Arthur speaks for Tennyson is left aside, it can still be said that Swinburne has made a strong case for the view that claims for the moral greatness of *Idylls of the King* are appreciably weakened because its central figure, 'the blameless King,' is indelibly stained with the moralistic scruples which led Swinburne to rename Tennyson's poem the 'Idylls of the Prince Consort.'

Swinburne's next comments on Tennyson were made indirectly in verse. In the early 1880s he published two excellent parodies of poems by the Laureate.[44] 'The Higher Pantheism in a Nutshell' (1880) answered 'The Higher Pantheism,' and 'Disgust: a Dramatic Monologue,' published in December 1818, followed the publication the previous month of 'Despair: a Dramatic Monologue.' In their different ways, both Tennyson's poems are tempting targets for any parodist. In addition, their muddled cosmic and theological cerebrations could not have been better calculated to draw Swinburne's annoyed attention.

'Despair' is one of a number of late Tennyson poems worked up from stories or suggestions provided by friends. It is written in long rhyming couplets like those of the Locksley Hall poems, a metre of which Tennyson was fond but which has the tendency to make whatever is said in it sound like rant. The poem's speaker has inadvertently survived a suicide pact as a result of which his wife has drowned. He addresses his rescuer, 'a minister of the sect he had abandoned.' We learn that the couple's faith had been destroyed by the minister's 'fatalist creed,' his insistence on 'a God of eternal rage' who had made for most men 'an everlasting Hell.' Husband and wife reasoned that if there were a God He must be a God of Love, but their occasional glimmers (that key Tennysonian term) of such a being were insufficient to sustain them. Agnostic literature, 'horrible infidel writings,' the disappointments of their children (one had forged his father's signature) help to confirm their view that there is no delight on earth, that 'the limitless Universe' of stars is maintained by 'No soul in the heaven above,' and that no 'earthly flower would be heavenly fruit.' Their most desolating perception is that love will end with death. Their present love consequently (according to the Tennysonian logic) turns to ashes in their mouths. At the end of the poem the speaker makes a fresh resolution to destroy himself as soon as circumstances permit.

If we look for sources and analogues for 'Despair,' the first glance, taking in the poem's subtitle, the cramped, dissenting background of the speaker, and the intimations of the need for a theology of a God of Love, suggests Browning. The second glance suggests Swinburne. The would-be suicides long for eternal sleep after reading the 'horrible infidel writings' of 'the new dark ages' which say (in the accents of the first *Poems and Ballads*) 'Why should we bear with an hour of torture, a moment of pain, / If every man die forever, if all his griefs are in vain.' As Curtis Dahl has said, the allusion to infidel writings 'almost certainly reflects Tennyson's antipathy to Swinburnian attitudes.'[45]

But if Browning and Swinburne helped Tennyson to bring his poem into focus, the thought that informs 'Despair' and the postulates that determine the speaker's decline into suicide are uniquely Tennyson's. As instanced in connection with 'Lucretius,' no belief of Tennyson's is more necessary to his psychological stability than the doctrine that human love implies divine Love, that if there is no immortality (the showing forth of divine Love) there can be no human love, only degrees of lust. Without Love, life is meaningless, the alternatives being, as in 'Lucretius,' suicide or bestiality. The locus classicus of this view is sections xxxiv and xxxv of *In Memoriam*:

My own dim life should teach me this,
  That life shall live for evermore,
  Else earth is darkness at the core,
And dust and ashes all that is;

This round of green, this orb of flame,
  Fantastic beauty; such as lurks
  In some wild Poet, when he works
Without a conscience or an aim.

What then were God to such as I?
  'Twere hardly worth my while to choose
  Of things all mortal, or to use
A little patience ere I die;

'Twere best at once to sink to peace,
  Like birds the charming serpent draws,
  To drop head-foremost in the jaws
Of vacant darkness and to cease.

...

> O me, what profits it to put
>   An idle case? If Death were seen
>   At first as Death, Love had not been,
> Or been in narrowest working shut,
>
> Mere fellowship of sluggish moods,
>   Or in his coarsest Satyr-shape
>   Had bruised the herb and crushed the grape,
> And basked and battened in the woods.

In *In Memoriam* this doctrine is of crucial importance. It provides a vital link in the chain of circular reasoning forged to provide an emotionally satisfying belief in immortality. If there is no immortality (no Love) – so the reasoning goes – there can be no human love. But I know that human love exists because I so loved Hallam; since I loved him he must still exist for there is a Love (known to me by my love) making him immortal.[46] Unlike the Tennyson of *In Memoriam*, the speaker of 'Despair' is not able to avail himself of the assuagements of this sophistry. Since he cannot believe in Love, love and life necessarily become meaningless for him and the jaws of vacant darkness open to receive him.

As a general statement about human experience, the belief encapsulated in the *In Memoriam* stanzas and dramatized in 'Despair' is of course specious. It is contradicted by ordinary human experience, for everyone knows people whose capacity to love is increased and intensified, and whose lives are enriched and ennobled, by an acceptance of mortality. Swinburne belongs at least to the latter group, and in 'Disgust: a Dramatic Monologue,' he beautifully undermines Tennyson's poem by calling attention to its arbitrary logic, melodramatic and rhetorical excesses, and stylistic lameness. The speaker of 'Disgust' is the female survivor of a marital suicide pact, saved by her eleventh-hour decision only to sip the strychnine which dispatches her husband, and by the subsequent 'application of the stomach pump.' She and her husband were brought up agnostics, knew about selection and evolution, and lived happily enough until their troubles began:

> …his cousin was wanted one day on the charge of forging a cheque –
> And his puppy died of the mange – my parrot choked on its perch.
> This was the consequence, was it, of not going weekly to church.[47]

Before destroying themselves they decide it is only 'rational' to give religion a chance, but the preacher at Little Zion is drunk. They also remember having once read an inspirational text, 'A reverend gentleman's work – the Conversion of Colonel Quagg,' but its Carlylean exhortations – ' "Vocation," says he, "is vocation, and duty duty" ' – finally suggest to them only that their present duty is to do each other in. Cosmic speculation is similarly unhelpful:

> Nothing that can't be, can, and what must be, must. Q.E.D.
> And the infinitesimal sources of Infinite Unideality
> Curve in to the central abyss of a sort of a queer Personality.
> Whose refraction is felt in the nebulae strewn in the pathway of Mars
> Like the parings of nails Aeonian – clippings and snippings of stars –
> Shavings of suns that revolve and evolve and involve and at times
> Give a sweet astronomical twang to remarkably hobbling rhymes.

In the deliberately banal conclusion we learn that what has determined the speaker not to attempt suicide again is no glimmer of higher things but a crude, and crudely expressed, *aviditas vitae*:

> Terrible, isn't it? Still, on reflection, it might have been worse.
> He might have been the unhappy survivor, and followed my hearse.
> 'Never do it again?' Why, certainly not. You don't
> Suppose I should think of it, surely? But anyhow – there – I won't.

The 'parings of nails Aeonian' passage in 'Disgust' echoes not only 'Despair' but also a number of late Tennyson poems devoted to cosmic speculation. 'The Higher Pantheism,' 'The Voice and the Peak,' 'De Profundis,' 'Vastness,' and 'The Ancient Sage' all display a pretty taste for paradox in tackling against a cosmic background the issues of knowledge versus faith, mortality versus immortality, immanence versus transcendence, chaos versus order, temporal versus eternal. 'The Ancient Sage' is the longest and strongest of this group of poems; 'The Higher Pantheism,' read at the first formal meeting of the Metaphysical Society in 1869, is the shortest and perhaps the best known. I quote it in toto:

> The sun, the moon, the stars, the seas, the hills and the plains –
> Are not these, O Soul, the Vision of Him who reigns?
>
> Is not the Vision He? though He be not that which He seems?
> Dreams are true while they last, and do we not live in dreams?
>
> Earth, these solid stars, this weight of body and limb,
> Are they not sign and symbol of thy division from Him?

Dark is the world to thee: thyself art the reason why;
For is He not all but that which has power to feel 'I am I'?

Glory about thee, without thee; and thou fulfillest thy doom,
Making Him broken gleams, and a stifled splendour and gloom.

Speak to Him thou for He hears, and Spirit with Spirit can meet –
Closer is He than breathing, and nearer than hands and feet.

God is law, say the wise; O Soul, and let us rejoice,
For if He thunder by law the thunder is yet His voice.

Law is God, say some: no God at all, says the fool;
For all we have power to see is a straight staff bent in a pool;

And the ear of man cannot hear, and the eye of man cannot see;
But if we could see and hear, this Vision – were it not He?

Swinburne's response to the poem was unequivocal. On 15 January 1870 he wrote to W.M. Rossetti: '... I looked at Tennyson's "Higher Pantheism" again – not bad verse altogether, but what gabble and babble of half-hatched thoughts in half-baked words! – and wrote at the tail of it this summary of its theology: "God, whom we see not, is; and God, who is not, we see: / Fiddle we know, is diddle: and diddle is possibly dee." I think it is terse and accurate as a Tennyson compendium.'[48] Ten years later the couplet in the letter to Rossetti, slightly changed, had become the last stanza of 'The Higher Pantheism in a Nutshell,' the opening parody in the anonymously published *The Heptalogia, or The Seven against Sense* (the poem should be read aloud, dead pan, in a tone of earnestness tempered by perplexity):

One, who is not, we see: but one, whom we see not, is:
Surely this is not that: but that is assuredly this.

What, and wherefore, and whence? for under is over and under:
If thunder could be without lightning, lightning could be without thunder.

Doubt is faith in the main: but faith, on the whole, is doubt:
We cannot believe by proof: but could we believe without?

Why, and whither, and how? for barley and rye are not clover:
Neither are straight lines curves: yet over is under and over.

Two and two may be four: but four and four are not eight:
Fate and God may be twain: but God is the same thing as fate.

Ask a man what he thinks, and get from a man what he feels:
God, once caught in the fact, shows you a fair pair of heels.

Body and spirit are twins: God only knows which is which:
The soul squats down in the flesh, like a tinker drunk in a ditch.

More is the whole than a part: but half is more than the whole:
Clearly, the soul is the body: but is not the body the soul?

One and two are not one: but one and nothing is two:
Truth can hardly be false, if falsehood cannot be true.

Once the mastodon was: pterodactyls were common as cocks:
Then the mammoth was God: now is He a prize ox.

Parallels all things are: yet many of these are askew:
You are certainly I: but certainly I am not you.

Springs the rock from the plain, shoots the stream from the rock:
Cocks exist for the hen: but hens exist for the cock.

God, whom we see not, is: and God, who is not, we see:
Fiddle, we know, is diddle: and diddle, we take it, is dee.

This splendid poem is less a parody in the usual sense of the term than a replaying in a different key of Tennyson's poem. (The one exception is the fourth from the last stanza: the reference to evolutionary progress is ungrounded in 'The Higher Pantheism,' although of course a number of other Tennyson poems do treat the subject; and the reference to God now being a 'prize ox' is too crudely overt to blend with the rest of the poem.) 'The Higher Pantheism in a Nutshell' does not apply the style of its parent poem to an incongruous subject, as Lewis Carroll did when he used the pro-contra thrust of the triplets of Tennyson's 'The Two Voices' to debate not whether to live or die but whether a certain meal was dinner or tea. Nor does it, like 'Disgust,' reveal the badness of the parent poem by being more overtly bad. Swinburne respects the style of 'The Higher Pantheism' ('not bad verse altogether'), showing one what to think about the poem by retelling it with slight but illuminating changes. There is a significantly larger proportion of declarative, as opposed to interrogative, sentences and a larger number of particulars which are deployed with demeaning effect: the fair pair of heels (the *Deus absconditus*), the tinker drunk in the ditch (man, the great amphibian), barley, clover, rye, cocks, and hens (humdrum, non-cosmic phenomena). Whereas Tennyson has given each of his antithetical assertions a stanza of its own, Swinburne places his antithetical pairs in revealing juxtaposition within the same line. The list of mutually inclusive opposites is extended to include truth and falsehood; Tennyson's blurring of the distinction between knowledge and faith is pointed up by the inclusion of mathematical concepts; and the confusion of deed and wish, datum and desideratum, is underlined in the verse 'Ask a man what he thinks, and get from a man what he feels.' In short Swinburne has identified 'The Higher Pantheism' as another example of those wearisome Victorian poems delivering themselves of 'half-hearted hope and half-incredulous faith,' and in his parody brought home to the reader the droll confusions of its tenor and the inappositeness of its vehicle.

Swinburne's last extended comment on Tennyson dates from the late 1890s when Tennyson, who had died in 1892, declaimed, so to speak, from beyond the grave. In his *Memoir* of his father, which came out in 1897, Hallam Tennyson included an epigram which Tennyson had written in late 1869 or early 1870:

> Art for Art's sake! Hail, truest Lord of Hell!
>   Hail Genius, blaster of the Moral Will!
> 'The filthiest of all paintings painted well
>   Is mightier than the purest painted ill!'
> Yes, mightier than the purest painted well,
> So prone are we toward that broad way to Hell.

Few poems can be less worthy of their author than this philistine six-liner is of Tennyson. Perhaps the most charitable response is simply to say it recalls Swinburne's description of the strain of 'beardless bluster' which he had earlier found in the Laureate's 'utterance on large questions of contemporary national history.'[49] But it is hard not to say more. If anyone could have been expected to exhibit a sympathetic understanding of the complex questions concerning the self-referential qualities of art and the poet's difficulties in reconciling the conflicting claims of art and life, it is the author of 'The Lady of Shalott,' 'The Palace of Art,' 'The Poet's Mind,' and 'The Hesperides.' Tennyson's poem deserved what it got when Swinburne scrutinized it in his late essay 'Changes of Aspect':

And, great as was the charm of his genius, the intelligence which could 'hail' a proposition or a definition of a principle common to all arts whatever as 'truest lord of hell' was simply putid: stupid is no word for it. It is unimaginable ... how any man imbued with so much as a smattering of scholarship in English or in French can have imagined that the law which bids an artist or a workman look first of all to the conditions of his work, think of nothing more seriously than the rules and the requisites of his art, bids him abstain from consideration of moral or political, patriotic or polemical subjects ... And whenever Tennyson himself was not serving this lord of hell, the law which compels every artist to do his very best in his own line, and not allow the very noblest intention or instinct or emotion to deflect or distort or pervert his hand, he drivelled: he drivelled as pitifully as in this idiotic eructation of doggerel.[50]

As Swinburne says more succinctly in another place: 'the doctrine of art for art is true in the positive sense, false in the negative; sound as an affirmation, unsound as a prohibition.'[51]

From the point of view of assessing Tennyson's poetic achievement, the important question is not whether Swinburne's excoriation of the 'Art for Art's sake' squib is warranted, but how frequently noble intentions, instincts, or emotions led Tennyson to break the law that compels every artist 'to do his very best in his own line.' Swinburne's emphasis in 'Changes of Aspect' is on integrity of craftmanship; in the case of Tennyson the question of fidelity to personal vision is closely analogous. In this regard Humphry House long ago pointed out that: 'Compared with Coleridge and Keats, say, Tennyson never felt on his pulses that the poetic activity, the exercise of creative imagination through words, contained the ground of its own justification.'[52] Without doubt Swinburne would have endorsed this view, for we have seen how he regretted the adulteration of aesthetic surface by obstrusive moralizing in 'Oenone' and *Idylls of the King*, and the dilution of the lyric expression of personal sorrow by 'pretentiously unpretentious philosophy' in *In Memoriam*. He would also have agreed with one of Tennyson's earliest and most insightful commentators, who in 1831 cautioned the young poet to remember a central aspect of his Romantic inheritance which in later years Swinburne on several occasions tried to keep the older poet from forgetting. In his review of Tennyson's 1830 *Poems, Chiefly Lyrical*, Arthur Hallam had written: 'That delicate sense of fitness, which grows with the growth of artist feelings, and strengthens with their strength, until it acquires a celerity and weight of decision hardly inferior to the correspondent judgments of conscience, is weakened by every indulgence of heterogeneous aspirations, however pure they may be, however lofty, however suitable to human nature.'[53]

And what of Swinburne's own poetry? One certainly cannot say that it is in danger of being too indiscriminately praised. Of all the major Victorian poets, Swinburne's reputation is still the most equivocal. A central reason is that criticism remains hampered by the same difficulty that bothered George Meredith as early as 1861: 'I don't see any internal centre from which springs anything that he does.'[54] But Swinburne's reflections on Tennyson and his works, though made over the span of three decades, clearly do have a consistency and coherence, which, as was instanced in the discussion of his response to 'Lucretius,' can help in locating the 'internal centre' of his finest and most characteristic poetry. Swinburne once told Ruskin that he preferred 'an indubitable and living lizard to a dead or doubtful god.'[55] This remark reminds one that Swinburne, with Meredith, is the most passionately and insistently naturalistic English poet between Keats and Lawrence, even though the natural world his poetry describes tends to be as bleak and comfortless as the waste area between land and sea to which he was particularly drawn. In several fundamental ways Swinburne has more in common with his Romantic predecessors and with certain twentieth-century poets in the Romantic tradition than with his contemporaries. There are no traces of doubt in Swinburne, no nostalgia for vanished certainties, no grasping at other-worldly straws, no confusion of poetry and heterogeneous aspirations. It was from under the shadow of these Victorian preoccupations that Swinburne's poetry had to struggle up into the sunlight; as we have seen, the deepest and longest shadow was cast by Tennyson.

2

Tennyson's Poetry 1830 to 1842

The 1820s and the 1830s were not propitious times for poets, especially for third-generation Romantic poets concerned with self-expression, vision, a life of immediate sympathy with the external world, and the apprehension and creation of beauty – poets, that is, whose imaginations wished to be indulged. In 1820, Thomas Love Peacock argued in 'The Four Ages of Poetry' that poets had no role to play in the civilized and enlightened community of an age characterized by rapid advances in knowledge and in the comforts and utilities of life. Poets were 'semi-barbarians' living in a past that had gone forever. Supernatural interventions and other phenomena essential to the production of poetry were no longer available to the poet; in Peacock's witty formulation, 'there are no Dryads in Hyde-Park nor Naiads in the Regent's canal.' Even if one thought of their production as merely ornamental, it did not follow that any more poems needed to be written: 'There are more good poems already existing than are sufficient to employ that portion of life which any mere reader and recipient of poetical impressions should devote to them, and these having been produced in poetical times, are far superior in all the characteristics of poetry to the artificial reconstructions of a few morbid ascetics in unpoetical times.'[1] It is true that Peacock's analysis was answered by Shelley's rhapsodic 'A Defence of Poetry,' perhaps the most extreme declaration ever written of poetry's power and efficacy. But this document, whatever it would have been worth to poets born in the infancy or the adolescence of the nineteenth century, remained unpublished until 1840.

While Peacock declared poets to be redundant, Thomas Babington Macaulay, in a similar analysis in his essay on Milton, claimed they were doomed to isolation and possibly to derangement. 'As civilisation advances,' said

Macaulay, 'Poetry almost necessarily declines.' Poetry flourished during the childhood of the race and poets had to be capable, as children are, of perception unadulterated by abstraction, and have the ability to 'abandon themselves without reserve to every illusion.' In a modern society characterized by the dominance of scientific and rational modes of intellection, the truth 'essential to poetry' could only be 'the truth of madness,' requiring 'a degree of credibility which almost amounts to a partial and temporary derangement of the intellect.' In a passage of extraordinary prescience, Macaulay predicted the fates of many Romantic visionaries from his day to our own:

He who, in an enlightened and literary society, aspires to be a great poet, must first become a little child. He must take to pieces the whole web of his mind. He must unlearn much of that knowledge which has perhaps constituted hitherto his chief title to superiority. His very talents will be a hindrance to him ... And it is well, if after all his sacrifices and exertions, his works do not resemble a lisping man or a modern ruin. We have seen in our own time great talents, intense labour, and long meditation, employed in this struggle against the spirit of the age, and employed, we will not say absolutely in vain, but with dubious success and feeble applause.[2]

Although he analysed the situation from a quite different perspective, Arthur Henry Hallam arrived at conclusions remarkably similar to Macaulay's. In his review of Tennyson's *Poems, Chiefly Lyrical* in the August 1831 *Englishman's Magazine*, Hallam had begun by stating his aesthetic premise: false art results whenever 'the mind of the artist suffers itself to be occupied, during its periods of creation, by any other predominant motive than the desire for beauty.' Wordsworth was 'frequently chargeable with this error, and ... much has been said by him which is good as philosophy, powerful as rhetoric, but false as poetry.' The poetry of Shelley and Keats was praised: they were 'both poets of sensation rather than reflection,' their poetry was 'a sort of magic,' and their delight in the 'simple exertions of eye and ear ... tended to absorb their whole being into the energy of sense.' In the present day, however, there was necessarily a 'barrier' between such poets and society in general: for 'How should they be popular, whose senses told them a richer and ampler tale than most men could understand? ... The public very naturally derided them as visionaries.' It was true that pleasure was derived by most men from Shakespeare, Dante, and Homer; but these writers had flourished 'in the most propitious eras' of their nations' literary development: 'In the youthful periods of any literature there is an expansive and communicative tendency in mind, which produces unreservedness of communion and reciprocity of vigour between different orders of intelligence.' But the age of Hallam and Tennyson 'comes late in our national progress.' The different powers of the poetic disposition, 'the energies of Sensitive, of Reflective, of Passionate Emotion,' formerly intermingled and mutually supportive, were now isolated from each other: 'intrinsic harmony,' unity, and community were no more:

Hence the melancholy, which so evidently characterises the spirit of modern poetry: hence that return of the mind upon itself, and the habit of seeking relief in idiosyncracies rather than community of interest. In the old times the poetic impulse went along with the general impulse of the nation; in these, it is a reaction against it ... Our inference, therefore, from this change in the relative position of artists to the rest of the community is, that modern poetry, in proportion to its depth and truth, is likely to have little immediate authority over public opinion.[3]

The young Tennyson was himself keenly aware of the reduced possibilities for poetry in his age and of the consequences for the artist. In 'Timbuctoo,' his Cambridge prize poem of 1829, the 'I' of the poem, standing on a mountain at evening (always in Tennyson the best time for vision) experiences one of those transfiguring moments of expanded consciousness and heightened perceptual awareness which are the raison d'être of Romantic meditation:

> I felt my soul grow mighty, and my Spirit
> With supernatural excitation bound
> Within me, and my mental eye grew large
> With such a vast circumference of thought,
> That in my vanity I seemed to stand
> Upon the outward verge and bound alone
> Of full beatitude. Each failing sense
> As with a momentary flash of light
> Grew thrillingly distinct and keen.

During this vision the speaker's thoughts, 'erstwhile so low, now felt / Unutterable buoyancy and strength.' But his brain begins to stagger 'beneath the vision,' night falls, and he collapses. He is raised up by an Angel, a version of Shelley's Apollo, not at all a Christian messenger, who explains what has happened:

> Lo! I have given *thee*
> To understand my presence, and to feel
> My fullness; I have filled thy lips with power.
> I have raised three nigher to the spheres of Heaven,

> Man's first, last home: and thou with ravished sense
> Listenest the lordly music flowing from
> The illimitable years. I am the Spirit,
> The permeating life which courseth through
> All the intricate and labyrinthine veins
> Of the great vine of *Fable* …

At the end of the poem, however, the Angel abruptly warns that the fabled city of the speaker's vision will soon lose its 'mystery of loveliness' because of civilization's advance:

> the time is well-nigh come
> When I must render up this glorious home
> To keen *Discovery*: soon yon brilliant towers
> Shall darken with the waving of her wand;
> Darken, and shrink and shiver into huts,
> Black specks amid a waste of dreary sand.

The moral of the end of 'Timbuctoo' is patent: as civilization advances, poetry declines; keen *Discovery* is antithetical to *Fable*; rational, scientific knowledge to the imagination; the march of progress to poetic vision.

One of Tennyson's early poems, 'The Poet,' does confidently picture a Promethean bard of total self-knowledge and divine powers who comes to redeem the world accompanied by Freedom, Hope, Youth, and Wisdom. But this poem is one of Tennyson's least characteristic performances, and one of his least sincere (in the sense of Ezra Pound's dictum that technique is the test of sincerity).[4] The poem that follows it in the *Poems, Chiefly Lyrical* of 1830, the very Keatsian 'The Poet's Mind,' is a better and a much more characteristic piece of verse, containing the germ of both 'The Hesperides' and 'The Lady of Shalott.' Here the poet is not active but passive, not omnipotent but threatened, defensive, fey. The poem develops an extended image of the poet's mind as 'holy ground,' a magical garden in the middle of which leaps a fountain

> Like sheet lightning,
> Ever brightening
> With a low melodious thunder.

The garden is described in incantatory rhythms which make the poem's recitation a charm to keep at bay the 'dark-browed sophist' (a rationalist, a keen Discoverer) with death in his eye and frost in his breath. "Philosophy" (rational thought), which in Keats' *Lamia* is said to conquer all mysteries by rule and line, empty the haunted air and unweave the rainbow, threatens in Tennyson's poem to kill the merry bird chanting in the heart of the garden of poetry and to 'shrink to the earth' the leaping fountain of imaginative activity.

Mention of Keats reminds one that Tennyson's generation was not the first to feel the weight of the considerations analysed from an anti-poetical viewpoint by Peacock and Macaulay. In 'The Fall of Hyperion,' for instance, Keats had tried desperately to win through to a conception of the poet as neither a fanatic nor a savage but 'a sage; / A humanist, physician to all men'; and in 'Resolution and Independence' Wordsworth had anticipated Macaulay's description of the modern poet as 'a lisping man or a modern ruin' in his melancholy reflection that

> We Poets in our youth begin in gladness;
> But thereof come in the end despondency and madness.

Such similarities can be over-emphasized, however, for the first of Wordsworth's famous lines on the fate of poets points up a significant difference between Tennyson's poetic development and that of Wordsworth and Keats: in Tennyson, there is no time of youthful gladness antedating despondency and madness. In what became the prospectus to *The Excursion*, the young Wordsworth had described his own mind (and the mind of man) as 'My haunt, and the main region of my song'; the 'fear and awe' which attended this probing of self were for him essentially wholesome and ennobling. The self-consciousness of the young Tennyson on the other hand was just as essentially morbid and sometimes horrifying. Similarly, in the famous 'simile of human life' in his May 1818 letter to Reynolds, Keats had imaged the time of youthful gladness as 'the Chamber of Maiden-Thought,' the intoxications of which made him think of 'delaying there for ever in delight,' until the chamber began to darken and its many doors, 'all leading to dark passages,' were set open.[5] This simile has been cited in an excellent discussion of the 'essentially Romantic basis' of Tennyson's development,[6] but its appositeness is limited by the undeniable fact that there is no 'Chamber of Maiden-Thought' period in Tennyson; 'dark passages' were the first rooms he entered as a poet.

Tennyson's contributions to the 1827 *Poems by Two Brothers*, which were written between his sixteenth and eighteenth years, are full of catastrophic occurrences, Byronic gloom, and a Poe-like fascination with death. In 'Memory,' 'Remorse,' 'The Outcast,' and 'I wander in darkness and sorrow,' the adolescent Tennyson uses the mask of age (as Paden long ago explained in *Tennyson in Egypt*) to give voice to growing feelings of sinfulness, despair, guilt, and sexual repression. The subject of the highly personal 'Supposed Confessions of a Second-Rate Sensitive Mind' of 1830 (a poem to which I shall return) is extreme self-consciousness paralysed by the fear of death. The poem answers point for point to Matthew Arnold's description of dialogue-of-the-mind-with-itself poems 'in which the suffering finds no vent in action; in which a continuous state of mental distress is prolonged, unrelieved by incident, hope, or resistance; in which there is everything to be endured, nothing to be done.'[7] And the two finest short poems of the 1830 Poems, Chiefly Lyrical both encapsulate the morbid subjectivity of much of Tennyson's early verse. 'A spirit haunts the year's last hours' distils the sombre landscapes and the midnight glooms of Poems by Two Brothers into a haunting evocation of the spirit of autumnal decay and mortality moving at eventide through the Lincoln-shire countryside. And if we choose to say something of an interpretative nature about 'The Kraken,' it must be that the fabulous sea monster asleep in the depths of the abysmal sea symbolizes a primordial horror submerged in the psychic depths of the poet, 'a latency so profoundly repressed that it can break free only in death.'[8]

One explanation for the differences between the poetic starting point of Wordsworth and Keats and that of Tennyson is genetic and environmental: the 'black blood' of the Tennysons and the exacerbations of family life at Somersby during the poet's formative years. In a letter of 1834, Alfred spoke of his younger brother Septimus' 'fits of the most gloomy despondency accompanied with tears,' and of his 'blindly resigning himself to every morbid influence.' Similar traits appear in varying degrees in most of the male Tennysons: Edward Tennyson, another brother, spent the last fifty-nine years of his life in an asylum; and their father's alcoholic broodings and self-lacerated sensibilities not only contributed to his premature death but made the home life of Mrs Tennyson and her children perpetually strained and frequently intolerable. In addition there were the Calvinistic intensities of Aunt Mary Bourne, who once declared to her young nephew: 'Alfred, Alfred, when I look at you I think of the words of Holy Scripture "Depart from me ye cursed into everlasting FIRE".'[9]

While family background is an unquestionably important factor in Tenny-son's poetic make-up, it is just as certainly not the whole story; for Tennyson's poetic beginnings (and subsequent development) are not unique; they are remarkably similar to those of other early Victorian writers of Romantic sensibilities who came from very different family backgrounds. The case of Browning is instructive: his first published poem, Pauline (1833), bears the same relationship to its Romantic precursors as do Tennyson's early poems, and is reminiscent of some of these poems in its employment of various strategies designed to distract attention from the rawly personal nature of the utterance.

Pauline is a Romantic confessional poem; its subject is the development of the poet's imagination. But this growth is more like that of a cancer than like the liberating maturation described in the *Prelude*, Wordsworth's poem on the growth of a poet's mind. John Stuart Mill described the poet of *Pauline* as 'possessed with a more intense and morbid self-consciousness than I ever knew in any sane human being.'[10] The emphasis throughout the poem is on the return of the speaker's mind upon itself and on his frustration, 'baffled hopes,' and feelings of guilt caused by his failure to emulate his ideal, 'the sun-treader' Shelley:

> For I have nought in common with him – shapes
> Which followed him avoid me, and foul forms
> Seek me, which ne'er could fasten on his mind.

Pauline ends with the speaker's desperate resolve to throw off the self-consciousness that is destroying him, to 'look within no more,' and with some unconvincing gestures in the direction of religious submissiveness which recall the end of Tennyson's 'Supposed Confessions.'

The similarities between Tennyson's early poems and *Pauline* suggest that the spirit of the age had something to do with the subjects and the shapes of the early creative efforts of both poets. The point can be made in another way. Like Browning in *Pauline* (the epigraphs, the footnote, the title, the pseudo-dramatic situation), Tennyson in a number of early poems uses framing devices designed to distance the reader (and himself) from the subjective, Romantic, and more often than not morbid content of his poems. This could be explained simply in terms of adolescent hypersensitivity, failure of nerve, and the lack of adequate technical resources. But when one reflects that the very same organizational device – the imposition of a qualifying, non-Romantic frame on patently Romantic content – is the informing structural principle of two of the masterpieces of early Victorian literature, Carlyle's *Sartor Resartus* and Emily Brontë's *Wuthering Heights*, one is led to recognize that the frames and other distancing devices of Tennyson's early poems, however crude or disingenuous, are part of the complex shift in sensibility that is nothing less than the mutation of Romantic into Victorian literature.

The supersession of a Romantic age by an un-Romantic one and the fate of a poet from the former (an age of unified sensibility and community) living on into the latter (the modern age described in Hallam's essay) was to be the central concern of the major poetic work of a younger contemporary of Tennyson and Browning. It is instructive to consider Matthew Arnold's *Empedocles on Etna*, first published in 1852, because it enacts a third version of the dilemma in which

Tennyson and Browning had found themselves. Arnold had begun his poetic career in his 1849 volume, *The Strayed Reveller, and Other Poems*, by employing masks to conceal a brooding self-consciousness ('Mycerinus,' 'The Sick King in Bokhara'), by rewriting poems of Wordsworth's in a way that contrasted the optimism and the possibilities for joy in the Romantic past with the stoic pessimism and shrunken possibilities for joy in the present ('To a Gypsy Child on the Shore,' 'Resignation'), and by insisting on the labour and pain inherent in poetic vocation ('The Strayed Reveller'). In *Empedocles on Etna*, the title figure is a Romantic poet who has known past days of joy, oneness with the natural world, and efficacious ministration to his fellow man. But Empedocles has lived on into an un-Romantic and unpoetical age; a swarm of sophists now rule the schools, the 'brave, impetuous heart' has yielded to the 'subtle, contriving head' and he has grown enervated, isolated, and misanthropic, and become thought's slave and 'dead to every natural joy.' Pausanius thinks the times vex Empedocles; Callicles says that 'The sophists are no enemies of his' and that the cause of malaise is 'some root of suffering in himself / Some secret and unfollowed vein of woe.' They are both right: it is a combination of external and internal pressures that afflicts Empedocles. He insists that stoic resignation and unself-consciousness are the keys to survival in the modern world, but cannot himself live without joy or repress introspection and so destroys himself. *Empedocles on Etna* is an imaginative projection of Arnold's own dilemma as a poet; the way in which he came to avoid the fate of his protagonist was to reject self-consciousness as the subject matter of his own art (a solution announced in his preface to the 1853 edition of his poems, which explains why he has chosen not to reprint *Empedocles*) and to turn from private to public concerns (from the self to society) and from subjective modes of expression to more objective literary forms (the prose essay in particular).

In his transformation from a Romantic poet into a Victorian sage, Arnold repeated the pattern of development observable in the careers of Browning and Tennyson. After much hammering, including repeatedly unsuccessful attempts to write for the stage, Browning finally forged himself into an objective poet of a particular sort, one who emphasized 'action in character,' not 'character in action,' and went on to write the great dramatic poems of his middle years. Tennyson's mutation from a Romantic into a largely Victorian poet was as protracted as Browning's, but its stages are less clear cut, the transition less complete, and the results much more equivocal. The general drift is clear and has been often described: Tennyson tended to move from dream visions towards more realistic and contemporary subjects, from confessional utterances towards more dramatic and less overtly personal forms, and from self-expression towards philosophical and ethical discourse. In the standard shorthand, from private to public, from art to life. The internal pressures which helped to effect this mutation are not difficult to discover, for they are the subjects of some of the best known of the poems of 1830 to 1842: the burden of isolation, the need to escape the sometimes frenzied oscillation between dream visions and horrific actualities and to lessen the intensity of a self-consciousness that seemed more often than not to lead only to the brink of the abyss. The external pressures helping to shape this transformation have long been known: they are the subject of Edgar Shannon's *Tennyson and the Reviewers: A Study of his Literary Reputation and of the Influence of the Critics upon his Poetry 1827–1851*. In his concluding chapter, Shannon summarized his findings in an oversimplified but helpful fashion:

Upon his poetic theory and practice the reviewers seem to have had a far-reaching effect. Late in life [Tennyson] told Knowles that from boyhood he had always felt the 'passion of the past.' 'It is the distance,' he said, 'that charms me in the landscape, the picture and the past, and not the immediate to-day in which I move.' But the critics had frowned upon this element in his work; and in spite of this undying feeling within him, after his first two poetical ventures he continually attempted to make his poetry reflect the 'immediate to-day,' which did not appeal to him, and to prophesy of the future, which did not beckon him. He began his career by writing poetry with little trace of the era of its genesis, but by 1845 he was telling Aubrey de Vere that 'a poem should reflect the time and place.' By his own admission, originally he took more delight in the beautiful than in the good. Yet in *In Memoriam* he cast a derogatory light upon the beauty created by a poet without a conscience or an aim. With the critics harping on the necessity for didacticism, his poetry eventually became infused with moral and religious teaching to such an extent that he was almost thought of as 'a writer of philosophical treatises.'[11]

With exceptions like Arthur Hallam, who died in 1833, the early Victorians who could see a future for poetry tended to feel that it lay not in the direction of self-expression and the creation of beauty for its own sake but in that of instruction and an active grappling with the problems of the age. In his 1834 preface to *Philip Van Artevelde*, for example, Sir Henry Taylor had called on poets not to follow the example of their Romantic predecessors but to 'thread the mazes of life in all its classes and under all its circumstances, common as well as romantic, and, seeing all things, to infer and to instruct.'[12] Exactly the same views were held by a trio of gifted friends. In 1843, Alfred Domett, who had emigrated to New Zealand (of which he would later become prime minister), received a long letter from his friend Joseph Arnould, which contained an excited discussion of Tennyson's recently published *Poems* of 1842, followed by some reflections on their author:

Browning says [Tennyson] is living in seclusion in a remote watering-place, seeing no man, and having his letters directed (of all conceivable beings) to a muffin-man … If 'tis true, 'tis pity, for the very thing Tennyson most wants is more intercourse with his fellow-creatures. One grand thing gained is that he has learnt that poetry consists in thought and passion more than in mere beauty of metre or airiness of imagination, and that the commonest things, people, and situations are full of poetry to the poet. What a pity he has not the intense vigour of Robert Browning.[13]

Arnould and Domett were of course intimate friends of Browning, who by 1843 had virtually completed his metamorphosis from a subjective into an objective poet. All three regarded 'Locksley Hall,' the most contemporary and engagé of the 1842 *Poems*, as the high point of the volume.

Emphasis on 'intense vigour' reminds one that the person most influential in promulgating a post-Romantic view of the artist's role was Thomas Carlyle. What made Carlyle so persuasive, in addition to his rhetorical powers, was that his own spiritual development bore witness to the necessity for artists to move beyond the dead ends of Romantic ambition and the hell of introspection to an unself-conscious, other-regarding life of practical activity. Carlyle had described his imaginative and spiritual growth in fictional form in *Sartor Resartus*, a work that dates from the same years as *Pauline* and Tennyson's early poems and is further evidence of how unconducive to the fulfilment of Romantic ambition the spirit of the times was. As George Levine has said, *Sartor Resartus*

marks the transition from the Romantics to the Victorians because it adds one quality to the Romantic vision which had not yet become dominant – desperation. Carlyle lived through the Romantics' period of greatness (having been born in the same year as Keats) without ever having been of it, and he watched as the great Romantic ideals were shattered by history. Instead of a universe integrated by love and a nature harmonious with man, instead of the artist as legislator or hero … he found a mechanical world governed by outmoded laws, by mere respectability ('Dilettantism'), by political economies and rational systems which seemed to attempt to justify the dehumanization of man he thought he saw all about him.[14]

Sartor Resartus was not only symptomatic of the times: its description in book 2 of Teufelsdröckh's passage from the Everlasting No of Romantic self-consciousness to the Everlasting Yea attained when he ceases to look within and begins to root himself in the real world of social struggle provided a paradigm of spiritual development that was to be repeated over and over again in the lives and the literature of Victorian writers. Since Jerome Buckley's influential study of *The Victorian Temper* in 1952, it has become common to use this 'pattern of conversion' as the model for examining Tennyson's poetic development.[15] There is certainly some justification for doing so. The speaker of 'Locksley Hall,' which appealed so strongly to Browning and his friends, undergoes a Carlylean progression from a self-consciousness characterized by frustration, anger, and disillusionment to an eventual affirmation rooted in his uniting himself with the future of his race. A similar pattern has been found in *In Memoriam* (1850) and in *Maud* (1855), and when the title figure of 'The Ancient Sage' (1888) urges the hedonistic younger poet (a Housmanish version of the Romantic bard) to 'Let be thy wail and help thy fellow men' it is patent that his advice owes more to Teufelsdröckh's 'Close thy *Byron*; open thy *Goethe*' than to the Chinese philosopher Lao-tze, the poem's ostensible subject.[16]

The trouble with seeing Tennyson's poetic development, particularly from 1830 to 1842, through the prism of a 'pattern of conversion' is that some of the best and/or strongest of the poems of these years became blurred or distorted when so viewed. This prism has also tended to foster the presumption that moralizing his song was more poetically beneficial to Tennyson than continuing to wander in fancy's maze would have been, that the present and the future were more appropriate poetical subjects for him than the past, and that something that is morally, socially, or spiritually preferable is also aesthetically superior. This over-emphasis on moral, instructional, and theological concerns can also lead one to over-simplify poems in which what is being said is sometimes at odds with how it is being said, and in which there appear to be discrepancies between intention and effect that force one to choose between trusting the teller or the tale. Matters are additionally complicated because in some of his after-the-fact comments Tennyson set an influential precedent for the employment of moral or theological paraphrase in interpreting his poems. He placed analogous difficulties in the way of his commentators by revising or expanding his poems, titling them, framing them, positioning them, concluding them, and not reprinting them, in ways that sometimes suggest a desire to draw attention away form the essentially Romantic and subjective ambiance of some poems, and to load others with a weight of ethical implication they were not designed to carry.[17]

For a long time it has been a commonplace for commentators to lament the one-sidedness of Harold Nicolson's brilliant 1923 study of Tennyson. Certainly one can agree that Nicolson went to an extreme in lowering the Victorian Tennyson so as to raise the 'morbid and unhappy mystic' of the early years who 'was afraid of death, and Sex, and God [and] endeavoured instinctively to sublimate his terrors by enunciating the beliefs which he desired to feel, by dwelling upon the solutions by which he would like to be convinced' and who, had he lived a generation earlier, would have been a great Romantic poet.[18] Today, however, the situation has become reversed, and it is the Victorian Tennyson, the moralist and seeker after religious faith, who has thrown into the shadow the morbid and unhappy Romantic of the early years who, as Douglas Bush put it, 'had consummate powers of expression and not very much, except as an emotional poet, to say.'[19]

Given the internal and external pressures on the early Tennyson, it is not surprising to find that the poems he published between 1830 and 1842, his major creative period (most of the *In Memoriam* lyrics also date from these years) are sometimes ambiguous, sometimes imperfectly resolved, sometimes contradicted by other poems, sometimes self-contradictory, and sometimes elliptical or parabolic. They are products of a baffled Romantic temperament on the verge of an inner abyss, and either are not susceptible to moral interpretation and theological inference or can be so considered only by ignoring what is most imaginatively exciting and vital in them. In the following account of a number of these poems I hope to point up some of the distinctive excellences of their obsessive themes: the depiction of self-conscious and unhealthily isolated states of mind (usually characterized by sexual or artistic frustration); the exploration of the nature of creative activity and of the costs of artistic vocation; the fear of death that freezes the heart; the longing for death that warms it; and the ambiguous attractions of a naturalistic vision of human existence.

II

'Mariana' (1830) and 'Mariana in the South' (1832; revised 1842) are both accomplished poems that can stand alone; but when considered in the light of the other each gains in richness of implication. The specific subject of both poems is morbid self-consciousness caused by isolation and sexual frustration. Their generic subject is loss, the yearning for what is past and gone. The broken sheds at the beginning of 'Mariana' are 'sad and strange' for the same reason that 'the earliest pipe of half-awakened birds' is 'sad and strange' to the dying man in 'Tears, Idle Tears'; both are charged with the mysterious power of absence: 'So sad, so strange, the days that are no more.' The southern Mariana dreams at noon of the mountain grass, breezes, and runlets of her native glen; but she wakes to the stillness, desiccation, and flatness of the present. Later her reading of old letters from her absent lover conjures up an apparition from the past, but it seems only clinically interested in her plight. Similarly, the old faces, footsteps, and voices that the northern Mariana hears and sees only serve to intensify her isolation from the past and suggest incipient derangement.

Thomas Carlyle said of the earlier poem that 'If Alfred Tennyson could only make that long wail, like the winter wind, about Mariana in the Moated Grange, and could not get her to throw herself into the ditch, or could not bring her another man to help her ennui, he had much better have left her alone altogether.'[20] The prescriptive part of this remark illustrates something of Carlyle's anti-Romantic assumptions concerning the proper subject matter of poetry and helps to place 'Mariana' in its historical context. The descriptive part is of course quite accurate; it is of the essence of 'Mariana' that nothing happens. The poem explores a static situation: the emotional withering and psychological deterioration caused by living 'without hope of change.'

Tennyson depicts Mariana's psychological condition through description of her external surroundings; the poem is among the purest examples in Tennyson's canon of what Hallam identified as one of the five 'distinctive excellencies' of his friend's poetic manner: 'his vivid, picturesque delineation of objects, and the peculiar skill with which he holds all of them *fused* ... in a medium of strong emotion';[21] and of what John Stuart Mill described as Tennyson's 'power of *creating* scenery, in keeping with some state of human feeling; so fitted to it as to be the embodied symbol of it, and to summon up the state of feeling itself, with a force not to be surpassed by anything but reality.'[22] The power of 'Mariana' lies in the skill with which Tennyson has suggested the phenomenological congruence between its subject and her surroundings – the dark fen, glooming flats and rounding grey, the lone poplar, the dilapidated farmyard, and the mouldering 'dreamy' house which are the sum total of Mariana's experiential reality. Over and over again in her refrain she reads her own condition in the world outside her; her sad equation is that 'The day is dreary,' 'The night is dreary,' 'My life is dreary': 'I would that I were dead.' The sluice with blackened waters, the blackest moss thickly crusted on the flower pots, the rusted nails, broken sheds, spent thatch, and the mouse shrieking behind the wainscot are all reflections of Mariana's stagnant, diseased consciousness, just as the single poplar standing alone above 'the level waste' is an emblem of her isolation.

Mariana hears as much as she sees: the creaking hinges, clinking latch, ticking clock, wind's rustle, night fowl's crow, cock's cry, oxen's low, sparrow's chirrup. But none of these everyday natural and domestic sounds has any wholesome associations for her, nor do they suggest the continuity of past and present. In *The Mill on the Floss*, even the broken Mr Tulliver had his exacerbations assuaged by familiar sounds: for 'All long-known objects, even a mere window fastening or a particular door-latch, have sounds which are a sort of recognized voice to us – a voice that will thrill and awaken, when it has been used to touch deep-lying fibres.'[23] But Mariana's morbid self-absorption is so intense that she has no ear for the sustaining aural particulars of her existence;

she hears only disconnected sounds, unnaturally amplified by her isolation, which finally 'confound her sense.'

The only movement in 'Mariana' is the cycle of the day which in the poem's most poignant moment (the only time Mariana is touched by anything outside herself) brings the shadow of the poplar 'upon her bed, across her brow.' The two times when the natural cycle of diurnal change is most noticeable are evening and dawn, and it is telling that these are the times of day that Mariana cannot abide. Evening and dawn are of enormous importance in Tennyson's poetry because they are charged with special consoling, liberating, and revelatory possibilities; they are the times when vision, insight, union, or release is most likely to occur. In the context of Tennyson's poetry, then, the most chilling indication of the terminal nature of Mariana's disease of self is that 'She could not look on the sweet heaven, / Either at morn or eventide' and that she most loathed the hour 'when the day was sloping toward his western bower.' Hardy's Tess, another isolated female, was able to allay her sorrow and isolation because 'She knew how to hit to a hair's-breadth that moment of evening when the light and the darkness are so evenly balanced that the constraint of day and the suspense of night neutralize each other, leaving absolute mental liberty.'[24] But Mariana can no more open herself to the liberating possibilities of union with the natural world than she can be moved by quotidian sounds. Like Arnold's Empedocles (or Melville's Ahab) she can see in what is outside her only reflections of her own inner deadness and isolation. If, remembering Carlyle's complaint, one imagines what would have happened if Tennyson had brought to Mariana 'another man to help her ennui,' the one thing that seems certain is that he would not have stayed long.

There is nothing intrinsic to the account of Mariana in the moated grange to relieve the grimness of her condition. Nor does Tennyson allow himself to move outside Mariana's point of view and suggest a larger context in which to place her tragedy. This is the major difference between 'Mariana' and Wordsworth's tale of Margaret in book 1 of the The Excursion (in earlier versions called 'The Ruined Cottage'), to which Tennyson's poem has often been compared. Wordsworth's narrator insists that the bleak facts of Margaret's irremissive silent suffering have 'a power to viture friendly,' blesses Margaret in 'the impotence of grief,' thereby illustrating the 'secret spirit of humanity,' and points up the powerful consolation of the 'calm oblivious tendencies / Of nature.' Tennyson's poem has for commentary only Mariana's repeated 'I would that I were dead.' If there is any consolation in 'Mariana,' any mitigation of her plight, it is the implied consolation of art, the aesthetic clarification implicit in the creation of a work of beauty with which, as Hallam insisted, the mind of the artist during creation had to be predominantly occupied.

'Mariana in the South' does not invite the same kind of aesthetic comment, partly because it is not so finely wrought a poem as 'Mariana,' but mainly because it contains within itself a powerful consolation. Hallam explained in a letter to a friend that 'Mariana in the South' expresses the 'desolate loneliness [and] forlorn feeling [of 'Mariana'] as it would exist under the influence of different impressions of sense.'[25] The scenery is not Lincolnshire but southern France, and it was perhaps the Mediterranean setting that made Tennyson feel free to play up the erotic longing of his second Mariana, whose utterance is more explicitly a sexual lament: 'And "Ah," she said, "but I wake alone."' 'Mariana in the South' has the same congruence of subject and setting as does 'Mariana,' but the poem is not so restricted to the heroine's point of view; as Carol Christ has noted, 'By giving a clear sense of the area's geography and of open space extending to the horizon, the poem creates a feeling of objectivity and freedom of movement totally lacking in the earlier poem.'[26] In addition, attention is less exclusively focused on the landscape; there is more sense of a background story; and more happens in the poem, especially at its conclusion when the southern Mariana shows herself more open to the liberating possibilities of evening than her northern namesake.

The cycle of the day is also more emphasized in 'Mariana in the South' than in 'Mariana.' The poem begins with the rising of the sun, the cause of the black shadow at the feet of the house mentioned in the opening line; it ends with the end of the day, the black shadow by then having rounded to the east as the sun moves westward. The descriptive touchstone in the poem is the absence of water. The opening stanza emphasizes the dryness and aridity of the landscape: the brooding heat, dusty vines, empty riverbed, and glaring sand. In the second stanza Mariana is seen to be as drought-stricken as her surroundings, for her eyes are 'The home of woe without a tear.' As the crimson of dawn changes to the deep orange of full morning, the day increases 'from heat to heat, / On stony drought and steaming salt,' while the metaphoric qualities of Mariana's 'streaming hair' and the 'liquid mirror' indirectly remind one of the actual absence of water. At noon Mariana sleeps. She dreams especially of water, the 'runlets babbling down the glen'; she wakes to the present reality:

>   the babble of the stream
> Fell, and, without, the steady glare
> Shrank one sick willow sere and small.
>   The river-bed was dusty-white;
>   And all the furnace of the light
> Struck up against the blinding wall.

Her afternoon lament is 'More inward than at night or morn': that is, more repressed and stifled, and Mariana is now led to take out and reread some old letters of her betrayer, presumably for the same reason that Tennyson rereads some of Hallam's letters at the beginning of the climactic ninety-fifth section of *In Memoriam*: in the attempt to create a consoling present image of the lost beloved. (The stanzas about the letters were not in the 1832 text of 'Mariana in the South,' which predates Hallam's death in 1833.) But neither of the 'images' evoked by reading the letters assuages Mariana; and at the end of the poem's penultimate stanza she is still as desolate as she has been throughout.

In the last stanza the day ends and evening comes. A 'dry cicala' begins to sing, but then water unexpectedly, almost apocalyptically, enters the poem. Mariana hears 'a sound as of the sea,' opens her lattice-blind to look out at the arriving night – something her northern counterpart could not bring herself to do – and begins to cry:

> There all in spaces rosy-bright
>   Large Hesper glittered on her tears,
>   And deepening through the silent spheres
> Heaven over Heaven rose the night.

As the 'ancient poetess [Sappho] singeth,' according to Tennyson in his 1830 'Leonine Elegiacs,' 'Hesperus all good things bringeth / Smoothing the wearied mind.'

What precisely has Hesperus brought to Mariana? What is the cause of her emotional release? If one were speaking of the 1832 text of 'Mariana in the South' the answer would be supernatural grace, for there it is said that 'on her soul' Hesperus 'poured divine solace,' a religious consolation prepared for by Mariana's repeated supplications to the Madonna and by the devotional ambiance of the poem's second stanza. But if one is speaking of the 1842 version (a much finer poem), the answer is that Hesper, the star of evening, has brought a powerful natural consolation, similar in kind to what happens to Tennyson himself in section xcv of *In Memoriam*. If only momentarily, Mariana has moved from anguished isolation to a sense of harmony and reciprocity with the external world; in looking at the vastness of the night sky she is moved outside of herself and listens for a moment to what the Angel in 'Timbuctoo' called 'The lordly music flowing from / The illimitable years.'

While the evening does bring a temporary emotional release, however, there is no suggestion in 'Mariana in the South' that the moment is the harbinger of a lasting mitigation of her isolated self-consciousness. But Mariana's last words (the closing lines of the poem) do suggest that her evening insight has left her with one hope which cannot prove false to her:

> And weeping then she made her moan,
> 'The night comes on that knows not morn,
> When I shall cease to be all alone,
> To live forgotten, and love forlorn.'

In the first Mariana poem, it was an indication of the heroine's diseased state of mind that she had repeatedly longed for death: the southern Mariana, while repeatedly lamenting being forgotten and left forlorn, had never wished for extinction. But at the end of her poem the evening congruence of subject and object, of self and natural world, reminds Mariana that just as in the natural world day ends in night so in her human cycle life will end in death, the 'night that knows not morn,' which can be the only lasting cure for her loss.

Death is also the only lasting cure for the best known of the early Tennyson's isolated maidens. While 'The Lady of Shalott' resembles the Mariana poems in obvious ways, it differs from them, as do 'The Hesperides' and 'The Palace of Art,' in its explicitly aesthetic concerns: with the conditions under which artistic creation becomes possible and with the relationship between the artist's work and his life. One of Tennyson's finest poems, 'The Lady of Shalott' is a simple ballad-like narrative possessing enormous suggestiveness and resonance. Complex processes are distilled into a concentrated parable. In some ways the poem 'The Lady of Shalott' most resembles is Keats' 'La Belle Dame sans Merci,' another elliptical fable which is simultaneously about the erotic life and the poetic life. Both poems have the same movement: the transition from life to some form of death, the passage from a sparkling springtime world to a cold autumnal world of dissolution; both are rich in implication but resistant to conceptualization; both demand interpretation while denying the reader the wherewithal for more than reductive paraphrases.

Some descriptive generalizations may nevertheless be made. 'The Lady of Shalott' is about the relationship of the artist to his art and to what is external to his art, and about the relationship of the artistic impulse to other impulses. The poem suggests that creative gifts are necessarily isolating, and that creative fulfilment entails the non-fulfilment of other human desires. This is of course a common theme in the work of nineteenth- and twentieth-century artists in the Romantic tradition. It appears in Keats and Swinburne, is the subject of Arnold's 'The Strayed Reveller,' figures in Wilde's *The Picture of Dorian Gray*, in Thomas Mann, and is ubiquitous in Yeats, one of whose poems begins: 'The intellect of man is forced to choose / Perfection of the life, or of the work.' Because of their changelessness, self-sufficiency, and wholeness, and because of their distance from the quotidian affairs of men, works of art may be said to exist in a timeless, immutable realm. Their creators, however, necessarily exist in the world of time and change. Among men it is artists who can respond most fully to the timeless perfection of art and most sharply experience a vicarious sense of mortal abolition. But at the same time artists are the ones whose energies are drained by the solitude and labour of their calling and who feel most sharply art's beautiful disdain for mortals, its passionless perfection – 'Cold pastoral' as Keats complains of his Grecian urn.

Complex questions such as these concerning the ambiguous blessings of creative vocation are the subject of 'The Lady of Shalott.' The poem is not reducible to either/or schemata like art versus life, private versus public, palace of art versus cottage in the vale. The poem's concerns are psychological, not moral; it deals with the inevitable, not the volitional, with what is fated, not what is chosen. It does not analyse a problem, it adumbrates a process, a passage from one state of being to another – from spring to fall, innocence to experience, gladness to despondency, life to death – which the Lady of Shalott is powerless to change. There is nothing judgmental about her 'curse': it is simply that she is mortal; her art may be timeless but she is not; she must participate in life and consequently in death. The most revealing stanza in the poem, the last in section 2, puts her dilemma succinctly:

> But in her web she still delights
> To weave the mirror's magic sights,
> For often through the silent nights
> A funeral, with plumes and lights
>   And music, went to Camelot:
> Or when the moon was overhead,
> Came two young lovers lately wed;
> 'I am half sick of shadows,' said
>   The Lady of Shalott.

Though 'She hath no loyal knight and true' (as the previous stanza had said) the Lady nevertheless 'delights' in her separation from life because it is also a separation from the process of life and death: for down there in the world are the funerals which pass under her window on silent nights. But quarantine from mortality also entails an emotional isolation, a separation from the human world of love, of 'the two young lovers lately wed.' It is seeing these lovers that makes her 'half sick of shadows'; that is, frustrated with seeing only the distant reflections of life through a mirror whose primary function is instrumental to her art.*

The reader is thus prepared for the Lady's frenzied response to the dazzling apparition of Lancelot in the poem's next section, which rends her web, cracks her mirror, and brings upon her the curse. Four-fifths of this section is devoted to a description of Lancelot, who symbolizes everything from which the Lady is separated by her calling. He is the epitome of all those on the road to Camelot glimpsed by the Lady from the window. He rides into the poem in the midday sunlight of a cloudless day, embodying the splendour of the natural world at its most vibrant and vigorous, just as the glitter of his gemmy bridle (like 'a branch of stars ... in the golden galaxy') suggests the awesomeness of the phenomenal world at its most transcendent. But what Lancelot most insistently represents is human love, idealized in the depiction on his shield of a red-cross knight kneeling to a lady, but elsewhere presented erotically: in the 'Tirra lirra' of Lancelot's song, which recalls Autolycus' randy paean to spring and summer in *The Winter's Tale*; in the 'bearded meteor, trailing light' through the dark heavens, which reminds one less of the star-like gems of the bridle than of the silent meteor that leaves a shining furrow in Tennyson's most radiantly erotic poem, 'Now sleeps the crimson petal'; and finally, in the splendid Swinburnean image of sexual union, 'The helmet and the helmet-feather / Burned like one burning flame together,' the only aspect of Lancelot's appearance which the Lady is explicitly said to see when she activates the curse by looking down to earth.[27]

In the fourth and last section, the Lady of Shalott comes down from her tower into the world of life, love, and death. At the beginning of the poem the reader had been introduced to the poem's landscape from the viewpoint of the tower. From that distanced perspective the spring fields, river, sky, and road had appeared ordered and harmonious. In Arnoldian terms, the Lady had seen as the gods see, not deeply but widely. At the beginning of section 4, the Lady enters directly into what is now an autumnal landscape of disorder and dissolution. The little breezes of the first section that dusk and shiver and tease the waves 'for ever' have become the stormy east-wind causing the leaves, which do not last forever, to fall around the Lady as she lies down in the boat to die. She no

---

* The purpose of the mirror is to allow the weaver to see the pattern of her tapestry from the right side. There is no reason to assume, as most commentators do, that the Lady's art is 'mimetic,' i.e. that it merely reflects or copies the outside world as seen through the mirror. The 'magic web with colours gay' is an emblem of the imagination rather than the fancy, and is no more representational of external reality than the fountain in 'The Poet's Mind,' the sisters' song in 'The Hesperides,' or the Lady's other imaginative productions, her two expressive songs.

longer sees the natural world from a distance: she has become part of its processes, the colours of her spirit merged with nature's colours, her waning and complaint that of the woods and water:

In the stormy east-wind straining,
The pale yellow woods were waning,
The broad stream in his banks complaining.
Heavily the low sky raining.

The congruence of self and nature suggests that the Lady's frequently over-interpreted 'last song' – sung at 'the closing of the day,' the time of release, the climactic moment – is simply a lament for the death of nature and of self.[28] It does not 'echo cheerly' or seem a 'fairy' utterance, as did her song in the first section, because it is sung by one who has begun to live only by beginning to die, who knows life and love only through their absence. The death song may be thought as poignant and moving as the stanzas of 'The Lady of Shalott' that describe the song and its singer's first and last journey – they and the whole poem being, like the Lady's dead body robed in snowy white, 'A gleaming shape' of haunting strangeness that remains incandescently in the memory of the reader.

'The Hesperides' is another 1832 poem on the subject of the creative imagination and its workings. In the best account of the poem, G. Robert Stange describes it as 'an interpretation of the spiritual conditions under which the poetic experience comes to life.' The epigraph to the poem – 'Hesperus and his daughters three, / That sing about the golden tree' – is from the closing speech of Milton's *Comus* in which the Attendant Spirit describes his celestial home. According to Stange, the chief resemblance between Tennyson's Hesperides and Milton's 'is in the parallel conception of the gardens as a restful abode for the privileged and as a source of creativity.'[29] But another point of resemblance has to do with virginity, for earlier in *Comus* the second brother had used the necessity of guarding the 'fair Hesperian tree / Laden with blooming gold' as a simile to emphasize his view that 'beauty' (his virgin sister) need 'defend her fruit' from those who would pluck it.

In its association of creativity with sexual isolation 'The Hesperides' resembles 'The Lady of Shalott.' Another point of resemblance is the emphasis on the timeless qualities of art: the song of the sisters is 'evermore … born anew' and if they fail to sing they 'shall lose eternal pleasure, / Worth eternal want of rest.' 'The Hesperides' differs from 'The Lady of Shalott,' however, not only because there is no curse but also because if there were there would seem little likelihood of its becoming operative: the garden is presented as unequivocally desirable and fully satisfying, and since the only man within sight is the silver-haired Father Hesper – the spirit of evening – there is no possibility of erotic temptation. The thirteen lines of introduction bring us only to the shore of the island; after that we have only the sisters' song. 'The Hesperides' is the magical incantation that the sisters continually chant in order to guard the tree with the golden apple that gives them the energy to chant forever. This is an image of art at its most esoteric and self-referential, and of self-consciousness at its most benignly solipsistic. There is no progress in the sisters' song and therefore none in 'The Hesperides'; there is only a single moment endlessly prolonged, the aesthetic moment in which the apple blossoms are 'evermore … born anew' as the sisters' music causes the 'liquid gold, honeysweet' sap continually to course through the sacred tree.

In the same way the natural setting and time of day are changeless. The Hesperides is an evening world of the west and the sisters repeatedly insist that this is the only time and place in which their art can exist. The apple of gold is 'sunset-ripened' and it is

> the western sun and the western star
> And the low west wind, breathing afar,
> The end of day and beginning of night
> Make the apple holy and bright.

While 'All good things are in the west,' all things inimical to poetry are in the east, the place of transience and strife, where 'Kingdoms lapse, and climates change, and races die' and the world is 'wasted with fire and sword.' 'The Hesperides' is Tennyson's most extreme statement of the aesthetic position espoused by Hallam in defending Tennyson's 1830 poems: that poetry of sensation is superior to poetry of reflection, that the 'delicate sense of fitness, which grows with the growth of artist feelings … is weakened by every indulgence of heterogeneous aspirations,' and that false art results whenever during periods of creation the desire of beauty is not, for Hallam the 'predominant motive,' for the sisters the exclusive motive.

Subsequent embarrassment over the presence in his canon of an extreme art-for-art's-sake position must have been a factor in Tennyson's choosing never to reprint this superbly evocative poem. The suppression is all the more regrettable because it was unnecessary. For while 'The Hesperides' is undoubtedly an accomplished poem it does not carry much conviction. In the poem's introductory lines the voices of the sisters sounded to Hanno like 'the voices in a dream,' and there is a recessive but abiding sense throughout that the sisters' song is wish-fulfilling fantasy, the depiction of an impossible place. And one senses in the song intimations that the days of the golden apple tree, or at least of the sisters' exclusive proprietorship of it, are numbered. One also senses that the sisters are a little sated, like their dragon whose 'ancient heart is drunk with overwatchings night and day,' a little weary, perhaps even a little bored, and that they feel they are nearing the end of something, perhaps the time when their lovely *Fable* will give way to the 'keen *Discovery*' of Hercules, or when, like Lancelot's eruption into the art world of the Lady of Shalott, 'one from the East' will bring the blinding midday sun into their afternoon world.

Finally, one notices that the fragile and listless music of the sisters' égoïsme à trois and the bliss of their 'secret smiles' are predicated on a dualistic view of human existence: their secrets cannot be told to all; 'the old wound of the world' must not be healed: in the poem's dominant symbolic contrast, 'Hesper hateth Phosphor, evening hateth morn.' As Tennyson will come to say in one of his finest lyrics, section cxxi of *In Memoriam*, Hesper and Phosphor are in fact not two distinct, opposed entities, but 'a double name / For what is one': Venus, the planet of love. To insist on their separation is to insist on the separation of the artist and his art from natural process. In shunning the change and death inimical to their lovely art the sisters necessarily shut out life and love. Despite the poem's undertones they are successful in doing so. But in another 1832 isolated-maiden poem on the subject of art and the external world something like the curse of 'The Lady of Shalott' returns.

'The Palace of Art' is nowhere near as fine a poem as the four we have just examined. One reason for this, as perusal of the 1842 revisions of the 1832 text points up, is that Tennyson is dawdling with the painted shell, indulging his technical and stylistic virtuosity in concocting and describing the palace's sumptuous objets d'art while paying insufficient attention to the structure and balance of his poem. Another reason is that despite the dawdling, heterogeneous materials have intruded themselves into the chamber/dungeon of Tennyson's maiden-thought. One example is the social concern with 'the selfish misuse of beauty by a privileged class.'[30] But the major impurity in 'The Palace of Art' is the admixture of moral and didactic concerns.

These are pointed up by Tennyson himself in the first and most influential reading of the poem. In some introductory verses addressed to his Cambridge friend R.C. Trench, Tennyson described 'The Palace of Art' as a moral exemplum, 'a sort of allegory' of 'A sinful soul possessed of many gifts ... That did love Beauty only,' to the exclusion of Good and Knowledge, and who eventually learned that one who

> shuts Love out, in turn shall be
> Shut out from Love, and on her threshold lie
> Howling in outer darkness. Not for this
> Was common clay ta'en from the common earth
> Moulded by God, and tempered with the tears
> Of angels to the perfect shape of man.

There is, to be sure, textual justification for such a sententious reading, especially the moralizing generalizations of the poem's narrator concerning what happens to his 'soul,' the female figure for whom he builds the palace of art. For example, when the Soul begins to crack up the narrator, in tones that recall the dedicatory poem, introjects this explanation:

> Lest she should fail and perish utterly,
>   God, before whom ever lie bare
> The abysmal deeps of Personality,
>   Plagued her with sore despair.

The trouble with this analysis is that it is partial and reductive, leaves too much out of account, and is misleading concerning the feel of the poem and all that happens in it. It is no more helpful than the comments of several other Christian choric figures in nineteenth-century works: the Abbot's on Manfred at the end of Byron's drama; Festus' on Paracelsus at the end of Browning's poem; Nelly Dean's on Heathcliff in *Wuthering Heights*; or Starbuck's on Ahab in *Moby-Dick*. Indeed, the statements in the dedicatory poem are so gratuitously moralizing as to suggest a post-factum attempt to supply a Victorian frame for a Romantic picture. For if 'The Palace of Art' is approached from the psychological and aesthetic point of view from which the four previous poems have necessarily been considered, it begins to look very different from the text described by Tennyson. It becomes a poem about the expansion of consciousness through the stimulus of art, and its eventual nemesis, the affliction of morbid self-consciousness caused by isolation from life.

In choosing as her home 'a lordly pleasure house / Wherein at ease for aye to dwell' the soul commits herself to an aesthetic philosophy close to that advocated later in the century by Walter Pater in his 'Conclusion' to *The Renaissance*. For Pater, success in life was 'to burn always with [a] hard, gemlike flame,' to cultivate isolated moments of sensation for their own sake and to maintain their ecstasy. This was the only way of keeping at bay the awareness of death and of salvaging something from the constantly perishing flux of life. 'We are all,' said Pater, 'under sentence of death but with a sort of indefinite reprieve';

and the soul in 'The Palace of Art' would agree that 'our one chance' to make something of our interval of life is to seek out sensations that yield the 'fruit of a quickened, multiplied consciousness,' the most potent stimulus to which is 'the poetic passion, the desire for beauty, the love of art for art's sake.'[31] To put it another way, the instinct which leads the speaker of 'The Palace of Art' to fill his soul's palace with works of art is the same that led Keats in the 'Ode to Psyche' to 'build a fane / In some untrodden region of my mind' and there dress the rosy sanctuary 'in the midst of this wide quietness' with 'all the gardener Fancy e'er could feign.'

The soul, a solitary singer like the Lady of Shalott and the sisters of 'The Hesperides,' at first delights to 'sing her songs alone' in her sanctuary and to hear them echo through her halls. She rejoices in her life and its self-communings. At evening – 'when young night divine / Crowned dying day with stars' – she claps her hands in delight at the 'Godlike isolation' that is hers and at her distance from the droves of swine outside who 'graze and wallow, breed and sleep.' And while 'the riddle of the painful earth' – the subject matter of many of her art objects – often troubles her, it does not make her repine or curdle her 'solemn mirth.' She is pleased to sit 'as God,' contemplating all but touching nothing. But unlike Keats' rosy sanctuary, Tennyson's palace of art (like the Lady of Shalott's tower) has no casement that can be opened 'To let the warm Love in.' One is surprised only by the abruptness – 'so three years / She prospered: on the fourth she fell' – of the soul's fall from expansion of consciousness in the heaven of art to egotistical self-absorption (soon souring into morbid self-consciousness) in the hell of self, as madness replaces gladness and dark passages the chamber of the soul's maiden-thought.

The most imaginatively exciting section of 'The Palace of Art' is not any of the cameo descriptions of the palace's furnishings (fine as many of these are) but the lines (217 to 288) describing the soul's breakdown. Here we are back in the world of the Mariana poems and 'The Lady of Shalott' as 'uncertain shapes' and 'phantasms' begin to impinge on a consciousness that has become 'a spot of dull stagnation,' 'A still salt pool, locked in with bars of sand.' Absence of sound intensifies the isolation: 'No voice breaks through the stillness of this world: / One deep, deep silence all.' The soul's condition is 'ever unrelieved by dismal tears'; shut up in the 'crumbling tomb' of self she yearns for the sights and sounds of the outside world; and is compared to a lost traveller finding a new land only to die in it. At last she howls aloud, 'I am on fire within.'

It is at this point – what William E. Fredeman and Christopher Ricks have taught readers of Tennyson to call the penultimate moment – that 'The Palace of Art' should have concluded, for the two-stanza coda that follows is poetically and conceptually weak, a half-hearted attempt to complete the frame of the dedicatory poem and thereby point a moral to adorn a harrowing tale of psychological affliction. In these eight lines the soul is said to leave the palace and repair to 'a cottage in the vale' to mourn and pray. As she leaves for this penitential place she asks of someone that her palace not be destroyed, on the chance that she may want to return with others when her 'guilt' is purged. The most obvious failure of the coda is quantitative. It says that the soul will be restored to health, but does not show it. Well over a hundred lines describe the palace of art, the cottage in the vale is given only one line; the soul's breakdown is rendered in seventy lines; her cure is predicted in just one. The more important failure is qualitative. The implied ease and the certainty of the cure tend to make the soul's psychological malaise seem in retrospect factitious. Her condition cannot have been that acute, one is led to think, if it could be so efficaciously purged by a stay in the country; she must have been shamming, one reflects, for if her state were really like Mariana's she could not be so easily cured, if cured at all. What has happened, one is forced to conclude, is that Tennyson has attempted to impose a simplistic moral resolution on a complex psychological exploration, to cure the hell of Romantic self-consciousness with the wand of Victorian earnestness and social commitment. The intentions may be admirable, but the base psychological metals out of which 'The Palace of Art' is made cannot be so alchemized into the gold of ethical discourse.

Like the soul in 'The Palace of Art,' the speakers of two other early Tennyson poems – the 1830 'Supposed Confessions of a Second-Rate Sensitive Mind not in Unity with Itself' (to use its original title) and the 1842 'The Two Voices' – are equally on fire within. In coming to consider these poems one moves from the extraordinary group of isolated-maiden poems to two confessional poems, dialogues of the mind with itself, in which the young Tennyson expresses himself without the mediation of female personae. Indeed, the main trouble with 'Supposed Confessions' is that Tennyson has confessed himself much too directly and unmediatedly: the poem's subject is the wild oscillations of a morbidly self-conscious youth in the grip of an overpowering imagination of disaster, whose shapeless utterance does little more than chart his frenzied vacillations.

At one point, the 'I' of the poem describes his state by saying he is 'moved from beneath by doubt and fear.' If one emphasizes the former emotion, the poem can be seen as one of the first in a long line of Victorian poems on the subject of the difficulties of religious belief in the nineteenth century, on 'How very hard it is to be / A Christian' as Browning was to put it in 'Easter-Day.' But 'Supposed Confessions' would be a more characteristically Victorian poem of doubt if the will to believe were stronger and the process of doubting more sustained. For it was only in the speaker's past, 'in my morn of youth,' that he had engaged in doubt (lines 139 to 177 recall this time), and he had done so only because of his presumption that the dice were loaded, that man's reasoning powers and his 'double nature' indicated he was made for higher things that the beasts (the lamb and the ox who merely romped, fed, and slept before being uncomprehendingly slaughtered), and that the rails of doubt led inevitably to the terminus of truth. 'It is man's privilege to doubt, 'he had said, 'If so be that from doubt at length, / Truth may stand forth unmoved of change.'

In the present time of the poem, the speaker has learned better: his doubting has become recessive; fear and horror in the face of personal extinction are now dominant. The speaker is in darkness lost, the darkness of the grave; having lost the sustaining sense of oneness with the maternal universe that he experienced as an infant on his mother's knee (lines 40 to 67), he had been unable to associate himself with other analogues of immortality. As Mark Pattison was to put it later in the century: 'Agnosticism has taken away Providence as death takes away the mother from the child and leaves us forlorn of protection and love.'[32] In the present time of the poem the speaker is in no condition to doubt; he is 'void, / Dark, formless, utterly destroyed.' To be again the trustful infant who knows nothing but his mother's eyes, who 'hath no thought of coming woes [and] no care of life or death' (the very condition of the lamb and ox he had earlier contemptuously dismissed) now appears most attractive.

So does the Christian community of believers, a world of peace and confidence, trust and 'hope till all things should cease, / And then one Heaven receive us all.' But in one of the poem's most striking moments, as the speaker re-creates in his fancy the soothing ambiance of supernatural belief, his idealizings are undercut from within, as what he is saying is simultaneously contradicted by how it is being said:

> How sweet to have a common faith!
> To hold a common scorn of death!
> And at a burial to hear
> The creaking cords which wound and eat
> Into my human heart, whene'er
> Earth goes to earth, with grief, not fear,
> With hopeful grief, were passing sweet!

The speaker begins by picturing in his mind an interment ceremony made 'sweet' and hopeful by shared belief in salvation. But in the very act of calling up this comforting image of what it would be like if … , his imagination is gripped by what is, the auditory particular of the creaking ropes lowering the coffin into the grave, the sound of which travels out from the concoctions of his head to lacerate his heart and emotions with the insistence that earth goes to earth and there is no beyond.

At the end of 'Supposed Confessions,' as at the end of *Pauline*, the speaker attempts to conclude on a positive, hopeful note by attempting to look no more within and by assuming the traditional Christian posture of submissiveness to the will of a benevolent God. But what he attempts notionally to assert is once again smothered by psychological and emotional realities; his imagination is again fixated by the grave as the hope of a divine Love yields to the reality of being beastly dead:

> Let Thy dove
> Shadow me over, and my sins
> Be unremembered, and Thy love
> Enlighten me. O teach me yet
> Somewhat before the heavy clod
> Weighs on me, and the busy fret
> Of that sharp-headed worm begins
> In the gross blackness underneath.

After this, the speaker abandons the attempt to end his poem; he stops with exhausted apostrophes to weary life, weary death, his desolate spirit and heart, and his 'damnèd vacillating state.'

After its first publication in 1830, Tennyson did not allow 'Supposed Confessions' to appear in print again for over fifty years. Just as the mature Browning felt 'extreme repugnance' for *Pauline*,[33] so Tennyson seems to have suppressed his early poem not only because of its technical and rhetorical immaturity, but also because of its radically subjective content. Yet for all its manifest imperfections and excesses, 'Supposed Confessions' is an intermittently powerful ramble of a poem. And for all its adolescent angst, it is certainly interesting and hardly deserving of its demeaning title, which seems designed to dissociate Tennyson from its rawly personal content. Arthur Hallam was not fooled by the title, however; understanding that modern poetry was necessarily characterized by 'the return of the mind upon itself,' he described the speaker's state as 'rather the clouded season of a strong mind, than the habitual condition of one feeble and "second-rate"' and thought the poem an inevitable product of its time, 'full of deep insight into human nature, and into those particular trials, which are sure to beset men who think and feel for themselves at this epoch of social development.'[34]

'The Two Voices' is a greatly more accomplished poem than 'Supposed

Confessions.' The random cogitations and repetitions of the earlier poem are structured and ordered by casting the later poem in the form of a debate between the two poles of the speaker's consciousness – a perplexed 'I' of idealizing tendencies, whose totem might be the supernal dove, and an alter ego, the 'still, small voice' prompting to suicide, a relentless de-idealizer whom we may associate with the 'sharp-headed worm.' And instead of the sprawling, irregularly rhyming tetrameters of the earlier poem, 'The Two Voices' is written in short, usually syntactically self-contained rhyming triplets, a rigorous, technically demanding form that encourages brevity, clarity and sharply etched images, and is excellently suited to the pro-contra thrust of the speaker's debate with himself.

In the body of the poem – its first 402 lines – the 'still small voice' urging suicide ('Why inch by inch to darkness crawl? / There is one remedy for all') over and over again seems on the verge of winning the debate. But in the much-lamented conclusion to 'The Two Voices' the demon of self-consciousness gives way to the Sabbath dawn, the tableau of the family on its way to church, and the piping up of a second voice urging the speaker to 'Be of better cheer.' Like the ending of 'The Palace of Art,' that of 'The Two Voices' is unrooted in what precedes it in a way that again suggests an eleventh-hour attempt on Tennyson's part to graft a happy ending with an uplifting moral on to a work of psychological exploration, an inference supported by the information that Tennyson's working title for the poem was 'Thoughts of a Suicide' and that its closing sections were added some time after most of the poem had been composed.

In the first 400 lines of 'The Two Voices' the urbane and always self-possessed first voice, a master ironist, repeatedly brings the speaker back from his sublimating fantasies and melioristic scenarios to the mortal world in which he lives and to the psychological données that wring tears from his eyes. In the poem's opening stanzas, when the 'I' argues that he should not take his own life because it would be to 'cast in endless shade / What is so wonderfully made,' the voice makes his first devastating rejoinder: he describes the wonderfully made dragonfly moving through the natural world like 'A flash of living light,' and allows the 'I' to make for himself the under-side of this connection: that, in the words of the fiftieth section of *In Memoriam*, men are like 'the flies of latter spring, / That lay their eggs, and sting and sing / And weave their petty cells and die.' This pattern of the voice's cool appeals to the observable answering the speaker's overheated theories is repeated again and again as the poem develops. The speaker desperately tries on a number of garments of Victorian cut designed to cover his existential nakedness: he argues, as Mill does in the fifth chapter of his *Autobiography*, that man can find meaning in life by devoting himself to a goal external to himself: 'In some good cause, not in mine own, / To perish'; like Arnold in 'Rugby Chapel,' he imagines the few who 'rowing hard against the stream' have in spite of great odds achieved calm; like Browning's Childe Roland he tries to raise 'One hope that warmed me in the days / While still I yearned for human praise'; and when he speaks of 'that heat of inward evidence / By which [man] doubts against the sense' we are reminded of the influence of Coleridge's religious writings on the Cambridge Apostles.

Over and over again the voice strips away these garments, forcing the speaker to confront without illusions the nature of his present state. And when the speaker laments:

> For I go, weak from suffering here:
> Naked I go, and void of cheer;
> What is it that I may not fear?

the voice replies with characteristic indirection, painting a superbly chilling picture of the one thing the speaker need not fear:

> 'Consider well,' the voice replied,
> 'His face, that two hours since hath died;
> Wilt thou find passion, pain or pride?
>
> Will he obey when one commands?
> Or answer should one press his hands?
> He answers not, nor understands.
>
> His palms are folded on his breast:
> There is no other thing expressed
> But long disquiet merged in rest.
>
> His lips are very mild and meek:
> Though one should smite him on the cheek,
> And on the mouth, he will not speak.
>
> ...
>
> He will not hear the north-wind rave,
> Nor, moaning, household shelter crave
> From winter rains that beat his grave.

> High up the vapours fold and swim:
> About him broods the twilight dim:
> The place he knew forgetteth him.'

At the climax of their dialogue the 'I' is at his most desperately impassioned, and his most sympathetic, when he speaks with pathetic vagueness of the 'something' out there or inside him, in his future or his past, which quickens his will to live:

> Moreover, something is or seems,
> That touches me with mystic gleams,
> Like glimpses of forgotten dreams –
>
> Of something felt, like something here;
> Of something done, I know what where;
> Such as no language may declare.

In reply, the voice is at its most flippantly cruel in once again recalling the speaker to the present:

> The still voice laughed. 'I talk' said he,
> 'Not with thy dreams. Suffice it thee
> Thy pain is a reality.'

And when the 'I' wretchedly cries out for more life and a fuller consciousness –

> 'Tis life, whereof our nerves are scant,
> Oh life, not death, for which we pant;
> More life, and fuller, that I want –

the voice speaks his ironic last, saying 'in quiet scorn / "Behold, it is the Sabbath morn".'

If it had ended at this precarious moment of balance, the penultimate moment, with the speaker's *aviditas vitae*, his agonized longing for something other than death, dominated but not yet totally suffocated by the suave reductiveness of the gentlemanly prince of darkness, 'The Two Voices' would have been a poetically complete and aesthetically satisfying poem. It would also have been a poem answering perfectly to Arnold's description of the poetry of Romantic self-consciousness 'in which everything is to be endured, nothing is to be done' and from which nothing to inspirit the reader or make him rejoice can be derived. 'The Two Voices' does not end at this point, however. It is followed by the sentimental optimism of the concluding section, which begins with the speaker hearing 'the sweet church bells [begin] to peal' and from his window watching a family on their way to 'God's house':

> One walked between his wife and child,
> With measured footfall firm and mild,
> And now and then he gravely smiled.
>
> The prudent partner of his blood
> Leaned on him, faithful, gentle, good,
> Wearing the rose of womanhood.
>
> And in their double love secure,
> The little maiden walked demure,
> Pacing with downward eyelids pure.
>
> These three made unity so sweet,
> My frozen heart began to beat,
> Remembering its ancient heat.

The first thing to say about this passage is simply that it is an example of Tennyson's occasional lapses in taste and decorum, like the similar attempts in *In Memoriam* (especially its epilogue) to poeticize domestic incidents and occasions. A more fundamental difficulty is that this image of matrimonial propriety is redolent of the moral platitudes and sentimental conventions of Victorian middle-class life and art.[35] One understands that at the end of this poem Tennyson wants an emblem of unself-consciousness, love, and purpose to counter the abyss of fruitless introspection, self-absorption, and over-intellectualizing. Such contrasts are found everywhere in nineteenth-century literature: the leech gatherer and brooding poet in 'Resolution and Independence'; the 'village churl' in *Empedocles on Etna* who 'feels the truth more than' Pausanias; the 'burly lovers on the village green,' of whom the tormented speaker of Meredith's *Modern Love* says: 'Yours is a lower, and a happier star!'; the common people carrying their daily burdens whom Dorothea Brooke sees from her window at dawn at the end of chapter 80 of *Middlemarch*; the peasant whose chance words change the course of Levin's life at the end of *Anna Karenina*. It is noteworthy that in each of these examples the representatives of endurance and unself-consciousness are simple rooted country people of immemorial callings and habits of thought and feeling. They are, if you will, pastoral types. In Tennyson's poetry, however, as *The Times'* reviewer of *In Memoriam* was among the first to note,[36] the traditional values of the pastoral tend to be assumed by the domestic. While this displacement does contribute to the distinctive felicities of a number of Tennyson's poems, the results are elsewhere much more equivocal. In the case of 'The Two Voices' the displacement is clearly unfortunate, for instead of an immemorial image of unself-consciousness and endurance like the 'hind' ploughing his allotted field in King Arthur's great speech at the end of *The Holy Grail* idyll, we have instead the angel-in-the-house iconography of the Victorian middle-class family.

After the family has passed by, 'a second voice' appears at the speaker's ear urging him to 'Be of better cheer.' One cannot really complain that the second voice is unprepared for or a deus ex machina; it is simply the naturally idealizing voice of the speaker pitched in a more effusively positive key now that the still small voice of the night has departed. But one can complain that the hidden hope of which it vaguely speaks, and its claim to 'see the end, and know the good,' are gratuitous, unconvincing because psychologically ungrounded in what has gone before, and as insubstantially rendered as the cottage in the vale in 'The Palace of Art.'

But the ending of 'The Two Voices' is not only unearned and ungrounded in the body of the poem; its most unfortunate feature is that, like the end of 'The Palace of Art,' it tends to make retrospectively factitious what has preceded it. In the conclusion the speaker blesses the church-going family as they pass by his window in a way that makes it hard not to recall the moment of release for Coleridge's Ancient Mariner, when 'unaware' he blesses the water snakes.[37] But it is the difference between the two moments, not their similarities, that is most suggestive: the difference between accepting into consciousness what had formerly seemed hostile and repellent, and assenting to a saccharine conception of human existence made no less didactically offensive for its being presented first iconographically and then vaguely. The difference between the moment of blessing in 'The Ancient Mariner' and that in 'The Two Voices' is the difference between the void growing luminous and the void being made to disappear by the magic wand of sentimentality. We have only to imagine the withering scrutiny that the first voice (had it been allowed into the poem's conclusion) would have brought to bear on the picture of husband, prudent partner, and little maiden or on the gushings of the second voice to realize that the ending of 'The Two Voices' resolves nothing and settles nothing: it merely substitutes asserted optimism and a cloying image of marital felicity and ethical propriety for the felt confusion of a searing dialogue of the mind with itself.

In 'The Vision of Sin,' one of the strangest and most intriguing of the

1830–42 poems, the concerns of the two confessional poems just examined are transmogrified from the conscious, ratiocinative level of the mind to the unconscious level of dream. Discursiveness and sententiae are replaced by symbol: the idealizing tendencies of the 'I' of 'The Two Voices,' his strainings toward something up there at the limit of his vision, become 'the awful rose of dawn' at the 'glimmering limit far withdrawn'; and the still small voice becomes the macabre figure of the 'gray and gap-toothed man as lean as death.'

The form of 'The Vision of Sin' is exemplary narrative made discontinuous, disproportionate and finally turned into something different by the unconscious force of the dream logic. As in 'The Two Voices' and 'The Palace of Art,' the mixture of moral parable and psychological exploration provides two imperfectly compatible foci. Tennyson's retrospective account of 'The Vision of Sin' (reminiscent of his verse preface to 'The Palace of Art') summarizes the ethical and religious interpretation: 'This describes the soul of a youth who has given himself up to pleasure and Epicureanism. He at length is worn out and wrapt in the mists of satiety. Afterwards he grows into a cynical old man afflicted with the "curse of nature", and joining in the Feast of Death. Then we see the landscape which symbolizes God, Law and the future life.'[38] The other focus, and the context provided by the poems we have been examining, make 'The Vision of Sin' look quite different, revealing it to be a much more interesting, if less straightforward text, and doing more justice to its most poetically exciting moments.

One of the first things the second lens reveals is that the dream logic of 'The Vision of Sin' also transforms some of the key images in the 1830–42 poems on art and the artist. In the poem's first two sections, images elsewhere associated with the workings of the creative imagination and its necessary isolation and virginity are given erotic connotations. Sexuality, recessive or known only through its absence in 'The Poet's Mind,' 'The Hesperides,' and 'The Lady of Shalott,' becomes dominant in 'The Vision of Sin,' just as the sexual repressions of the waking mind often find expression in dreams. The vision opens with a youth on a horse with wings, not taking flight but alighting at a palace and being led in by 'a child of sin.' The brows and lips of the sodden company within are suffused by a sleepy light 'As when the sun, a crescent of eclipse, / Dreams over lake and lawn and isles and capes.' This simile recalls the late-afternoon, listless world of the virginal sisters of 'The Hesperides'; and just as the sisters of the western evening hate Phosphor, emblem of the east and the morning, the voluptuaries of 'The Vision of Sin' are heedless of the livid phosphorescence of God's awful rose of dawn in the east. The company begins to pant and sigh as 'low voluptuous music' grows louder, becoming 'As't were a hundred-throated nightingale,' while the fountain in the centre of the scene begins to spout, 'showering wide / Sleet of diamond drift and pearly hail.' Is this not a dreamlike magnification and debasement of the fountain ('like sheet lightning') in the garden of 'The Poet's Mind,' just as the hundred-throated nightingale is a dark enlargement of the merry bird chanting in the same poem? And the music itself, 'woven in circles' and synesthetically mixing with the pyrotechnics of the fountain to produce a 'torrent rainbow' of 'purple gauzes, golden hazes, liquid mazes': what is this but a lurid metamorphosis of the Lady of Shalott's 'magic web with colours gay'?

As the music grows louder and the strobe-light effects of it and the fountain more pyschedelic, the company comes to life, the spouting of the fountain having given them their cue:

Then they started from their places,
Moved with violence, changed in hue,
Caught each other with wild grimaces,
Half-invisible to the view.
Wheeling with precipitate paces
To the melody, till they flew,
Hair, and eyes, and limbs, and faces,
Twisted hard in fierce embraces,
Like to Furies, like to Graces,
Dashed together in blinding dew:
Till, killed with some luxurious agony,
The nerve-dissolving melody
Fluttered headlong from the Sky.

In this remarkable passage, the most sustained and explicit orgasmic imagery in Tennyson's canon, the moment of climax, its intensity oxymoronically under-lined ('luxurious agony') and ambiguously assessed (Furies or Graces?), is followed by the abrupt post-coitum fadeout that ends section 2.

In the transitional third section the dreamer looks upward to a mountain tract where he sees both God's awful rose of dawn and a 'heavy vapour' (a transformation of the erotic haze of sections 1 and 2) which is equally unheeded as it begins to float down from the mountain. When it touches the palace gate the lower scene is transformed: the palace becomes the ruined inn, the child of sin the 'wrinkled ostler, grim and thin,' the horse with wings the 'brute' whose ribs the ostler is told to 'stuff ... with mouldy hay'; the youth becomes the 'gray and gap-toothed man as lean as death'; the company with heated eyes become the 'scarecrows' of the old man and the 'bitter barmaid, waning fast,' and the skeletons whose danse macabre inverts the bacchic riot of section 2, just as the chanting of a 'wicked stave' to raise drooping courage and set rheumy eyes aglimmer is a geriatric parody of the palpitating, voluptuous music. There is no equivalent to the fountain, unless we take it to be the spouting of the old man whose utterance comprises section 4.

This section is the jingly dance-of-death of a natural man grown old, a relentless de-idealizer whose speech is a demotic rescoring of that of the urbane still, small voice of 'The Two Voices.' The old man's rant systematically mocks and negates 'name and fame,' friendship, God, religion, virtue, politics, freedom, first love, youthful hopes, 'visions of a perfect state,' and all appeals to a melioristic future. For him all ideals, institutions, and aspirations 'Are but dust that rises up, / And is lightly laid again,' and every heart 'when sifted well … a clot of warmer dust, / Mixed with cunning sparks of hell.' For him 'Death is king,' every face is 'but modelled on a skull,' and though he may remember his 'half divine' youth he knows that in the present he is rotting just as the year is rotting:

> Wine is good for shrivelled lips,
>   When a blanket wraps the day,
> When the rotten woodland drips,
>   And the leaf is stamped in clay.

Despite the grimness of his view of human existence and despite his recognition of his imminent extinction, the old man does not repine and, however grotesque, is not without a certain engaging vitality. Wine and the flesh and bones of the barmaid, the 'glow-worm of the grave' glimmering in her rheumy eyes, are enough for him. He is totally unregenerate and unrepentant: for him the only wisdom is bodily decrepitude, and destiny only the inevitabilities of the natural cycle:

> Every moment dies a man,
>   Every moment one is born.
>
> We are men of ruined blood;
>   Therefore comes it we are wise.
> Fish are we that love the mud,
>   Rising to no fancy-flies.

The deconstructive energy of section 4, which comprises sixty-five per cent of its text, throws 'The Vision of Sin' quite out of proportion. F. E. L. Priestley, among the best of Tennyson's idealizing commentators, has recognized this and argued that 'something like ten or twelve of the best' of the thirty-six quatrains would have been more appropriate to Tennyson's exemplary purpose. This criticism is to the point if the poem is regarded as 'an allegorical vision ... related, however distantly, to both *The Vision of Piers the Plowman* and *The Pilgrim's Progress.*'[39] But if the poem is regarded as a treatment from a pathological viewpoint of the natural man, and as a work of which Tennyson is not in complete artistic control because the sources that energize it are tensions and conflicts deep within him that can find only imperfect and indirect expression in a dream atmosphere, a different kind of commentary becomes necessary.

As instanced in the previous chapter in connection with 'Lucretius' and sections xxxiv and xxxv of *In Memoriam*, whenever the elements of sexuality and naturalism are brought together in Tennyson's poetry the resultant combination is extremely volatile and poetically unstable: uncontrollable eruptions are liable to occur, like the nightmares of Lucretius or the cataclysm at the end of the third section of 'The Lady of Shalott'; discontinuities or discrepancies may cause fissures in the text, as in the presentation of Vivien and Tristram in *Idylls of the King*; cherished images of the imagination may become weirdly perverted, as at the beginning of 'The Vision of Sin.' These eruptions, discontinuities, and perversions are ultimately traceable to the strength of Tennyson's attraction/revulsion to sexuality, which persist throughout his long career, from the mask-of-age pieces in the *Poem by Two Brothers* of 1827 to *Balin and Balan* in 1885. The presence of sexuality can cause Tennyson abruptly to turn away from a naturalistic vision of human existence, to which he was intensely attracted throughout his career, and to fix his gaze not on what is out there in the natural world but what is up there beyond the limit of the visible. In the case of 'The Vision of Sin,' it is clear that the voice in section 5 crying 'Is there any hope?' to the summit, beyond which God's awful rose of dawn appears, is the yearning for a glimpse of a life beyond the natural which will supply supernatural sanction for sexual repression, the foundation of moral convention.

From this psychological perspective, it is not section 4 but section 5 that becomes the weak link in 'The Vision of Sin.' Not only does it introduce the quantitatively insignificant line and a half describing what the speaker of 4 would call the 'fancy-fly' of God's awful rose of dawn at the 'glimmering limit' (the supernatural transformation of the glimmer in the rheumy eyes of the barmaid), it also introduces judgmental and moralistic hypotheses of marked impercipience. In a hideous landscape of men and horses pierced with worms, three voices each offer different but equally moralistic interpretations to account for the appalling reality of the speaker of 4. For the first, the old man's crime was one of sense avenged by sense; for the second, the crime of sense became the crime of malice; for the third, the old man's sourness was the hopeful sign of a little grain of conscience sprouting within. That Tennyson himself realized the partiality of these interpretations is clear from the fact he had originally included in his poem a fourth voice, which in answer to the first had offered a quite different perspective: 'But a crime of sense? / Give him new nerves with old experience.' This non-judgmental, de-moralizing answer, which according to Palgrave Tennyson omitted from the poem only 'from fear of overlength,'[40] is surely the correct one, just as it is certainly the least comforting one. For everything we learn about the garrulous, decrepit, and hideously leering old man suggests that if he had his life to live over again he would live it in exactly the same way.

In addition to female laments in enclosed settings and dialogues of the mind with itself, Tennyson also developed a third kind of poem in the years between 1830 and 1842 through which he sought to give expression to his deepest feelings, tensions, and longings. The poems on classical subjects are for Douglas Bush (short lyrics aside) Tennyson's best work: 'For the classical themes generally banished from his mind what was timid, parochial, sentimental, inadequately philosophical, and evoked his special gifts and his most authentic emotions, his rich and wistful sense of the past, his love of nature, and his powers of style.'[41] In the different but cognate terms of this chapter, the classical poems were written by a poet of sensation, not reflection, quarreling with himself and not with his society, and giving full voice to his quintessential poetic concerns, which were so little attuned to the spirit of the age: the power of the past, sympathy with the natural world, the workings of a luxuriant imagination, and the attractions of an aesthetic philosophy. This is not to say that the classical poems are free of the internal contradictions and discrepancies found elsewhere in the earlier poetry. Even if one does not agree with Swinburne's description of them as 'magnificent hashes and stews of old and new with a sharp sauce of personality,' one cannot deny that 'Oenone' and 'Ulysses' are notorious as examples of poems not fully in control of the meanings they generate. In the two finest of the 1830–42 classical poems, however, Tennyson is completely in control of his texts. 'Tithonus' is virtually without peer in sustaining a single, unequivocal mood; and in 'The Lotos Eaters' the imperfectly controlled and resolved dialectic of other poems is masterfully handled.

The classical poems also gave Tennyson the opportunity to explore another of his authentic emotions: the longing for death. In 'Tiresias,' the speaker uges his son not to fear 'to plunge / Thy torch of life in darkness.' As for himself: 'I would that I were gathered to my rest, / And mingled with the famous kings of old.' And in her poem, Oenone, deserted like the two Marianas, prays:

O death, death, death, thou ever-floating cloud,
...
I pray thee, pass before my light of live,
And shadow all my soul, that I may die.
Thou weighest heavy on the heart within,
Weigh heavy on my eyelids: let me die.

One reason Tennyson's classical personae are able to give full voice to their
longing for death is that they live in a pagan world which has not experienced
the Christian revelation of a life beyond the grave: 'Death closes all,' as
Tennyson's Ulysses insists; 'Death is the end of life' as his mariners chant in
'The Lotos Eaters.' That the classical setting allowed Tennyson to indulge
feelings otherwise unacceptable to a Christian culture should not be construed
to mean what Christopher Ricks thinks it does: that Tennyson sought poetically
to indulge his 'impulse to suicide.'[42] Self-destruction is on the minds of the
speaker of 'Supposed Confessions' and the 'The Two Voices'; but the death
longed for in the classical poems is the release and completion intimated at the
end of 'Mariana in the South.' It is a purely naturalistic and not unwholesome
longing, and it receives definitive expression in 'Tithonus,' which was written in
the 1830s but remained unpublished until 1860 when Tennyson retrieved it
from his notebooks for the first number of the *Cornhill*.

In approaching this poem, a preliminary point should be made. 'Tithonus'
not only contains a wholly naturalistic vision; it also provides Tennyson with
an opportunity for such extraordinarily delicate and affective renderings of
erotic attraction (superior even to 'Now sleeps the crimson petal') as to make
one wish that the times and his own temperament had provided a more
congenial ambiance for the exercise of his surpassing talents as a poet of sexual
invitation. In a superlative passage, the rising of Eos, goddess of the dawn, is
simultaneously Eos the woman becoming erotically aroused, as Tithonus'
yearning for mortality dissolves into a renewed yearning for the sexual yoke of
his beloved:

Once more the old mysterious glimmer steals
From thy pure brows, and from thy shoulders pure
And bosom beating with a heart renewed.
Thy cheek begins to redden through the gloom,
Thy sweet eyes brighten slowly close to mine,
Ere yet they blind the stars, and the wild team
Which love thee, yearning for thy yoke, arise,
And shake the darkness from their loosened manes,
And beat the twilight into flakes of fire.

Since sexuality and naturalism fuse in 'Tithonus,' why is the result not volatile and poetically unstable? For compared with 'Ulysses,' its more famous partner, and with all but one or two of the poems examined in this chapter, the tone of 'Tithonus' is sustained and unequivocal; even the above passage does not break, though it deliciously stretches, the spell of elegiac lament cast by the single voice in a poem fully in control of itself. The answer to this question is that in 'Tithonus' the possible dissonances of naturalism linked with eroticism are enveloped, indeed overwhelmed, by an even more deeply felt Tennysonian emotion: the passion of the past, the longing for what is gone, the sense of the Virgilian 'tears of things' that makes 'Tithonus' the closest of all Tennyson's poems to 'Tears, Idle Tears.'

In the classical story on which the poem is based, Tithonus, a mortal in love with Eos, goddess of the dawn, is granted by the gods immortal life, for which he has asked, but not immortal youth, for which he has neglected to ask; this background is recapitulated in the least interesting lines of the poem (11 to 23). Since 'The Gods themselves cannot recall their gifts,' Tithonus has come to realize that his gift is in reality a curse which has cut him off from the human cycle of life and death, where alone release is to be found. If this makes Tithonus sound like the Lady of Shalott, it is with good reason, for Eos is not only a desirable woman; she is also a symbol of aesthetic beauty and poetic vision. Her beauty is evermore born anew like the golden apples of 'The Hesperides,' and when he had kissed Eos in the past, Tithonus, 'Changed with thy mystic change,' had become like a god and could hear on her lips sounds 'Like that strange song I heard Apollo sing / While Ilion like a mist rose into towers'; that is, like the visionary in 'Timbuctoo,' he was raised 'nigher to the spheres of Heaven' and 'with ravished sense / Listenest the lordly music flowing from / The illimitable years.'

But Eos not only represents the creative imagination. She at the same time represents the timelessness of natural process, which is in Tennyson the content of poetic vision. For a mortal to fall in love with a goddess is seldom in his best long-term interest, however intense the short-term benefits. In the case of Tithonus, his love for Eos has led him to seek to rise above his mortal limitations to a timeless state antithetical to his human nature. Eos is a nature goddess and her immortality is that of natural process, deathless in the sense that it is perpetually recurrent, every spring and every dawn as fresh and vigorous as the one before: 'Lo, ever thus thou growest beautiful.' Uniting himself with natural process had brought Tithonus a period of intense fulfilment and happiness; but now the dewy-warm kisses of his dawn goddess have changed their aspect and become her tears falling on his cheek. The correspondence of natural and human process necessarily brings the awareness that the night of life is death and that in the individual life cycle there is a no second dawn – 'Death closes all.' To become fully naturalistic is to accept death as the necessary end of life, as inevitable and self-completing as an apple falling to the autumnal ground. Not to do so is to wither in the grip of a 'cruel immortality.' In the present time of his poem, Tithonus has come to realize his mistake:

> Why should a man desire in any way
> To vary from the kindly race of men,
> Or pass beyond the goal of ordinance
> Where all should pause, as is most meet for all?

The warmth of youth has vanished; he is old and cold and the return of dawn can only heighten his sense of contrast with her youth and warmth. It is time for Tithonus to leave the never-changing east, to be released and restored to the ground, to become merged – like the Lady of Shalott and the old man of 'The Vision of Sin' – with the autumnal decay and mortality made to sound so maturely attractive in his poem's famous opening lines:

> The woods decay, the woods decay and fall,
> The vapours weep their burthen to the ground,
> Man comes and tills the field and lies beneath,
> And after many a summer dies the swan.

'The Lotos Eaters,' first published in 1832 and subsequently much revised for its republication in the 1842 *Poems*, has clear affinities with 'Tithonus,' as it does with most of the other poems discussed in this chapter. Certainly it recalls 'The Hesperides,' which it followed in the 1832 *Poems*, particularly in its introductory stanzas which describe the lotos land, a western domain of changelessness and listlessness, 'In which it seemèd always afternoon,' where the mountain pinnacles stood 'sunset flushed' while the 'charmèd sunset lingered low adown / In the red West.' It is a land in which 'all things always seemed the same,' and the 'sweet music' of the opening stanza of the mariners' 'Choric Song' is only a slightly drowsier and mellower version of the lilting chant of the three sisters. There is, however, a fundamental difference between the sisters and the afternoon men that the mariners have become, a difference to which Tennyson himself calls attention in the opening lines of 'The Hesperides' when it is said that what Zidonian Hanno heard when he passed the land of the golden apple was not the 'melody o' the Lybian lotosflute.' The Hesperides was a garden of imaginative activity in its purest and most innocent state, innocent because untainted by the world of experience, that is by the East. In 'The Lotos

Eaters,' on the other hand, the mariners have brought this taint with them to the lotos land and cannot rid themselves of it. The world from which they have come seems far away but it is present in their memories, just as in 'The Palace of Art' the outside world is the subject matter of the soul's objets d'art.

For 'The Lotos Eaters' also recalls 'The Palace of Art' and 'The Vision of Sin' in its contrast of an exclusive naturalistic/aesthetic mode of human existence with a more sombre and other-regarding mode. In 'The Lotos Eaters' this contrast is much more effectively managed than in the other two poems because the latter position is implicit throughout, not tacked on at the end, and the conflict is presented dramatically through what the mariners unconsciously reveal about themselves in their song, particularly in the richly complex last section of the poem, which is an enormously more satisfying ending than the empty didactic emblems of the rose of dawn and the cottage in the vale.

In the even-numbered stanzas of the lotos eaters' song, memories of the world they have left behind, and feelings of guilt about so doing (instanced in their exasperated questions), force themselves to the surface of their minds. In these stanzas we learn that the fallen world they have left – it is of course our world – is a place of brutality and suffering, solitary toil and 'perpetual moan' as man is 'from one sorrow to another thrown.' It is a world where (in the mariners' one Arnoldian turn of phrase) 'There is no joy but calm'; a world of transience, in which 'All things are taken from us, and become [part] of the dreadful Past'; a world of death in which (in the words of Shakespeare's Ulysses)

> vigor of bone, desert in service,
> Love, friendship, charity, are subjects all
> To envious and calumniating Time.[43]

In the odd-numbered stanzas, the contrasting attractiveness of the lotos land is evoked: the 'amber light' of afternoon, not the 'hateful' dark blue of midday; the crisping ripples and creamy spray of the beach, not the ever-climbing wave and seething surge of mid-ocean; living again in memory, at one with a past no longer dreadful. It is true that there is a hallucinatory quality to the particularized vividness with which the land is described, but this hardly to say that the mariners' song is simply the perceptual record of a drug-induced trance. It is rather a naturalistic vision of human existence, of human process as coextensive with natural process. In the lotos land there is no disfiguring tension between Eros and Thanatos; no compulsion to look before and after and pine for what is not; and death is seen as the inevitable, easeful culmination of life. This is best instanced in the leaf that 'takes no care' and the apple that 'hath no toil' in third stanza of their song:

Lo! in the middle of the wood,
The folded leaf is wooed from out the bud
With winds upon the branch, and there
Grows green and broad, and takes no care,
Sun-steeped at noon, and in the moon
Nightly dew-fed; and turning yellow
Falls, and floats adown the air.
Lo! sweetened with the summer light,
The full-juiced apple, waxing over-mellow,
Drops in a silent autumn night.
All its allotted length of days,
The flower ripens in its place,
Ripens and fades, and falls, and hath no toil,
Fast-rooted in the fruitful soil.

But while this splendid passage intimates a naturalistic vision of life, it would never be mistaken for one of Swinburne's tenacious insistences that the phenomenal given can suffice, or one of D.H. Lawrence's vitalist, living-in-the-present celebrations. It is too highly 'poetic' and stylized to be considered simply a naturalistic credo. It is an aesthetic credo as well, and its verbal luxuriance (a little 'over-mellow' like the apple) and the slow-motion, tableau-like quality suggest the distancing and softening quality of reverie and dream, not the penetrative insight of the imagination. The apple of the mariners' song has nothing in common with the apples that fall 'like great drops of dew / to bruise themselves an exit from themselves' at the beginning of Lawrence's death poem, 'The Ship of Death.'[44] Their apple is less like those of the orchard than like the golden apple of 'The Hesperides,' which grew only in an aesthetic and non-human atmosphere. For what is significantly missing from the natural scene of which the mariners chant is the human element, a sense of the human cycle and its 'enduring toil,' which makes all the difference between their naturalistic vision and that of Tithonus, who saw man tilling the field and lying beneath as part of the natural cycle of decaying woods, weeping vapours, and dying swans. Tennyson's mariners, that is to say, do not so much desire to live in a natural present as to burn with the gemlike flame of the aesthetic, its colour the pale rose of evening.

In the final, even-numbered stanza of the choric song the guilty memories of the lotos eaters and the implied insufficiency of the aesthetic naturalism of their evening land have the last word, just as the cottage in the vale and the awful rose of dawn do in their poems. But because the concluding stanza is psychologically grounded in what has gone before and is presented dramatically, not emblematically, 'The Lotos Eaters' is able to end in a tremendously exciting manner. This was not the case with the original 1832 ending of the poem. There the mariners' final utterance was an 'Hesperides'- like incantation which suggested that they had come to find a prelapsarian contentment in the lotos land:

> With the blissful Lotoseaters pale
> We will abide in the golden vale
> Of the Lotos-land, till the lotos fail.

This ending was not a satisfactory conclusion to the poem because it did not bring together the antithetical themes of the odd- and even-numbered stanzas, and made the survivors of the Trojan War and the enmity of the sea sound like the fey virgins of 'The Hesperides' who had never known the harsh light of midday.

In the revised ending, a strange psychological energy, an urgency and an insistence enters the mariners' utterance. It is as if they were trying desperately one final time fully to convince themselves that their decision to remain in the lotos land is the correct one. Their speech becomes turbulent and violent; like the soul in 'The Palace of Art' they are on fire within, and like her they come to detest ordinary humanity. Their earlier longing to live like a leaf or an apple is now revealed to be really the anti-human longing to live as 'Gods together, careless of mankind' in an Epicurean 'gleaming world' (like Tithonus in the halls of Eos) where they can barely hear and are heedless of the human song wafted up from below which speaks of a life of 'enduring toil.' At the end of the poem, when they say that 'Surely, surely, slumber is more sweet than toil, the shore / Than labour in the deep mid-ocean,' we say that they would not be so over-insistent if they were really sure; and the echo of their final words – 'we will not wander more' – rings as strangely hollow in our ears as the equally insistent assertions of Tennyson's Ulysses that he will never cease to wander. The reader thus finishes 'The Lotos Eaters' with a sense similar to that with which he leaves so many of Tennyson's 1830 to 1842 poems: not with the sense that a moral order has been affirmed or a higher purpose intimated (despite some endings that seem engineered for this purpose); but with a sense of deep inner anguish, of conflicting tendencies that again and again prove incapable of resolution, and of longings that only death can satisfy.

3

The Natural Magic of *In Memoriam*

A sense of loss, of the irrecoverability of the past and of diminution in the present, runs through the poetry of the nineteenth century. 'Whither is fled the visionary gleam? / Where is it now, the glory and the dream?' asks Wordsworth in the *Intimations of Immortality* ode. Browning asks the same question in the 'Prologue' to *Asolando* in comparing his earlier perception of the Italian countryside to his present one: 'And now? The lambent flame is – where? / Lost from the naked world.' Hardy and Swinburne ring countless changes on the subjects of loss and diminution. Arnold speaks in 'The Buried Life' of the longing to re-contact 'a lost pulse of feeling' which would put us again in touch with our buried self – 'the unregarded river of our life' deep within. Similarly, Emily Dickinson, in 'A loss of something ever felt I' (No. 959), speaks of the feeling that there exists in the past an ennobling richness which is her birthright but of which she has never come into possession, even though she has never ceased to be haunted by a sense of deprivation which leaves her in present time a 'Prince cast out / ... still softly searching / For my Delinquent Palaces.' And Whitman, while he claimed in 1855 that his poetry came from a full expansion of consciousness in the present, by 1860 had come to say that his own songs 'awakened' from the hour when he had first experienced loss and deprivation.

The attitudes to loss in nineteenth-century writers differ widely, but they may be grouped under three headings. In Hardy, Swinburne, and (with a significant exception) Arnold, the response is simply that loss and deprivation are the human condition and must be accepted: there are no 'radiant hints of times to be,' says Hardy in 'A Sign-Seeker,' 'nor whisperings / To open out my limitings'; 'There is no help for these things,' says Swinburne in 'Ave atque Vale'; 'we are here as on a darkling plain,' says Arnold in 'Dover Beach.' A second response, which one might call more characteristically Victorian and which Hardy, Swinburne, and Arnold all repeatedly gainsaid, is the transcendental alternative: the supernatural 'golden echo' answering the tumbling-to-decay 'leaden echo,' to recall Hopkins' poem; the Voice from beyond that at the end of *Asolando*'s prologue subsumes the discrepancy of past and present by asserting that 'all's in ken' and 'God is it who transcends'; the 'saint's voice in the palm-trees' of 'God's Eden-land unknown,' who at the end of Elizabeth Barrett Browning's 'The Lost Bower' assures the poet that the secret garden of her childhood, with its sublime music and 'Mystic Presences,' has at last been recovered: 'All is lost ... and *won*!'

The third alternative involves neither accepting the données of the tragic present nor turning to a melioristic future or a world beyond. It is the Wordsworthian 'abundant recompense' for loss through repossession of the past in memory. While the visionary gleam of childhood, 'the radiance which was once so bright,' is gone for good, the renovating power of memory (which reconnects us with the days when we felt immortal), human sympathy, and continued intimacy with the natural world bring a 'perpetual benediction.' George Eliot, the most Wordsworthian of English novelists, offers a fictional version of the saving power of the past in *The Mill on the Floss*. Early in the novel the narrator several times emphasizes the abiding importance of the special perceptions of childhood in a rooted environment – in the 'home-scene' which is 'the mother tongue of our imagination,' where everything 'is known, and *loved* because it is known.' Such early rootedness later stabilizes us: 'heaven knows where ... striving might lead us, if our affections had not a trick of twining round those old inferior things – if the loves and sanctities of our life had no deep immovable roots in memory.'[1] And in Arnold's 'Thyrsis,' despite the anti-Wordsworthian bias of his earlier poetry, a similar pattern is found. The rediscovery of the signal-elm in the countryside around Oxford is a recapturing of the past, the re-contacting of a pulse of feeling which gives a sustaining sense of wholeness and continuity. It is a purely naturalistic renewal, and we should not be led to think otherwise by the red herring of the poem's fifteenth stanza, which introduces onward-and-upward imagery of mountain tops and the throne of Truth. Such imagery is common to other late poems of Arnold but is grossly intrusive in a deeply meditated (despite the conventional trappings) poem on the theme of self-renovation through re-contacting the past in a known and loved natural setting (there are no mountain-tops in the Cotswolds).

In the case of Tennyson, the central post-Romantic poet of the nineteenth century, loss and the power of the past are fundamental subjects. 'Tears, Idle Tears' is the century's most intense lyric distillation of the Virgilian 'tears of things,' of the desolating awareness of 'the days that are no more,' the absence of which makes the speaker's present state a 'Death of Life.' The same mood is evoked again, less sharply focused but almost as hauntingly, in 'Far-Far-Away' and in these lines from 'The Ancient Sage':

Today? but what of yesterday? for oft
On me, when boy, there came what then I called,
Who knew no books and no philosophies,
In my boy-phrase 'The Passion of the Past.'
The first gray streak of earliest summer-dawn,
The last long stripe of waning crimson gloom,
As if the late and early were but one –
A height, a broken grange, a grove, a flower
Had murmurs 'Lost and gone and lost and gone!'
A breath, a whisper – some divine farewell –
Desolate sweetness – far and faraway –
What had he loved, what had he lost, the boy?
I know not and I speak of what has been.

Of the three responses to loss outlined above, there is no equivalent in Tennyson of the bite-the-bullet stoicism of Hardy and Swinburne. For the two Marianas and Oenone, the sense of loss is so incapacitating that the only alternative is longing for the release of death; and in his own voice Tennyson said many times what we have seen him saying in the thirty-fifth section of *In Memoriam*: that if he thought man were not immortal he would either kill himself or live like a beast. There are of course many examples in Tennyson's canon of the futuristic/transcendental alternative, of what Hardy called 'radiant hints of times to be.' In the previous chapter we saw examples of this alternative at the end of 'The Two Voices' and of 'The Vision of Sin,' and in the first chapter other examples were examined from Swinburne's de-idealizing and de-mystifying point of view. In his parodies of Tennyson poems, Swinburne's generic point was that the Laureate was at far from his poetic best when his gaze was turned onward and upward, and no one would deny that much of this body of verse is of inferior poetic quality compared with the consummate mastery of such downward-and-inward works as 'Tears, Idle Tears,' 'The Lady of Shalott' and the Mariana poems. 'The Ancient Sage' illustrates the point, for on one side of the 'Passion of the Past' section lies the Sage's fatuous advice for today:

Cleave ever to the sunnier side of doubt,
And cling to Faith beyond the forms of Faith!
She reels not in the storm of warring words,
She brightens at the clash of 'Yes' and 'No,'
She sees the Best that glimmers through the Worst,
She feels the Sun is hid but for a night,
She spies the summer through the winter bud,

> She tastes the fruit before the blossom falls,
> She hears the lark within the songless egg,
> She finds the fountain where they wailed 'Mirage'!

And on the other side lies the poem's embarrassing ending concerning tomorrow, in which the Sage develops a version of Arnold's mountain-top imagery, and of the 'awful rose of dawn' of 'The Vision of Sin,' in urging his interlocutor to pull himself together:

> ... curb the beast would cast thee in the mire,
> And leave the hot swamp of voluptuousness
> A cloud between the Nameless and thyself,
> And lay thine uphill shoulder to the wheel,
> And climb the Mount of Blessing, whence, if thou
> Look higher, then – perchance – thou mayest – beyond
> A hundred ever-rising mountain lines,
> And past the range of Night and Shadow – see
> The high-heaven dawn of more than mortal day
> Strike on the Mount of Vision!

As in these passages, much of what one might call Tennyson's futuristic/ transcendental verse tends to be strident, rhetorical, and over-insistent, and to use natural objects and processes merely as grist for the moral and spiritual mill; while other texts, like 'The Higher Pantheism,' tend towards vagueness and blurriness. It is hard not to conclude that tomorrow was not a naturally congenial poetic subject for Tennyson. One recalls Hallam's 1830 caveat: that 'heterogeneous aspirations, however pure they may be, however lofty, however suitable to human nature,' weaken the 'delicate sense of fitness' of a poet of sensation rather than reflection, and go against the grain of his natural poetic gifts. For however much his intellect and will tend to pull him in onward-and-upward directions, Tennyson's imagination is likely to be at the same time, drawing him back into the past. One thinks of course of 'Ulysses,' with its heroic tenor 'about the need of going forward, and braving the struggle of life'[2] coupled with an elegiac vehicle which seems to move in the other direction. As the Victorian critic Goldwin Smith noted long ago, Ulysses says 'he intends to roam, but stands for ever a listless and melancholy figure on the shore.'[3]

One may also think of Tennyson's greatest work, *In Memoriam*, for one of the two informing principles of this poem of loss and recovery is the Wordsworthian process of 'abundant recompense' for loss through memory and the ministration of the natural world. This has hardly been recognized even by the best commentators on the poem,[4] for almost since the day it was published critical attention has been concentrated on the other informing principle: the futuristic/transcendental alternative, the onward-and-upward movement from despair, through doubt and hope to faith in A.C. Bradley's famous formulation. (For at least a generation this fourfold division has been the one thing, in many cases the only thing, that every graduate student in English literature could be relied on to know about the poem.) Much too little recognition and attention have been given to what may be called the 'natural magic' of *In Memoriam*.

The phrase 'natural magic' comes from Matthew Arnold's essay on Maurice de Guérin, in which he distinguishes between the two ways in which poetry interprets: the naturalistic and the moral. (The distinction is a more mature and balanced version of Hallam's distinction between poets of sensation and poets of reflection.) Concerning the former Arnold says:

The grand power of poetry is its interpretative power; by which I mean, not a power of drawing out in black and white an explanation of the mystery of the universe, but the power of so dealing with things as to awaken in us a wonderfully full, new, and intimate sense of them, and of our relations with them. When this sense is awakened in us, as to objects without us, we feel ourselves to be in contact with the essential nature of those objects, to be no longer bewildered and oppressed by them, but to have their secret, and to be in harmony with them; and this feeling calms and satisfies us as no other can. Poetry, indeed, interprets in another way besides this; but one of its two ways of interpreting, of exercising its highest power, is by awakening this sense in us ...

...

I have said that poetry interprets in two ways; it interprets by expressing with magical felicity the physiognomy and movement of the outward world, and it interprets by expressing, with inspired conviction, the ideas and laws of the inward world of man's moral and spiritual nature. In other words , poetry is interpretative both by having *natural magic* in it, and by having *moral profundity*. In both ways it illuminates man; it gives him a satisfying sense of reality; it reconciles him with himself and the universe.

Arnold goes on to say that (unlike Keats and Guérin, 'in whom the faculty of naturalistic interpretation is overpoweringly predominant, the natural magic is perfect') the greatest poets (like Aeschylus and Shakespeare) unite in themselves both kinds of interpretation.[5] Arnold would certainly not have included Tennyson in the second group; and one doubts that he recognized fully the qualitative dominance of naturalistic interpretation in his poetry. There is no need here to pronounce on the 'moral profundity' or otherwise of those aspects of *In Memoriam* which make the poem a nineteenth-century theodicy; and we have already heard Swinburne's views on the 'pretentiously unpretentious philosophy' of the elegy. But we can hardly remain unaware of the discontinuity in *In Memoriam* (similar to that in other Tennyson poems) caused by the incompatability between a naturalistic acceptance of death and the desperate need for some kind of supernatural belief. And we shall later have to examine carefully the point at which naturalistic and supernaturalistic readings of the poem necessarily conflict: the interpretation of the experience of union with Hallam's 'living soul' in section xcv, the most crucial single lyric in *In Memoriam*.

For the present, we should begin consideration of the elegy's natural magic by turning to a much earlier poem, the 1830 'Ode to Memory.' For however fully and freshly Tennyson renders the natural world and sees into the life of things so as to awaken in us a sense of their restorative, harmonizing power, the world out there in *In Memoriam*, as in 'Tears, Idle Tears,' is viewed through the memory as well as through the eyes and is always tinctured with a sense of the past. While the 'Ode to Memory' is stylistically and formally immature, occasionally confused and forced, and even seems not wholly sincere, it is Tennyson's most explicitly Wordsworthian poem and his most explicit statement on the relation of memory to nature; and in several important, even uncanny ways it looks forward to the great Hallam elegy.

The ode opens with an invocation to memory to stir the 'low desire' of the poet's present state, and with the first of three repetitions of the refrain that will end the poem:

Strengthen me, enlighten me!
I faint in this obscurity,
Thou dewy dawn of memory.

In the next stanza we learn that the speaker's present memories are turbulent and involve only the recent past, 'the gloom of yesternight.' He would prefer memory to come as she once did, 'as a maid' of the morning mist, a Primavera figure carrying blooms and shoots of orient green, a 'safe pledge' of the fruits of a fulfilled future.

In the third stanza we learn that in the past memory has also come with 'the evening cloud' and in 'sweet dreams softer than unbroken rest,' at which time she was accompanied by her infant Hope. Memory (or Hope – the pronominal references are imprecise) had then brought recollections of visionary insight into 'the half-attained futurity, / Though deep not fathomless.' For in the childhood past there was not only 'small thought ... of life's distress'; there was also access to what in Wordsworthian terms the poem later calls 'Emblems or glimpses of eternity' ('like emblems of infinity' in the 1842 text) and what the third stanza calls 'the lordly music flowing from / The illimitable years.'

One is initially astonished by this phrase, for these very same words are used by the angel in 'Timbuctoo' to describe part of the content of the visionary rapture of the poet raised by his imagination 'nigher to the spheres of Heaven' (this phrase also occurs again in the ode). It is not possible to determine which account of the astral music – the Wordsworthian or the Shelleyan – was adapted from the other, though one may reflect that while Tennyson had not visited the vicinity of Gibraltar, the setting of 'Timbuctoo,' he certainly had been a child. Perhaps priority does not matter greatly, for both poems are similar in placing this vision in the past – 'Timbuctoo' in the childhood of the race, 'Ode to Memory' in the childhood of the man – and both emphasize the impending or already accomplished fall into the present whereby the vision is lost: in 'Timbuctoo' visionary *Fable* is superseded by keen *Discovery*; in 'Ode to Memory' the shades of the prison house of perceptual diminishment close on the growing boy. There is, however, one important difference between the accounts of the loss of the visionary gleam and its aural equivalent, the lordly music. In the historical myth of 'Timbuctoo,' the vision would appear permanently irrecoverable because of the march of progress, or recoverable only through apocalypse; in the psychological myth of 'Ode to Memory' the vision is at least potentially recoverable through memory – through memory and, as the ode now goes on to explain, through the mediation of the known and loved natural settings of childhood.

This element enters the poem in the fourth stanza, which begins by relocating the proper setting for imaginative reverie, just as the previous section had relocated the source of the lordly music. The speaker admonishes memory not to come 'with shows of flaunting vines' for she was not 'nursèd by the waterfall'

> Which ever sounds and shines
>   A pillar of white light upon the wall
> Of purple cliffs.

That is to say, memory and its saving operations are dissociated from the exotic, timeless settings in which the imagination finds its home in early poems like 'The Hesperides,' 'The Lotos Eaters,' and even 'Recollections of the Arabian Nights,' which precedes 'Ode to Memory' in the 1830 *Poems, Chiefly Lyrical*. It is not in these esoteric settings but in the simple rustic scenes of childhood, à la George Eliot or Wordsworth, that memory and its restorative powers are to be found:

Come from the woods that belt the gray hill-side,
The seven elms, the poplars four
That stand beside my father's door,
And chiefly from the brook that loves
To purl o'er matted cress and ribbèd sand.
...
Pour round mine ears the livelong bleat
Of the thick-fleecèd sheep from wattled folds,
    Upon the ridgèd wolds,
When the first matin-song hath wakened loud
Over the dark dewy earth forlorn,
    What time the amber morn
Forth gushes from beneath a low-hung cloud.

The setting is the countryside around the rectory at Somersby where Tennyson grew up, and includes the very elms, brook, and amber dawn that figure in section xcv of *In Memoriam* when memory, bringing with it a sense of the dead Hallam's 'living soul,' and the sound of the illimitable years' lordly music, does come to the grieving Tennyson to strengthen and enlighten him.

Indeed, at the end of the 1830 ode – I am skipping over the strained image of memory as a great artist elaborately framing her earliest sketches, and the descriptions of the landscape of Mablethorpe, where the Tennyson family had a cottage, and of the rectory garden – Hallam is himself addressed in a way that seems uncannily anticipatory of the climactic sections of *In Memoriam*:

My friend, with you to live alone,
Were how much better than to own
A crown, a sceptre, and a throne!

It was Tennyson himself who subsequently said it was to his friend, then alive, that these lines were addressed. But no one would ever have thought this without the authorial gloss, for in context the lines seem clearly and naturally to refer to memory. It is hard not to agree with Culler's suggestion that Tennyson, subsequent to the writing of them, came to associate these lines with his then dead friend.[6] As Culler does not go on to say, it is not at all surprising that Tennyson would come to make this association, for in *In Memoriam* childhood memories of Somersby are overlaid and mixed with memories of the times when Hallam visited the Tennyson family there, and it is the natural world, particularly the Somersby setting, and the operation of memory that restore to the poet a sense of Hallam's living presence.

While formally and structurally a poem of marked originality, *In Memoriam* is basically an elegy and the literary tradition on which it draws most heavily is that of pastoral elegy. A number of conventions of this ancient genre appear in Tennyson's poem: the fiction of the poet as a shepherd lamenting his dead mate, the celebration of the idyllic time of shared friendship before the disaster, the invocation to the muses, the choice of flowers.[7] In addition there are echoes of earlier elegies, both classical and English.[8] But most important, the general pattern of *In Memoriam* is that of pastoral elegy. There is the initial expression of sorrow and grief, troubled reflections on the meaning and purpose of human existence, questioning of the powers in the universe that have allowed such a gifted man to die, recollection of the happy days now gone, the tempering of grief into resignation, the sudden turn or change in which the poet announces that the dead one has not totally perished but survives in some other form, and the consolation, which describes the form of this survival and joyfully celebrates it.

The elegy which most closely resembles *In Memoriam* is 'Lycidas.' In an insightful paper, Joseph Sendry has illuminated Tennyson's indebtedness to Milton's elegy, pointing up close 'thematic echoes' and arguing that Milton's 'intrusions of metaphysical and theological statements into a song of personal lament' served as a valuable precedent for Tennyson.[9] But Sendry is not concerned to do more than intimate some of the significant differences between the two poems, which are even more striking than their resemblances. This is particularly true of the poem's closing sections. At the end of Milton's poem, Lycidas is said to undergo a metamorphosis into 'the Genius of the shore,' a kind of classical nature deity who becomes the tutelary spirit of the natural setting in which he perished. But the entire source of Milton's consolation in the poem, and the cause of Lycidas' apotheosis, his entry into 'the blest Kingdoms meek of joy and love' in the poem's magnificent conclusion, is Milton's Christian belief in the resurrection of the dead, the immortality of the soul, and the soul's participation in the everlasting bliss of heaven. For these reasons, natural consolation cannot ultimately play more than a strictly subordinate role in 'Lycidas.' And natural facts, like 'the day-star' sinking in 'the Ocean bed' only to reappear flaming 'in the forehead of the morning sky,' ultimately have positive value because of the way in which they symbolize spiritual facts (death and spiritual rebirth, 'Through the dear might of him that walk'd the waves,' in the case of the setting and rising sun). Milton is explicit concerning the inadequacy of the natural world to effect by itself any permanent consolation, for he ends the lovely catalogue of flowers section with a terse admission of its limited role in his elegy: 'For so to interpose a little ease, / Let our frail thoughts dally with false surmise.'

The case is quite different with *In Memoriam*. It is a commonplace to say that Tennyson, like other Victorian writers, lacked the secure religious faith of earlier centuries and could no longer find support for his need to believe in the traditional sanctions of such faith. The implications of this changed situation are superbly encapsulated in Emily Dickinson's poem (No. 1551) on the subject of the disappearance of God in the nineteenth century:

> Those – dying then,
> Knew where they went –
> They went to God's Right Hand –
> That hand is amputated now
> And God cannot be found –
>
> The abdication of Belief
> Makes the Behavior small –
> Better an ignis fatuus
> Than no illume at all –

In many places in Tennyson's poetry gleams and glimmerings provide moments of spiritual illume, and in the closing poems of *In Memoriam* there are a number of apotheoses and affirmations which are designed to shed brighter and more lasting light. These various illuminations, however, are not necessarily compatible with each other and not always subjected by Tennyson to careful scrutiny. A / There is the domestic epiphany of the epilogue, with its detailed description of a marriage celebration and its confident anticipation of the new life which will result from this union. Reminiscent of the church-going family at the end of 'The Two Voices,' this image functions as a positive resolution of the anguished introspection and self-consciousness of the poet who, 'moulded in colossal calm,' is finally able to look within no more. B / In the pealing of the wild new year's bells in section cvi there is heard the prophecy of a political and social millennium ('Ring in the thousand years of peace'), which is associated with the survival of Hallam's spirit (the last line of the section, 'Ring in the Christ that is to be,' being followed by the first of cvii: 'It is the day when he was born,' i.e. 1 February, Hallam's birthday). C / There is the optimistic view of evolutionary process (in cxviii and the epilogue) which enables Tennyson to see Hallam as a prefigurement – a 'type' (the word has both biological and biblical overtones) – of the 'crowning race' to be, the 'one far-off divine event / To which the whole creation moves.' This evolutionary faith is thoroughly mixed with the residual Christian belief which allows Tennyson to describe Hallam as 'That friend of mine who lives in God.'[10] And D / there is the pantheistic rapture of section cxxx, modelled on stanzas 42 and 43 of Shelley's 'Adonais,' in which Tennyson says, 'Though mixed with God and Nature thou, / I seem to love thee more and more,' thereby again mixing incompatibles; for Tennyson does not keep separate, nor does he want to, the pagan and Christian consolations clearly distinguished in 'Lycidas.'

This state of affairs is made additionally complicated by the flowering in the closing sections of *In Memoriam* (in cxv and cxxi) of another consolation and affirmation which has its roots earlier in the poem. This pattern of natural consolation and renewal may initially seem less prominent or noteworthy than the poem's futuristic/transcendental patterns because it completes itself less spectacularly and less rhetorically as the poet's initial separation from the natural processes of cyclic change and his initially numbed memory finally culminate in celebrations of identity with natural process and of the continuity of past and present. Another reason it that there are two different 'natures' in *In Memoriam* which have not been sufficiently distinguished. One is the discovery of nineteenth-century science, Nature with a capital N. Its manifestations include the 'phantom' Nature of iii, 'A hollow form with empty hands'; the 'streams that ... / Draw down Aeonian hills, and sow / The dust of continents to be' in xxxv; the Nature, 'red in tooth and claw / With ravine' of lvi; Time, a 'maniac scattering dust' in section l, but in cxviii the positive evolutionary force that began in 'tracts of fluent heat,'

> grew to seeming-random forms,
> The seeming prey of cyclic storms,
> Till at the last arose the man;
>
> Who throve and branched from clime to clime,
> The herald of a higher race,
> And of himself in higher place;

and the force that in cxxvii is imagined to cause the sustaining crags to tremble, the spires of ice to topple down and 'molten up, and roar in flood,' while

> The fortress crashes from on high,
> The brute earth lightens to the sky,
> And the great Aeon sinks in blood.

The other nature is simply the immemorial sights and sounds of the English landscape, the processes of seasonal change and of the daily passage from light to dark, all of which are wonderfully evoked throughout the poem: the lonely fold, low morass, whispering reed, simple stile, 'sheepwalk up the windy wold,' and 'hoary knoll of ash and haw / That hears the latest linnet trill' of section c; in section lxxxv,

> Summer on the steaming floods,
> And Spring that swells the narrow brooks,
> And Autumn, with a noise of rooks,
> That gather in the waning woods;

the naturalized Christmas bells that 'from hill to hill / Answer each other in the mist' in xxviii; the February ice of section cvii that makes 'daggers at the sharpened eaves':

> And bristles all the brakes and thorns
> To yon hard crescent, as she hangs
> Above the wood which grides and clangs
> Its leafless ribs and iron horns;

the flowers of spring catalogued in section lxxxiii: orchis and

> the foxglove spire,
> The little speedwell's darling blue,
> Deep tulips dashed with fiery dew,
> Laburnums, dropping wells of fire;

the serenity of summer of section lxxxix, when

> brushing ankle deep in flowers,
> We heard behind the woodbine veil
> The milk that bubbled in the pail,
> And buzzings of the honied hours;

and the autumn of section xi, with 'the chestnut pattering to the ground,' the

> dews that drench the furze,
> And all the silvery gossamers
> That twinkle into green and gold.

As the above examples indicate, Nature in *In Memoriam* has a linear, progressive direction, extending from the remote geological and zoological past, of which Victorian scientists like Lyell and Darwin did so much to make their contemporaries aware, through the present to either a melioristic or catas-trophic future, which in either case tends to be envisaged in rhetorical and declamatory terms. Small-n nature, on the other hand, has a cyclical or ebb-and-flow movement and is non-progressive; indeed, as in 'Tears, Idle Tears,' it has the tremendous capacity to evoke the past, and the style appropriate to it tends, with important exceptions, to the non-declamatory and non-pyrotechnical quiet loveliness of the elegiac.

We may recall the two muses who address the poet in xxxvii, and say that those parts of *In Memoriam* which treat of Nature were written under the inspiration of Urania, who, as in *Paradise Lost*, is the muse of divine poetry. Those parts of the elegy in which Tennyson grapples with the data of nineteenth-century science are part of his struggle to find a viable religious faith which will guarantee the soul's immortality, and as such should be associated with Urania, the 'high muse.' Melpomene, on the other hand, is 'but an earthly Muse,' 'unworthy even to speak' of Urania's mysteries. She is the elegiac, this-worldly figure who may be said to be the spirit of nature in *In Memoriam*. It is she who in section lvii may be said to lead the tortured poet away from the brink of the 'scarpèd cliff' of Victorian doubt and horror in the face of Nature's fierce randomness, and with 'her earthly song,' a 'song of woe,' to bring peace by helping him to remember his personal loss ('The passing of the sweetest soul / That ever looked with human eyes') and once more, like Catullus at his brother's grave, to bid the dead one hail and farewell. It is she who in section cviii may be said to counter the poet's corrosive thought that the results of his scaling heaven's height and diving below the wells of Death may be merely solipsistic with the naturalistic determination to take instead 'what fruit may be / Of sorrow under human skies' – human skies, not vistas of unfolding supernatural good. Finally, recalling section xlviii, we may say that Urania is the intellectual muse of a poet of reflection whose province is 'Grave doubts and answers.' Melpomene, on the other hand, is the muse of the emotions of the poet of sensation who eschews the 'larger lay' and

> rather loosens from the lip
> Short swallow-flights of song, that dip
> Their wings in tears, and skim away.

While the majority of *In Memoriam*'s 'short swallow-flights of song' have a cyclical shape, or describe a part of nature's cycle, two sections have a distinctive ebb-and-flow shape; both make a good introduction to the subtleties of the natural magic of *In Memoriam* and to the clarifications and satisfactions afforded by an intimate sense of natural things and of our relations with them. In the case of sections xix and lxvii what is quietly sensed is the human participation in what Emerson called 'that great principle of Undulation in nature, that shows itself in the inspiring and expiring of the breath; in desire and satiety; in the ebb and flow of the sea; in day and night; in heat and cold.'[11]

The first of the four stanzas of xix states that Hallam's corpse ('The darkened heart that beat no more') was interred in the church at Clevedon near the shore of the Severn and within hearing of its waves. The next stanza describes a natural occurrence. As twice a day the tidal Severn 'fills,' its water moves up into the Wye (which joins the Severn above Clevedon) and 'hushes half the babbling Wye,' making 'a silence in the hills' – the sound of the shallow stream falling over rocks being silenced when its level is raised by the tidal incursions. The next two stanzas, with a point-for-point precision which Alan Sinfield has well described,[12] discover an analogy between this natural ebb and flow and the ebb and flow of grief within the poet lamenting the dead friend interred within hearing of what he cannot hear. As the Wye is hushed when full, so when the poet's sorrow fills him song is drowned and the possibility of emotional release curtailed: like the southern Mariana, he is then 'filled with tears that cannot fall.' But as the tide flows down and the shallower Wye is again 'vocal in its wooded walls,' so too the poet's 'deeper anguish *also* falls, / And I can speak a little then' (my italics). To be able to speak a little is not much, but it is something of positive value. The poet has been enabled to speak, or (almost as important) realized his ability to do so, through sympathetic identification with natural process, for the *also* of the penultimate line intimates not simply that there is an analogy between the rhythms of the Wye and the poet's internal rhythms, but that there is a reciprocity, a causal connection, between them.

Section lxvii, which also involves the church at Clevedon and repeats the falls/walls rhyme, is a more subtle and complex poem than xix:

> When on my bed the moonlight falls,
>   I know that in thy place of rest
>   By that broad water of the west,
> There comes a glory on the walls;
>
> Thy marble bright in dark appears,
>   As slowly steals a silver flame
>   Along the letters of thy name,
> And o'er the number of thy years.
>
> The mystic glory swims away;
>   From off my bed the moonlight dies;

And closing eaves of wearied eyes
I sleep till dusk is dipt in gray:

And then I know the mist is drawn
    A lucid veil from coast to coast,
    And in the dark church like a ghost
Thy tablet glimmers to the dawn.

One feels that this poem owes something to that species of love poem in which
the lover, separated from his beloved, attempts to overcome their separation
through creating more a numinous world – a superior reality – within which
they are in communion. Such a resonance adds to the pathos of lxvii, for the
euphemistic 'thy place of rest' conceals only for a few lines the realization that
the beloved whom the poet wishes vicariously to contact is in fact dead, and that
the spatial separation momentarily dissolved by the shared moonlight does
nothing to lessen the temporal distance between life and death, but only brings
the lover to the dark burial place of his beloved.

Or rather the bright-in-dark burial place, for when the moonlight falls on
the sacred place to which the poet is transported in imagination, a 'glory' and
then 'mystic glory' are said to be produced by the operation of the furtive 'silver
flame.' In this heightened moment of vision, the stark fact of Hallam's early
death, the pathetically small number of his twenty-two years, is momentarily
illuminated and enveloped in the aura of a higher ('mystic') reality. But only for
a moment, for the flow of moonlight 'swims away' (that is, ebbs) from the West
Country church, just as it leaves Tennyson's bed in Lincolnshire. It is succeeded
by the dismal morning dusk and the mist greyly shining across the country.

For all its pathos, however, the poem does not end with a feeling of greyness
and desolation, or a renewed sense of loss. For the moonlight which united the
two places of rest has left behind a positive residue intimated in the oxymoronic
'lucid veil' and imaged in the poem's last line and a half: 'like a ghost / Thy
tablet glimmers to the dawn.' A glimmer is enormously less than the 'silver
flame' of which it is the afterglow, just as the ghost-like tablet (that is, the tablet
which seems an apparition of a human form) glimpsed in the imaginative alembic
of the grey dawn is enormously less than the living presence of the loved one
who is no more. But as Faulkner said: 'Between grief and nothing, I will take
grief.' And in addition, despite the vicariousness, transience, and even illusori-
ness of what it describes, the assured, peaceful, and richly controlled tone and
movement of lxvii suggest that something more positive than the measured
expression of grief has been achieved. Through intimate sympathy with the
natural world, the flow and ebb, the brightening and darkening, of the poet's
longing for union with his beloved have been naturalized and a stabilization and

harmonization have been effected, as the after glow of vision remains to glimmer through the grey mist of grief.

The larger patterns of the workings of natural magic in *In Memoriam* tend to be cyclical rather than to ebb and flow: the cycle of the day and the turning of the seasons of the year. For about the first half of the poem, however (with exceptions like section xix), the poet's isolating and initially numbing grief has served to sever his life of immediate sympathy with the world of things and to cut him off from any rapport with nature's cyclic process. The day of Hallam's death is said to have 'sickened every living bloom, / And blurred the splendour of the sun' (lxxii), while in section xxxviii the poet confesses that the blossoming season and the 'herald melodies of spring' bring him no relief. It is only 'in the songs I love to sing' that 'A doubtful gleam of solace lives.' The stasis of grief and the process of nature appear incompatible. In section ii, it is only with the bleak, 'sullen' yew tree, its roots reaching down into the coffined bones of a corpse, that Tennyson is able to associate himself. In xxxix it is said that a 'golden hour' of bloom, 'When flower is feeling after flower,' comes even to this tree, but the state is short-lived and seems unnatural. The abiding condition of the yew seems a barren darkness, implicit even in its transitory blossoms: 'Thy gloom is kindled at the tips, / And passes into gloom again.' In lxix the poet dreams 'there would be Spring no more,' in liv he has only a minimal and plaintive hope that, as every winter changes to spring, his grief too will eventually change. And in section viii, 'every pleasant spot' known and loved because of its associations with Hallam is said to have lost its 'magic light': 'For all is dark where thou art not.'

Sections ix, xv, and xvi form a triad through which Tennyson describes the extreme forms his grief takes. In the first, the poet's 'calm despair' has its correlative in the chilling quiet of an autumn morning, while the opposite emotional state of 'wild unrest' is symbolized by the violent evening storm of xv in which the 'forest cracked, the waters curled, / The cattle huddled on the lea.' In xvi, a reconciliation of these opposites is effected in that both poles of the poet's grief are said to be 'tenants of single breast,' and to stem from the psychic imbalance and near delirium caused by his loss. Later in *In Memoriam*, in sections xcv and cxxi, the pattern of the opposed states of dawn and dusk, day and night, being brought out of strife and into an harmonious unity will be associated with the corresponding reconciliation on a human level of life and death, just as the dark places of viii will in later poems come regain their 'magic.' By the end of the elegy, then, one will have come to see that the dialectic of ix, xv, and xvi is an unhealthy inversion, a negative image, of the restorative processes through which later in the poem Tennyson's grief is assuaged and then healed.

After the second Christmas section (lxxviii), which Bradley rightly regarded as the 'turning point in the general feeling of *In Memoriam*,'[13] the poet's attitude to nature begins to change and at the same time memory, through the stimulus of the natural world, begins its repossession of the past. In section lxxix, for example, which is addressed to his older brother Charles, Tennyson speaks of the hills and woods and fields, the winds and especially the 'cold streamlet' – it is the same Somersby landscape described in the 1830 'Ode to Memory' – which 'did print / The same sweet forms' in the mind of each brother. And soon after this come three lovely poems which bespeak a decided change in Tennyson's relation to the natural world. They are poems of petition and invocation, which ask different aspects of the restorative force of natural process to bring to bear on the poet's grief their powers of assuagement and revivification. Section lxxxiii appeals to the new year not to delay but to bring on the 'sweetness' of spring: 'Can trouble live with April days, / Or sadness in the summer moons?' The answer is 'no,' for the changes of the earth will produce a corresponding change within the poet which will let him speak more vocally than did the fall of the Wye in xix:

> O thou, new-year, delaying long,
>   Delayest the sorrow in my blood,
>   That longs to burst a frozen bud
> And flood a fresher throat with song.

In section lxxxviii, the nightingale, the 'wild bird' whose liquid-sweet song rings paradisically through the hedgerows of hawthorn, is beseeched to make known the secret of its harmonious resolution in song of conflicting passions:

> O tell me where the senses mix,
> O tell me where the passions meet,
>
> Whence radiate: fierce extremes employ
>   Thy spirits in the darkening leaf,
>   And in the midmost heart of grief
> Thy passion clasps a secret joy.

And in the finest of this trio of poems (lxxxvi) the west wind is invoked:

> Sweet after showers, ambrosial air,
>   That rollest from the gorgeous gloom
>   Of evening over brake and bloom
> And meadow, slowly breathing bare

The round of space, and rapt below
  Through all the dewy-tasselled wood,
  And shadowing down the hornèd flood
In ripples, fan my brows and blow

The fever from my cheek, and sigh
  The full new life that feeds thy breath
  Throughout my frame, till Doubt and Death,
Ill brethren, let the fancy fly

From belt to belt of crimson seas
  On leagues of odour streaming far,
  To where in yonder orient star
A hundred spirits whisper 'Peace.'

Bradley and Sinfield are wrong in thinking that this poem is 'the answer to the prayer of lxxxiii' and that it describes an attained 'peace of mind';[14] for the poem is itself a prayer asking for peace. One can understand why such excellent commentators could mistake the wish for the deed. For one thing, the poem's verbal opulence, appropriate to its subject – the 'sweet ... ambrosial air,' the 'gorgeous gloom,' 'dewy-tasselled wood' 'crimson seas,' and 'leagues of odour' – suggests satiety rather than desire. And in the controlled onrush of this one-sentence poem (none of its first three quatrains is end-stopped, and there are syntactic or breath pauses at the end of only six of the sixteen lines, and three of these occur in the final stanza), the simple, one-syllable verbs of supplication (*bare, fan, blow, sigh*) tend not to be noticed as the poem moves unimpededly outward from brake, meadow, wood, and river to 'crimson seas' (the evening sky with ranks of crimson-coloured clouds) and to the orient (i.e. rising) star of evening beyond.

What the poet asks for is a macrocosmic version of what was effected by the rise and fall of the Wye in xix and by the moonlight in lxvii. Emotional release is sought, and renewal through becoming naturalized, through having one's human rhythms merged with those of a renovating and cleansing natural process. As the west wind clears the sky (the round of space) of rain clouds, so may the same force blow the fever from the poet's cheek, and sigh 'The full new life that feeds *thy* breath / Throughout *my* frame' (italics mine), free his imagination from the grip of loss, and carry it up to Hesper, the star of evening, and its sotto voce intimations of the harmony of lordly music in the hundred spirits whispering 'Peace.' It is the same natural consolation and release that the southern Mariana experienced at the end of her poem (as we saw in the previous chapter) when at the climax of evening 'in spaces rosy-bright' (that is, crimson) 'Large Hesper glittered on her tears' and 'Heaven over Heaven rose the night.'

There is another poem of Tennyson's with which we should also associate the ending of lxxxvi, for the belts (or stripes) of crimson cloud in the gloom of evening also recall the 'Passion of the Past' section of 'The Ancient Sage':

> The first gray streak of earliest summer-dawn,
> The last long stripe of waning crimson gloom,
> As if the late and early were but one ...

Here the crimson cloud is associated not with natural consolation and renewal but with the power of the past and the fusion of present and past (late and early, evening and dawn). The two apparently different associations are not mutually exclusive, however, any more than the different accounts noted earlier of the source of the 'lordly music.' In *In Memoriam*, natural consolation and the fusion of past and present through memory are the two sides of a single coin – a double name for what is one. Indeed, the point can be made without reference to 'The Ancient Sage,' for in the last nine lines of section cxxii Tennyson recalls in detail the setting of lxxxvi and addresses the same prayer not to the west wind but to Hallam (the past he wishes present to him). Hallam is asked to 'enter in at breast and brow,' quicken the poet 'with a livelier breath' and help him to 'slip the thoughts' of (the ill brethren of) life and death.

And if we stand back from the trio of poems just examined, we notice that they are found in the interstices of longer sections recalling Hallam as he was when alive. In section lxxxv, the longest in *In Memoriam* (save for the Epilogue) what is recalled is not so much the Hallam that was as the poet's constant sense – one is in places reminded of Heathcliff in *Wuthering Heights* talking about his sense of the continued presence of the dead Catherine – that everything in the world out there is charged with a sense of the dead loved one:

> And every pulse of wind and wave
>   Recalls, in change of light or gloom,
>   My old affection of the tomb,
> And my prime passion in the grave.

But while the poet had been left 'To wander on a darkened earth, / Where all things round me breathed of him,' the content of lxxxv is different from the numbed emptiness of the earliest sections of the elegy. In his loss, Tennyson now finds a compensatory 'image comforting the mind'; and now, 'though left alone,' he feels Hallam's being 'working in mine own, / The footsteps of his life in mine.' And like the trio of natural lyrics, the mood of lxxxv is anticipatory, despite the dying fall of its ending.

In lxxxvii, Tennyson describes a return to the 'reverend walls' of Trinity College, Cambridge, where his friendship with Hallam had begun and ripened, and goes on to remember his friend, the leading light of their undergraduate circle, with a vividness and fondness that contain no hint of grief or of obsession with loss, but rather suggest the quiet repossession of the past. So does lxxxix, which describes with a loving fullness of natural detail Hallam's summer visits to Somersby. There are recollections of his reading Dante and Petrarch on the lawn, of picnics in the woods, discussions of books, a sister's singing to the accompaniment of her harp — all suffused with the pastoral sounds of milk bubbling into the pail, bees buzzing, the sweep of a scythe in morning dew, and the tumbling to the ground of mellowing pears. There is also reference to the 'ambrosial dark' and the 'crimson-circled star' of evening, for in a way that recalls the cross-country imaginative flight of lxvii Tennyson has transported the gorgeous images from Barmouth on the Welsh coast, the setting of lxxxvi, to Lincolnshire and again linked natural consolation and renewal with the fusing of past and present through the operation of memory in a known and loved natural setting.

We also notice that the invocations of lxxxiii, lxxxvi, and lxxxviii are paralleled by three sections (xc, xci, and xciii) which invoke not various manifestations of natural process but the spirit of Hallam, and movingly beseech him to 'come thou back to me' and to 'Descend and touch and enter.' The answer to these two sets of petitions — the one asking for a natural, the other for a seemingly supernatural, revelation — is exactly the same: the experience that Tennyson undergoes in the climactic ninety-fifth section.

With reference to the pattern of pastoral elegy, the ninety-fifth section of *In Memoriam* corresponds to the turn, or reversal, in which the poet announces that the subject of his lament is not dead, but in some way lives on. With reference to the pattern of natural consolation and restoration, the section is the answer to the petitions of lxxxiii, lxxxvi, and lxxxviii and describes the experience that makes possible the celebrations of the identity of natural and human process in sections cxv and cxxi. With reference to the repossession of the past through memory, this is the section in which the veil between past and present is fully rent. In coming to understand what happens in this poem, it is essential to realize what kind of poem it is, and to recall the uses to which the Romantic version of the pastoral elegy has characteristically been put. This has not previously been done, perhaps owing to the fact that critical attention has been concentrated on the elusive content of the poem, rather than on its form.

Section xcv is an almost paradigmatic example of a kind of lyric which has played an extremely important role in English poetry since the very early nineteenth century. Its best known examples include Coleridge's conversation poems, Wordsworth's 'Tintern Abbey,' Keats' 'Ode to a Nightingale,' Whitman's 'Crossing Brooklyn Ferry,' and Yeats' 'The Wild Swans at Coole.' M.H. Abrams calls this kind of poem the 'greater Romantic lyric' and describes its characteristic features as follows:

They present a determinate speaker in a particularized, and usually a localized, outdoor setting, whom we overhear as he carries on, in a fluent vernacular which rises easily to a more formal speech, a sustained colloquy, sometimes with himself or with the outer scene, but more frequently with a silent human auditor, present or absent. The speaker begins with a description of the landscape; an aspect or change of aspect in the landscape evokes a varied but integral process of memory, thought, anticipation, and feeling which remains closely intervolved with the outer scene. In the course of this meditation the lyric speaker achieves an insight, faces up to a tragic loss, comes to a moral decision, or resolves an emotional problem. Often the poem rounds upon itself to end where it began, at the outer scene, but with an altered mood and deepened understanding which is the result of the intervening meditation.[15]

In Tennyson's poem, the silent human auditor is replaced by the remembered Hallam, and the reading of his letters substituted for 'an aspect or change of aspect in the landscape.' Tennyson suggests the intimate connection between the natural setting and the letters by describing the latter as 'those fallen leaves which kept their green.' The 'altered mood and deepened understanding' at the conclusion are conveyed through the natural description of the last three stanzas.

Section xcv opens with four stanzas of particularized description of a specific natural setting at a specific moment in time:

By night we lingered on the lawn,
　　For underfoot the herb was dry;
　　And genial warmth; and o'er the sky
The silvery haze of summer drawn;

And calm that let the tapers burn
　　Unwavering: not a cricket chirred:
　　The brook alone far-off was heard,
And on the board the fluttering urn:

And bats went round in fragrant skies,
  And wheeled or lit the filmy shapes
  That haunt the dusk, with ermine capes
And woolly breasts and beaded eyes;

While now we sang old songs that pealed
  From knoll to knoll, where, couched at ease,
  The white kine glimmered, and the trees
Laid their dark arms about the field.

The setting is the environs of the Tennyson family home at Somersby. The singing of old songs by a family gathering recalls the time when Hallam, who had been engaged to one of Tennyson's sisters, was a virtual member of the family, just as did the family singing of Christmas songs in section xxx. And the natural setting itself (as we saw in section lxxxix) is charged with associations and memories of the former visits of Hallam, who had come to love the place almost as much as Tennyson. For during one of his visits he had written that 'If I die I hope to be buried here: for never in my life, I think, have I loved a place more. I feel a new element of being within me ...'[16] And at another time something uncannily anticipatory of the poet's experience in xcv had occurred: 'Once the two friends [Tennyson and Hallam] sat talking in the garden all night until dawn came upon them unawares, when, thinking it too late to go to bed, they walked eastward over the wolds to meet the sunrise.'[17] But the natural setting has even deeper associations for Tennyson than it could have had for Hallam, for, as the elms and the brook remind us, it is also the haunt of childhood Memory, which the 1830 ode had invoked to come from the natural setting and strengthen and enlighten the poet. The particular time is also exceptional: it is a night at the height of midsummer, when evening seems never entirely to fade, for over the night sky is drawn the 'silvery haze of summer.' During this unique interval, the natural world is still and silent, 'calm,' 'genial,' and 'fragrant.' The trees lay 'their dark arms about the field,' the kine are at ease and the night moths richly apparelled – they and the wheeling bats reminding one that is nothing exotic or lotos-landish about this rural home-scene which is, to borrow George Eliot's phrase, 'the mother tongue' of Tennyson's imagination.

In the next four stanzas, the others go indoors 'one by one,' leaving the world to darkness and the poet. Tennyson is not quite alone, however, for in response to a 'hunger' which has seized his heart he takes out some old letters from Hallam and reads 'Of that glad year which once had been.' The silent-speaking words of the dead friend's letters break 'strangely on the silence' and vividly and 'strangely' recall Hallam's faith and vigour, and his boldness in confronting doubts (qualities previously recalled in the Cambridge visit of lxxxvii). In the next four stanzas, the centre of the poem, 'word by word and line by line, / The dead man touched me *from the past*' (my italics) and it suddenly 'seemed at last' that Hallam's 'living soul was flashed on mine.' This moment of illumination is accompanied by the feeling of being caught up and 'whirled / About empyreal heights of thought' and of coming into contact with 'the deep pulsations of the world, / Aeonian music' in which the random bludgeonings of human existence, 'the shocks of Chance – / The blows of Death,' are measured out and seem part of an harmonious cosmic pattern. This is of course the 'lordly music flowing from / The illimitable years' of the 'Ode to Memory,' which the poet of section xcv, 'raised nigher to heaven's spheres' than at any other place in *In Memoriam*, is now able to hear. Presently, the 'trance' is 'cancelled, stricken through with doubt,' and in the stanza which follows its termination Tennyson laments the inability of language (the 'matter-moulded forms of speech') or of intellect to reach 'Through memory that which I became.'

In the final four stanzas, the poem returns ot its starting point, the Somersby night landscape, and through intimate sympathy with the loved and carefully observed natural setting his 'doubt' concerning the efficacy of what he had through memory become is dispelled. For while Hallam had dealt with doubts boldly and actively, keenly tracking 'Suggestion to her inmost cell,' Tennyson here deals with his doubts in his own way, not as a man of action or a poet of reflection, but as a poet of sensation waiting upon the sympathetic correspondences and ministrations of the natural world. In the aftermath of vision the dusk, 'doubtful' like the speaker, reveals the trees to be still laying their dark arms protectively about the field while the white kine still 'glimmer' in the darkness of what is now the end of night, the latter image recalling and having the same positive, reassuring value as the white tablet glimmering like a ghost in the dark church at the end of lxvii.

And in the last twelve lines, the poet witnesses and describes a richly suggestive natural correlative to his mysterious and liberating inner experience. As in section cxxi (as we shall see), the achieved union of past and present, of what is dead and what is alive, is identified with the union of night and day:

> And sucked from out the distant gloom
> A breeze began to tremble o'er
> The large leaves of the sycamore,
> And fluctuate all the still perfume,

And gathering freshlier overhead,
  Rocked the full-foliaged elms, and swung
  The heavy-folded rose, and flung
The lilies to and fro, and said

'The dawn, the dawn,' and died away;
  And East and West, without a breath,
  Mixt their dim lights, like life and death,
To broaden into boundless day.

Like the vespertinal breeze invoked in lxxxvi, the matutinal breeze of the end of xcv blows through its landscape with a rich revitalizing motion which releases and disseminates the perfumes of nature. And as the earlier breeze had been beseeched to take the poet to the star of evening with its hundred voices whispering 'Peace,' so the breeze of xcv announces the extraordinarily suggestive moment of a midsummer dawn in a northern land, in which evening (the West), never having wholly vanished, seems to merge with the East (the rising dawn) and then to exfoliate into the fullness of day. The breeze blows through a previously still landscape, bringing it to life and announcing the moment when the apparent opposites of East and West are revealed to be the two complementary parts of one process, a process necessary for the return of full ('boundless') day.[18] This wind (as at the beginning of Wordsworth's *Prelude*) is the natural equivalent of a correspondent breeze of renewal and revelation within the poet. The 'dim lights' of dawn and dark, East and West, mix together, just as earlier in section xcv past and present, the dead Hallam and the live Tennyson, have become joined through the agency of the winds of memory blowing from out of the past. The prayer of section lxxxvi has at last been answered, as has that of the 1830 'Ode to Memory.' The dewy dawn of memory has raised the poet from the obscurity (dimness) of the present, strengthened and enlightened him.

Thus, like 'Tintern Abbey,' xcv describes an experience that is effected through natural magic and through memory. What Tennyson has experienced is a Proustian moment of rapturous fulfilment during which the seemingly dead past is recaptured. We may describe this experience as religious in the sense that the vision or 'trance' is accompanied by feelings of awe, reverence, and transcendence, and gives to Tennyson's existence a holistic or 'sacred' dimension as opposed to his fragmented, 'profane' existence as a grieving survivor in a purposeless universe.[19] And we may call the experience mystical if by this we mean that it is fortuitous, fleeting, and extraordinarily different from normal experience, and involves some kind of union. But if by religious is meant the traditional Christian beliefs in a personal God and the immortality of the soul (as Tennyson himself said, 'The cardinal point of Christianity is the Life after Death'),[20] and if by mystical is meant the attainment of a direct and unmediated experience of union with God before death, then there is nothing in xcv to justify the application of these terms.[21] It is a breach between two parts of Tennyson's being, and between the poet and the natural world, that is healed in xcv; not a breach between the poet and God or life beyond the grave.

A main reason why more than this has been claimed, or vaguely asserted, for xcv is that commentators primarily interested in the religious and intellectual aspects of *In Memoriam*, in *moral profundity* rather than *natural magic*, have necessarily sought to find a turning point in Tennyson's quest for religious faith and an emotionally satisfying belief in the soul's immortality.[22] This belief can only be founded on personal experience, as Tennyson makes clear at several places in his elegy, particularly in section cxxiv which speaks of 'A warmth within the breast' melting the cold doubts of reason, and of the heart's standing up to affirm God's existence with a resounding 'I have felt.' If xcv does not provide the experiential foundation for supernatural belief, where in *In Memoriam* is it to be found? Thus, a poem which rightly belongs to Melpomene has been wrongly pressed into the service of Urania.

One must add that the first and most influential person to attempt to raise the experience described in xcv to the status of a genuinely supernatural experience was Tennyson himself. More than twenty years after its first publication in 1850, and about thirty years after its probable date of composition, Tennyson introduced two crucial pronominal changes into the central part of xcv. 'His living soul was flashed on mine, / And mine in his was wound' was changed to 'The living soul was flashed on mine, / And mine in this was wound.' Tennyson subsequently went on to gloss 'The living soul' as 'The Deity, maybe. The first reading, "his living soul" troubled me, as perhaps giving a wrong impression.'[23] This is most exasperating. As many of the sections previous to xcv – particularly xc to xciv – make clear, it was solely Hallam's spirit which Tennyson wished to contact. 'If "the living soul" is not Hallam's,' as one commentator has said, 'the lines are without meaning.'[24] 'The Deity, maybe' seems patently an afterthought which attempts to substitute a later wish for the previous deed.

The intent of Tennyson's emendations and of his annotations may be associated with the composition in 1849 of the prologue to *In Memoriam*, which is addressed to the 'Strong Son of God, immortal Love,' insists on the necessity of a supernatural faith in what we 'cannot know,' and speciously argues that 'Thou wilt not leave us in the dust' because You made man, man thinks 'he was not made to die,' and You who have made him are just. The prologue leads one to expect that what follows will be much more exclusively concerned with matters of supernatural belief than is actually the case. It is belied by several features of *In Memoriam*, most notably by its pattern of natural consolation and renewal through memory, which reaches its climax in xcv. For what the later Tennyson feared was the 'wrong impression' is the very impression that section xcv powerfully conveys: not of an experience which encompasses an apprehension of a supernatural God but rather of a moment of fusion in which, through the beneficent ministration of nature, past and present are brought together into a living unity.

Section xcv is thus the positive climax of *In Memoriam*; but despite the apocalyptic overtones of its 'empyreal heights' and 'Aeonian music' passage, it would be wrong to think that a permanent transfiguration of either the poet or the subject of his elegy had been effected. (I am speaking, as always, of the Melpomene parts of *In Memoriam*, not those belonging to Urania, like the late sections in which the apotheosized Hallam becomes a Christ figure and a 'type' of the ideal man of the future.) In section xcix, for example, the extraordinary midsummer dawn of xcv has given way to the autumnal 'dim dawn' of the second anniversary of Hallam's death and the 'full-foliaged' trees of the earlier poem have had a 'fiery finger' laid upon them. The first of a lovely, under-noticed cluster of four poems on the past, the Somersby landscape, and change, xcix poignantly speaks of the 'meadows breathing of the past, / And woodlands holy to the dead.' But the renewed sense of loss is very different from what it was two years before in the immediate aftermath of Hallam's death. Then, in section vi, the thought that 'Loss is common to the race' was rejected by Tennyson as 'vacant chaff'; for 'That loss is common would not make / My own less bitter, rather more.' In xcix he is in contrast sustained by the Words-worthian 'primal sympathy' of humanity, by the soothing thoughts that spring out of the recognition of the shared commonalty of human suffering. 'Today,' Tennyson says, those similarly bereaved 'count as kindred souls; / They know me not, but mourn with me.' In the one hundredth section the poet climbs a hill, surveys the Somersby landscape spread before him, lovingly enunciates the simple particulars that had also pleased Hallam's eye, and recalls the 'kindlier day' of the past in a way that quickens the sense of loss: 'leaving these, to pass away, / I think once more he seems to die.' In ci, the poet reflects that because of his family's imminent removal to southern England the particulars of the natural setting – especially the brook to which in *In Memoriam* as in the 'Ode to Memory' Tennyson is particularly drawn – will be 'unwatched,' 'uncared for,' and (three times repeated) 'unloved,' until with the passage of time another child of another family becomes habituated to the seasonal rhythms of the landscape, while the memories of the Tennysons fade year by year. And in section cii, just before leaving 'the well-belovèd place,' Tennyson wonders which of two spirits of memory dominate his thoughts: the childhood memories (those of the 'Ode to Memory') or the later associations of Hallam with the landscape. The answer is unsurprising, for the question involves a distinction without a difference: neither has priority; they rather 'mix in one another's arms / To one pure image of regret.'

The removal from Somersby, soon followed by the third Christmas section (civ) which the family celebrates in 'new unhallowed ground,' does suggest a movement away from the past and the natural sources of memory, as does the peculiar dream of section ciii. But in leaving Somersby behind, it should not be thought that natural consolation and intimate sympathy with nature's cyclic processes are also left behind. For among the closing sections of *In Memoriam* are two surpassingly fine lyrics which celebrate the identification of natural process with the process of human change and cyclic renewal.

In section cxv, the positive answer to the prayer of lxxxiii, it is no longer necessary to beseech the new year to come; spring has arrived (as the five times repeated *now* joyfully reiterates); the poet's sorrow has burst its 'frozen bud' and floods 'a fresher throat with song.' The natural world now breaks into colour and sound: now 'fades the last long streak of snow, / Now burgeons every maze of quick / About the flowering' fields. The vernal sun makes distances lovelier, and makes whiter both flocks and sails, as its light dances over the natural landscape and as seamews dive in sea's 'greening gleam' (a splendidly suggestive image). In the breast of the poet,

> Spring wakens too; and my regret
> Becomes an April violet,
> And buds and blossoms like the rest.

Just as in the first stanza nature's violets blossom 'by ashen roots' (recalling that in section xviii Tennyson had thought it well that Hallam's body was returned to England for burial, for 'from his ashes may be made / The violet of his native land'), so from the ashes of the poet's grief springs the flower of joyous renewal and release. Section cxv hardly represents what some readers of *In Memoriam* think it does: a natural analogue for a more than natural change in the poet. It is rather than the poet's loss has been finally compensated for through its becoming fully naturalized. Tennyson here does not have to petition, nor does he look before and after and pine for what is not. He has here become one with

> The happy birds, that change their sky
> To build and brood; that live their lives

> From land to land.

He has now become able to accept change as the sine qua non of human, as of natural, existence, and thereby to flourish in the present.[25]

Section cxxi, one of the latest written parts of *In Memoriam*, is the other late lyric which celebrates both a purely naturalistic and a fully satisfying consolation. The section, which Hopkins called 'divine, terribly beautiful' and cited as an example of 'the language of inspiration'[26] (his phrase for what Hallam called poetry of sensation and Arnold natural magic), is addressed to Hesper, the evening star, and to Phosphor, the morning star, both of which are in reality the one planet Venus, seen at two different times. They are a 'double name / For what is one.' The opening two stanzas describe the coming on of night, the cessation of the day's labour, and the onset of sleep, with its intimations of human death:

> Sad Hesper, o'er the buried sun
> And ready, thou, to die with him,
> Thou watchest all things ever dim
> And dimmer, and a glory done:
>
> The team is loosened from the wain,
> The boat is drawn upon the shore;
> Thou listenest to the closing door,
> And life is darkened in the brain.

The next two stanzas, in equally homely, immemorial images, quietly celebrate the return of day. The natural world returns to light, and the human world to life and activity:

> Bright Phosphor, fresher for the night,
> By thee the world's great work is heard
> Beginning, and the wakeful bird;
> Behind thee comes the greater light:
>
> The market boat is on the stream,
> And voices hail it from the brink;
> Thou hear'st the village hammer clink,
> And see'st the moving of the team.

The last stanza brings together the night and the day, revealing them to be the two aspects of one process, and identifying this process with the cycle of an individual man's life:

Sweet Hesper-Phosphor, double name
  For what is one, the first, the last,
  Thou, like my present and my past,
Thy place is changed; thou art the same.

This fusion of Hesper and Phosphor, dawn and evening, East and West, is an extraordinary moment in Tennyson's canon, for over and over again in his pre-*In Memoriam* poetry (as we have seen) these natural states had been used to symbolize antithetical human states: 'Hesper hateth Phosphor, evening hateth morn,' as the sisters had insisted in 'The Hesperides.' In the exceptional moment of psychological integration described in cxxi (and at the end of xcv), dawn and evening, and the day and night which follow them, are seen to be not opposed, but mutually inclusive states. Like the stars which are their emblems, they are an inseparable unity, each part of which implies the other. On the human level, the corresponding states are life and death. On the more personal level of Tennyson's separation from Hallam, the corresponding states are 'my past' and 'my present,' the happy past when Hallam was alive, and the diminished present without him. Tennyson has here come to see that these are not mutually exclusive and irreconcilable states. They are the two parts of an individual's life cycle, the alpha and omega of his existence, the one implying the other, and unthinkable without the other. In this section Tennyson does not attempt (as he does elsewhere in *In Memoriam*) to overcome the apparent dichotomy between these two states by positing a third future state where the dead Hallam of the past and the living Tennyson of the present will eventually be reunited. Tennyson is here content with naturalistic acceptance, with the realization that past and present, life and death, are not antagonistic, but the two parts of one reality.

4

Sexuality and Vision in
Idylls of the King

Idylls of the King has always had its admirers, from the late Victorian commentators who promulgated its moral, social, and religious messages to the authors of the five full-length critical studies published during the last fourteen years. Roughly speaking, these five studies made three major claims: *Idylls of the King* is a poetic whole displaying a remarkable unity; it contains Tennyson's mature thought, his profound probing of central intellectual and spiritual questions; and it is a deeply moral poem which powerfully dramatizes fundamental ethical concerns.[1]

The first of these claims is unsurprising. The piecemeal composition of the *Idylls*, its generic and thematic discontinuities, and its plural title make a strong prima facie case for its composite, inorganic nature. But since it is a iron rule of most modern literary criticism that unity is a prerequisite for a successful, let alone a great work of art, critics seem to have felt themselves under the obligation of demonstrating the unity of the poem.[2] As John Bayley has remarked: 'The usual critical instinct is to show that the work under discussion is as coherent, as aware, as totally organized, as the critic desires his own representation of it to be.'[3] One trouble with arguments for the unity of a work of art is that they can easily have their origin in the eye of the beholder. Another is that they tend to make one forget that the presence or absence of unity (especially in literary works of extended length) does not necessarily tell one very much about a work's quality, or its intrinsic interest. And not only is the criterion of unity a sometimes misleading measure of quality; the search for a whole can also direct attention away from the more imaginatively vital parts of a work, what Swinburne, referring to Tennyson's *Idylls*, called 'splendid flashes of episodical illumination.' A final danger is that unifying patterns perceived in extended works of literary art often tend to be structures of meaning, patterns of paraphrastic ideas, or moral dicta which are primarily if not exclusively cognitive. Such emphasis can lead one to ignore the affective, confessional, and therapeutic aspects of a work, and the psychological pressures and contradictory impulses which energize it.[4]

With regard to the second claim, the profundity of Tennyson's poetic thought, commentators are on firmer ground. *The Holy Grail, The Coming of Arthur,* and *The Passing of Arthur* (which I propose to call the Holy Grail group) powerfully dramatize epistemological and spiritual issues central to nineteenth- and twentieth-century thought. A line from Merlin's 'riddling triplets' – 'And truth is this to me, and that to thee' – identifies a major preoccupation of these poems: the impossibility of absolute belief, the relativity of truth to point of view, and the consequent epistemological, religious, and political dilemmas. The relationship of the temporal to the transcendent and the cyclic to the apocalyptic, the qualities and kinds of religious experience, and the tension between man's longing for permanence and the inevitability of change are cognate matters which these idylls explore in such original and striking ways that it is easy to understand Rosenberg's hyperbole in calling the *Idylls* 'the subtlest anatomy of the failure of ideality in our literature.'[5] These three idylls, to which I shall return, were all first published in *The Holy Grail and Other Poems* in 1869, and make up a cluster that is largely discontinuous in both theme and technique with the other nine parts of the *Idylls* (except for the passage on Camelot and its founding interpolated into *Gareth and Lynette,* where it is clearly out of place), just as the Arthur who makes the vibrantly positive speech on the sacred dimensions of ordinary human experience at the end of *The Holy Grail* is a strikingly different figure from the Arthur who speaks so sententiously and moralistically to his adulterous Queen in *Guinevere.*

The largest cluster within the *Idylls* consists of *Gareth and Lynette* (1872) and the idylls published together in 1859: the two Geraint and Enid poems (originally published as one), *Merlin and Vivien, Lancelot and Elaine,* and *Guinevere.* In these idylls, the Guinevere group, moral considerations are dominant. It is true that a recurring motif in them is 'taking true for false, or false for true'; but this refers to the moral difficulties and trials of various characters and has little to do with the epistemological uncertainties of the Holy Grail group. When we examine the ethical dimensions of these poems we discover that they are principally concerned with sexual purity and fidelity, with the Swinburne called 'the Albertine ideal.' 'To lead sweet lives in purest chastity, / To love one maiden only, cleave to her' is presented as the highest of virtues, the charioteer of the others and the corner-stone of social stability. As Arthur explains during his final interview with his 'sinful Queen':

> for indeed I knew
> Of no more subtle master under heaven
> Than is the maiden passion for a maid,
> Not only to keep down the base in man,
> But teach high thought, and amiable words
> And courtliness, and the desire of fame,
> And love of truth, and all that makes a man.

Sexual incontinence and adultery correspondingly become the most heinous of sins: they are made the foremost cause of the destruction of the Round Table and of the ideals it embodies. One is even allowed to think (though the feel of the *Idylls* is quite different) that if Arthur, 'selfless man and stainless gentleman,' could gave found 'A woman in her womanhood as great / As he was in his manhood' the twain might well have changed the world.

I believe Tennyson's artistic achievement in the idylls of the Guinevere group is open to serious question; for with the best will in the world I have never been able to regard these poems as other than largely inert, dull, and so 'Victorian' (in the pejorative sense) as to be of predominantly social-historical interest. One can hardly 'prove' this to be so, however; and there would be little point in either briefly bearing witness to their comparative inferiority or adumbrating a sympathetic explanation of their weakness were it not helpful in bringing into a fresh perspective and a sharper focus the distinctive excellences of the other two groups of idylls.

Of course it is not surprising to find a major English poet placing such primary emphasis on chastity. This virtue is the subject of the third book of *The Faerie Queene* and of *Comus*, works which the allegorical overtones and the exemplary and didactic functions of the Guinevere idylls bring to mind. But we have only to continue this comparison beyond a certain point – the point at which practical criticism begins – for the deficiencies of the idylls of the Guinevere group to become patent. Compared with Spenser's legend of chastity or with Milton's masque, the treatment of moral virtue in the Guinevere group seems rooted more in Victorian conventions and anxieties than in perennial questions concerning the relation of flesh and spirit and the status of the erotic.

Gareth and Lynette, the two Geraint and Enid idylls, and *Lancelot and Elaine* are over 4,500 lines long, comprising over forty per cent of the text of *Idylls of the King*. There are some superlative lollipops in these poems, particularly the iconic configurations about which John Dixon Hunt has written.[6] There are some morally impressive and emotionally compelling moments, such as Lancelot's soliloquy at the close of his and Elaine's idyll, or the account of Elaine's derangement and death, including her limpidly pre-Raphaelite 'Song of

Love and Death.' But these are the exceptions. More characteristic of these idylls are the cardboard obstacles which Gareth must overcome to win the hand of a haughty maiden, the feeble symbolism of the wounded Geraint bleeding 'underneath his armour secretly' to signify the debilitating nature of his jealousy, and the soap-opera paradoxes of 'His honour rooted in dishonour stood, / And faith unfaithful kept him falsely true.'

Merlin and Vivien and *Guinevere* are a good deal more interesting. The debate in the former between the wicked seductress and the melancholy seer is dramatically vivid and intermittently powerful, as in Vivien's comparison of Love and Fame:

> Love, though Love were of the grossest, carves
> A portion from the solid present, eats
> And uses, careless of the rest; but Fame,
> The Fame that follows death is nothing to us;
> And what is Fame in life but half-disfame,
> And counterchanged with darkness.

On the whole, however, the vividness of *Merlin and Vivien* is that of melodrama, not of great art. We have seen that Swinburne complained of 'the utterly ignoble quality of Vivien which makes her so unspeakably repulsive and unfit for artistic treatment.' It is difficult not to agree. Vivien is too reptilian and Merlin too doddering in his geriatric passion to allow for more than a sensationalistic reponse on the reader's part. *Guinevere*, the strongest poem in its group, is full of fine things. Among them are the tableau of the 'moony vapour' above the dead earth enveloping the King as he rides off to his last battle; the maid's song about the coming of the bridegroom and the foolishness of the virgins; the interruption of Guinevere's remembrance of the first time she saw Arthur – she had found him 'High, self-contained, and passionless, not like him, / "Not like my Lancelot"' – by the entrance of the King who has come to speak to her, with great passion, for the last time; and the power of much of Arthur's address to her.

Of much, but not of all. The first thing we notice about the meeting of King and Queen is (as so often in Tennyson) the pictorial arrangement of scene: Guinevere grovels 'with her face against the floor,' while Arthur stands above her speaking in a voice 'Monotonous and hollow like a Ghost's / Denouncing judgment.' It is the iconography of the Victorian fallen woman, shamed by the presence of the upright man she has betrayed. This hints at an inappropriate topicality at odds with the parabolic drift of the idyll and does prepare one somewhat for Arthur's explanation of why he cannot allow his continued love for Guinevere to lead to a reconciliation: a man who for whatever reason allows a wife whom 'he knows false [to] abide and rule the house' is 'the worst of public foes.' For, allowed her station, the wife's disease of sexuality will infect others, sap the fealty of our friends, stir the pulse with devil's leaps, and poison half the young. In reading this extraordinary passage, in which the house referred to is unmistakably a nineteenth-century domicile, one experiences the same unpleasant aesthetic shock as in turning from the original stained glass of a medieval English church to a window containing those stiffly pious and garishly coloured figures which are immediately recognizable as the work of Victorian restorers. Reminiscent of Pallas Athene's speech in 'Oenone,' this passage from Arthur's speech to his wife is so prudishly Victorian and didactically offensive as to spoil what might have been the finest scene in *Idylls of the King*.

The implications of the stained glass analogy suggest a partial explanation of why the idylls of the Guinevere group are so unsatisfactory in comparison with their Renaissance counterparts: Spenser wrote in the sixteenth and Milton in the seventeenth century; Tennyson wrote in the nineteenth. God disappeared in the nineteenth century, taking with Him the religious certainties of centuries and the supernatural sanctions of morality. The Renaissance conception of a hierarchically ordered universe, rich in correspondences and analogies among its levels, which provided the organizing principles and the typological potency of *The Faerie Queene* and *Comus*, also disappeared. For most nineteenth- and twentieth-century poets all that is left is the ego and the world outside it; values and beliefs must be discovered through experience and are necessarily tentative and problematic. Revelatory correspondences can be found only in the relationship of the self to what is *out there*, not to what used to be *up there*. Thus, two of the key themes of nineteenth-century literature (which dominate such generically different works as Wordsworth's *Prelude*, Carlyle's *Sartor Resartus*, Thoreau's *Walden*, Melville's *Moby-Dick*, and Swinburne's 'By the North Sea') are the search for truth and fulfilment out there in the phenomenal world and, for the same reason, a simultaneous inward probing of what is *down there* in the depth of one's being.[7]

What was particularly difficult for many Victorians to accept were the relativistic moral implications of all this. A classic reponse is George Eliot's, who said God was inconceivable, Immortality unbelievable, but Duty peremptory and absolute.[8] No Victorian was more deeply concerned with these implications than Tennyson, and one cannot but admire him for grappling with them in the Guinevere group of idylls, however much one may feel that in doing so he was channelling his enormous talents in an unnatural direction. But Tennyson was not content to be diagnostic; he tried to be remedial as well, and his prescription is largely a characteristically Victorian over-emphasis on sexual conduct, an answer which touches little upon the perplexities of modern man's having to live (in Auden's phrase) 'in freedom by necessity.' Those parts of the *Idylls* which are most artistically successful and imaginatively exciting are the two groups where moral concerns are not dominant: the Holy Grail group, which explores epistemological and spiritual questions concerning what is out there; and the Tristram group, in which, as in a number of his 1830 to 1842 poems, Tennyson explores what is down there in the darker recesses of his being.

The poems of the Tristram group – *Balin and Balan*, *Pelleas and Ettarre*, and *The Last Tournament* – are usually viewed by commentators from the moral perspectives provided by the Guinevere group. F.E.L. Priestley, for example, argues in an influential article that Tristram and Vivien embody 'the ethics of materialism, naturalism, and utilitarianism' which undermine Arthur's 'higher ethical system.'[9] But if one examines the Tristram group without reference to the other groups of idylls it looks rather different. In urging readers of *Idylls of the King* to consider as a discrete group idylls long perceived as three parts of a group of twelve, one is tempted to begin with an abrupt over-simplification and say the poems of the Guinevere group were written by the public, laureate Tennyson; those of the Tristram group by the private, introspective Tennyson, so many of whose finest poems are articulations of psychological conflicts within himself. None of these conflicts is more fundamental or long-lived than his simultaneous attraction to and repulsion from a naturalistic acceptance of life, of which erotic fulfilment – the 'Free love, free field' of Tristram's song – can be a major constituent. In some poems – 'The Lotos Eaters' and 'Demeter and Persephone' for example – a purely naturalistic acceptance of death is presented as both fulfilling and inadequate. In others, like 'The Vision of Sin' and 'Lucretius,' the actualization of erotic potential is shown to be both intoxicating and destructive. From this perspective, *The Last Tournament* can be seen as one of the most extraordinary poems Tennyson ever wrote, and Tristram, its central character, as the most vivid and dramatic figure in the *Idylls*. And *Balin and Balan* and *Pelleas and Ettarre* begin to look like de-idealizing and de-moralizing studies in the destructive potential of sexuality.

Balin and Balan, the last-written and last-published of the *Idylls*, was unquestionably placed by Tennyson at the beginning of the middle of his poem because it contains the first concrete illustrations of the two principal forces (both set in motion by causes ultimately traceable to Guinevere's adultery) which bring Arthur's kingdom to ruin: the asceticism instanced in King Pellam, who has made his castle into a sort of Mount Athos, and the unbridled sexuality incarnated in Vivien. But the most important point about *Balin and Balan* is that, unlike the Geraint and Enid idylls which precede it and *Merlin and Vivien* which follows, it is not concerned with ethical *exempla* or moral conduct. The poem is a psychological romance comparable to those of Tennyson's American contemporary Hawthorne.[10] Its concerns are with psychological necessity, not with conscious virtue.[11]

Balin, called 'the Savage,' is a man who 'Had often wrought some fury on myself / Saving for Balan,' his twin brother and better half, who in several ways recalls the Freudian super-ego, just as the 'demon in the woods,' whom Balan sets out to slay and with whom Balin identifies his inner self, recalls the Freudian id. This fiend is said to live in a cavern-chasm which further suggests the dark subterranéan energies of the self. Within this cave

> The whole day died, but, dying, gleamed on rocks
> Roof-pendent, sharp; and others from the floor,
> Tusklike, arising, made that mouth of night
> Whereout the Demon issued up from Hell.

Balin is right in insisting that his 'violences' are psychological in origin, not ethical:

> My father hath begotten me in his wrath.
> I suffer from the things before me, know,
> Learn nothing.

Since his 'violences' are rooted in his nature, not his nurture, the moral ideals of Arthur are powerless to mitigate them:

> These be gifts,
> Born with the blood, not learnable, divine,
> Beyond *my* reach.

Like the 'boy lame-born' who longs 'to see the peak / Sun-flashed, or touch at night the northern star' but cannot climb up out of his valley, Balin is psychologically crippled and cannot actualize within himself the ideals of the Round Table. His sunsets are those of the cavern-chasm, not the peak. Arthur's pious moralizing is never more ineffectual than when in forgiving Balin for having beaten a thrall half to death he says: 'As children learn, be thou / Wiser for falling.' We remember this simile at the end of the poem when the brothers' 'dark ... doom' is fulfilled. Balan hears a shriek, thinks it 'the scream of that

Wood-devil I came to quell,' and engages in mortal combat with Balin from whose throat the 'weird yell' had come. The brothers mortally wound each other and die a bloody death in each other's arms while fondly saying goodnight *as if* they were children going to sleep.

The self-destructive irrationality latent in Balin, 'that chained range, which ever yelpt within,' is stimulated by sexuality. Upon his return to Arthur's court after a three-year banishment, he comes hopelessly to idealize Guinevere, whom he thinks a light with no shadow and a 'golden earnest of a gentler life.' Through her he feels he may 'forget / My heats and violences' and 'live afresh.' But Balin soon overhears a conversation between Guinevere and Lancelot in which the Queen identifies herself with 'this garden rose / Deep-hued and many-folded,' not with the spiritual lily redolent of 'stainless maidenhood' praised by her tormented lover. Balin's reaction to this scene is startling: he says he is 'not worthy to be knight,' but is 'A churl, a clown.' He rushes off 'mad for strange adventure,' and upon hearing of 'the Devil of these woods' longs for an encounter, for 'To lay that devil would lay the Devil in me.' We cannot properly understand Balin's self-revulsion simply by saying with one commentator that 'he supposes that it is his own imagination imputing evil in what is really innocent speech.' The speech is not innocent, and such an interpretation of Balin's response leads only to the limp moral that 'Running from evidence that might make us doubt our beliefs is no way of insuring them.'[12] Balin's reaction reveals psychological necessity, not moral immaturity, and is reminiscent of the moment in Tennyson's 'Lucretius' when the frenzied Roman poet beseeches the 'million-myrtled wilderness, / And cavern-shadowing laurels' to hide from his gaze the fornication of nymph and satyr, while at the same time asking himself if in fact he actually wishes 'that the bush were leafless.' As Rosenberg says, Balin rushes from the garden 'as if recoiling from [his] own suppressed desires.'[13]

In the woods Balin subsequently encounters Vivien, who makes her first appearance in the *Idylls* singing a 'savage and splendid hymn to Eros':[14]

> The fire of heaven has killed the barren cold.
> And kindled all the plain and all the wold.
> The new leaf ever pushes off the old.
> The fire of Heaven is not the flame of Hell.

> Old priest, who mumble worship in your quire –
> Old monk and nun, ye scorn the world's desire,
> Yet in your frosty cells ye feel the fire!
> The fire of Heaven is not the flame of Hell.

The fire of Heaven is on the dusty ways.
The wayside blossoms open to the blaze.
The whole wood-world is one full peal of praise.
The fire of Heaven is not the flame of Hell.

The fire of heaven is lord of all things good,
And starve not thou this fire within thy blood,
But follow Vivien through the fiery flood!
The fire of Heaven is not the flame of Hell.

This celebration of natural process, equating seasonal fruition and erotic fulfilment, is one of Tennyson's most direct and powerful lyrics, and his most Lawrencian. It may be thought a palinode to 'Tears, Idle Tears,' the vibrant assertion of the passion of the present in the former answering the enormously poignant evocation of the passion of the past in the latter. In the context of *Balin and Balan*, Vivien's song identifies the sexual and generative energies which, because he is unable to come to terms with them, fuel Balin's self-destructive violences. But we can hardly say that there is anything immoral about the song: it is amoral and it looks forward much more to the Tristram of *The Last Tournament* than to the Vivien of the closing scenes of *Balin and Balan* and of *Merlin and Vivien*, which reveal her to be a 'Victorian Duessa,'[15] a cruel liar, a cynic, an immoralist devoted to the destruction of the good.

The truth is that 'The fire of heaven' song deserves a better singer, and that there is a discontinuity between its bold amorality and Vivien's immoral machinations. We can see this discrepancy more clearly if we assess dispassionately Vivien's subsequent conversation with Balin. Although her story about seeing Lancelot and Guinevere declare their love at Caerleon is specifically a lie, her general point is true: the King's first knight and his Queen are lovers, and their adultery does undermine the basis of Arthur's code of conduct. Ought Vivien to be condemned for not being a team player and suppressing the truth? It is disingenuous of commentators to argue that Vivien is here telling more than a white lie because at this point in the *Idylls* Guinevere and Lancelot have yet to consummate their adultery. There is no evidence for this wistful assumption, and in any event the point is a quibble. It seems equally disingenuous for Tennyson to encourage his readers to think this way, for it tends to make us feel that there is something 'wrong' with Vivien's song, and this in turn may lull us into missing the last savage irony in a harrowing tale about the destructive power of sexuality. Balan's terminal assertion to his dying brother at the end of the poem is 'Pure as our own true Mother is our Queen.' This statement is simply not true; it tells one nothing about Guinevere, but it does suggest how desperately the brothers cling to the fantasy of an asexual childhood realm in which the erotic is subsumed by the maternal. The unreality of this realm is brutally pointed up by Vivien's raw comment on the failure of Balin and his *Doppelgänger* to come to terms with their sexuality:

> They might have cropt the myriad flower of May,
> And butt each other here, like brainless bulls,
> Dead for one heifer!

It is hard to account for the discrepancies in *Balin and Balan* unless one argues that they are caused by Tennyson's need to distance himself from his own insight into the relationship of sexuality and conduct, and from the boldness of his celebration of naturalistic potency. We remember that he had 'Tears, Idle Tears,' a wholly naturalistic and personal lyric, sung by one of the *Princess'* maidens; and we remember his choosing to follow in 'Lucretius' the legend sponsored by St Jerome, which claimed that the author of the sublime invocation to *Venus genetrix* was driven first to frenzy and then to suicide by a love philtre. In *Pelleas and Ettarre* and *The Last Tournament*, Tennyson's presentation of the same subject matter is more overt, though at the end of the latter poem one again encounters traces of the disingenuous.

    Pelleas and Ettarre is the ninth of the *Idylls*, coming just before *The Last Tournament*. It is usually discussed in terms of its contrast with *Gareth and Lynette* (the second idyll) and there are to be sure a number of parallels-with-a-difference between the two.[16] It is much more rewarding, however, to read the poem in the context of *Balin and Balan* and of *The Last Tournament*, to which it may be regarded as a prologue. The subject of *Pelleas and Ettarre*, like that of 'Lucretius' (the poems were originally collected in the same volume in 1869), is the destructive power of sexuality, and its form, like that of *Balin and Balan*, is psychological romance, not moral exemplum. Vivien's 'Fire of Heaven' song is recalled at the idyll's opening, for Pelleas is first encountered reeling from the blaze of the noon sun. He takes refuge from its power on a shady mound, sleeps, dreams of an ideal love, but wakes to find himself surrounded by a group of lascivious 'Damsels in diverse colours like the cloud of / Sunset and sunrise,' chief among whom is the beautiful Ettarre. From then until the end of the poem, when Pelleas rushes from Camelot into the dark to become the Red Knight of *The Last Tournament*, we witness his shattering and irreversible passage from innocence to experience, from daydreams of an ideal woman to the realization that love and sexuality are inextricably linked. When Pelleas first sees Ettarre, 'The beauty of her flesh abashed the boy, / As though it were the beauty of her soul.' Pelleas' attraction to Ettarre intensifies, but while the reader comes more and more to see her baseness, the knight comes more and more to idealize her. When he leaves Ettarre his face shines 'like the countenance of a priest of old.' He regards Ettarre's ignominious treatment of him as merely the trial of his faith in her and scorns Gawain's aid in combat because 'He needs no aid who doth his lady's will.'

While Pelleas idealizes her, Ettarre comes to loathe the young knight because she cannot stomach his idealizing love. She is 'affronted by his fulsome innocence' and says she would prefer some rough worldly knight, 'Albeit grizzlier than a bear.' Exasperated by his continued devotion, she reflects that 'He is not of my kind. / He could not love me, did he know me well.' Ettarre is wrong at least on her first point, for by the end of the idyll it will have become clear that Pelleas and she are of the same 'kind.'

The night of the climax of the sexual initiation of Pelleas is hot and silent; all is hushed below the mellow moon and nothing moves 'but his own self, / And his own shadow.' Pelleas sets out to look for Ettarre, passing through 'a slope of garden, all / Of roses white and red,' which recalls Balin's observation of Guinevere and Lancelot in a garden physically different but symbolically identical. In the last of three pavilions Pelleas finds Gawain, the brother knight who has promised to further his suit, sleeping with Ettarre, who is still wearing the golden circlet Pelleas had won for her in the Tournament of Youth. Pelleas recoils from his discovery 'as a coward slinks from what he fears / To cope with, or a traitor proven, or hound / Beaten.' He leaves as his calling card his 'naked sword athwart their naked throats' and rides off crushing 'the saddle with his thighs.' His speech of bitter disillusionment ends with his reductive insistence that 'I never loved her, I but lusted for her.'

He rides on until night begins to end as Phosphor, 'the star above the awakening sun, / ... Glanced from the rosy forehead of the dawn.' In this special Tennysonian moment Pelleas gazes up at what he calls the 'sweet star, / Pure on the virgin forehead of the dawn.' He 'would have wept' but his eyes, like the southern Mariana's , are the home of woe without a tear, drier than a fountain bed in summer to which 'the village girls ... will come no more' until it is again filled with 'living waters in the change / Of seasons.' But no revivifying change will be able to restore Pelleas to psychological health. The dawn may be virgin, so too the village girls of a poetic conceit; but his view of human nature has been unalterably fixed by what he has seen in the third pavilion. Pelleas' last actions in his poem are to hiss at Guinevere 'I have no sword' and run out into the dark. He has no sword because he has left it, together with his innocence and ideals, at his idyll's version of the primal scene.

Pelleas' rite of passage destroys him. He becomes in *The Last Tournament* the demonic immoralist who swears 'by the scorpion-worm that twists in hell, / And stings itself to everlasting death.' He founds a Round Table in the North insisting that his 'tower is full of harlots' like Arthur's, and his 'knights are all adulterers' like the King's, but that his are 'truer' because 'they profess / To be none other.' As such, Pelleas is in sharp contrast to Tristram, who is able to accept his sexuality and its relativistic consequences, who is not dazed by but flourishes in the naturalistic warmth of the sun. What Pelleas is shattered by, Tristram celebrates; what makes Pelleas monstrously immoral makes Tristram intelligently amoral.

This view of Tristram is by no means that of other commentators on the *Idylls*. Robert W. Hill describes Tristram as a 'cynical materialist'; J. Philip Eggers sees him as 'little more than a backwoods cynic.' For John R. Reed he 'amply illustrates the importance of moody pride and self-indulgence in the soul's demise,' while Priestley says, with evident distaste, that 'he is the type of those who talk about making morality "conform to the facts of human nature."'[17] The major reason for this condemnation is that these critics have assessed Tristram in terms of the ethical criteria of the Guinevere group. But if we content ourselves with taking Tristram as he is presented to us, we find that moral evaluation is the least adequate and least approrpiate response. Too much is lost if we take Tristram on other than his own terms; for he is a more complex (and more attractive) figure than critics have realized.

Tristram is the most 'modern' character in the *Idylls*. He has more in common with certain twentieth-century fictional and cinematic heroes and anti-heroes than he does with King Arthur or Prince Albert, whom Tennyson identified as Arthur's contemporary avatar. Tristram is highly intelligent, but for him all ideas, ideals, or conceptions are as nothing compared to the truths of perception. As he rides from Camelot to Lyonesse he tries to keep in his thoughts Queen Isolt, to whom he must 'explain' his marriage to the other Isolt, but she 'evermore' passes from his mind

> as a rustle or a twitter in the wood
> Made dull his inner, keen his outer eye
> For all that walked, or crept, or perched, or flew.
> Anon the face, as, when a gust hath blown,
> Unruffling waters re-collect the shape
> Of one that in them sees himself, returned;
> But at the slot or fewmets of a deer,
> Or even a fallen feather, vanished again.

Tristram acknowledges no responsibilities except those from moment to moment proved upon his pulses; for him even love has no meaning except in the context of present desire. Isolt of Britanny had

> loved him well, until himself had thought
> He loved her also, wedded easily,
> But left her all as easily.

For Tristram the ethical ideals of Arthur and the moral perplexities of Lancelot are incomprehensible, and his cool judgments make both the King and his first knight look rather public-schoolish. The jousts, for Arthur the physical testing of moral valour, are for Tristram merely 'the pastime of our King.' He responds to Lancelot's unwillingness to award him the Last Tournament's prize with the seasoned frankness of the professional addressing the amateur:

> Strength of heart
> And might of limb, but mainly use and skill,
> Are winners.

Tristram knows nothing of the Victorian agenbite of inwit, and what he next tells Lancelot is devastating: 'Great brother, thou nor I have made the world, / Be happy in thy fair Queen as I in mine.'

Tristram's existential nonchalance (which in places takes on a somewhat absurdist colouration) is not idealized by Tennyson. Certain of the things he says seem most unpleasant. In an exceptional moment we find him perplexed and hesitant: 'I know not what I would.' This is when he sees weeping near a cross a lone woman whose man 'Hath left me or is dead,' and who reminds Tristram of the wife he has abandoned and of the complexity of his situation. The brutal candour of his advice to the woman repels: 'Yet weep not thou, lest, if thy mate return, / He find thy favour changed, and love thee not.' Similarly, his dismissal of Dagonet's wisdom is both reductive and self-serving:

> but when the King
> Had made thee fool, thy vanity so shot up
> It frighted all free fool from out thy heart.

These instances, however, are the exceptions, not the rule. On the whole Tristram manifests a disinterested and unconditioned vitalism that should not be called immoral or cynical because, unlike the conduct of the Red Knight, it does not define itself in opposition to the moral or the idealistic. To realize this fully, the reader must learn to distinguish between some of the things Tristram says to Dagonet and Isolt, and what he actually believes. There is no question of insincerity or dissimulation; it is simply a matter of arguing with others in terms which they can understand. Responding to Dagonet's charge that he has broken the King's music, Tristram *is* relativistic and reductive: he judges ethical and spiritual ideals from a purely pragmatic viewpoint: 'Fool, I came late, the heathen wars were o'er, / The life had flown, we sware but by the shell.' Later, in defending himself to Isolt, he says that Arthur's vows served only an expedient, utilitarian purpose. They were

> the wholesome madness of an hour –
> They served their use, their time; for every knight
> Believed himself a greater than himself.

That Tristram speaks as he does only because of his interlocutors should not keep us from realizing the shrewdness of his analysis. But we must also realize that he speaks only to convince others: he does not need to convince himself, nor to rationalize his breaking of Arthur's vows. His very physical being negates the ideals of chastity, courtesy, and 'sublime repression' of self. His 'flesh and blood' must 'perforce' violate the vows. In a powerful speech he tells Isolt to

> feel this arm of mine – the tide within
> Red with free chase and heather-scented air,
> Pulsing full man; can Arthur make me pure
> As any maiden child? lock up my tongue
> From uttering freely what I freely hear?
> Bind me to one? The wide world laughs at it.
> And worldling of the world am I, and know
> The ptarmigan that whitens ere his hour
> Woos his own end; we are not angels here
> Nor shall be: vows – I am woodman of the woods,
> And hear the garnet-headed yaffingale
> Mock them: my soul, we love but while we may.

Tristram is no more a cynic or a materialist than was Orpheus, to whom Dagonet rightly compares him. The mysteries he celebrates are Orphic not Christian, ecstatic not ethical, as in his celebration of a free love authenticated by nature's great cycle of change (a song which closely resembles Vivien's):

> Free love – free field – we love but while we may:
> The woods are hushed, their music is no more:
> The leaf is dead, the yearning past away:
> New leaf, new life – the days of frost are o'er:
> New life, new love, to suit the newer day:
> New loves are sweet as those that went before:
> Free love – free field – we love but while we may.

Tristram's last meeting with Isolt begins with her noting the difference between his bold step and her husband Mark's 'catlike' stealing through his own castle. It ends with Mark silently stepping from the darkness and splitting open Tristram's head. It is the climactic scene of *The Last Tournament*, and its dramatic tautness, suspense, and psychological insight make it the finest single scene in *Idylls of the King*. It crackles with an excitement and a tension lacking in Arthur's portentous final meeting with Guinevere. During the scene, Isolt, who had contemplated suicide during Tristram's absence, so intolerable was he life with the fiendish Mark, shows herself to be more than a little neurotic. Her vacillating responses to Tristram's sudden return, her hunger to be the exclusive object of his love, which culminates in her begging to be lied to, contrast with Tristram's ability to live only for the present. It is she, not he, who seeks warrant for her adultery in the adultery of Guinevere and Lancelot. That her husband is repellent and vicious and that she deeply desires Tristram are not sufficient reasons to quell her residual moral scruples. Tristram is content to let her believe what will allow her some portion of happiness and pleasure:

> If here be comfort and if ours be sin,
> Crowned warrant had we for the crowning sin
> That made us happy.

But when Isolt pleads with him to 'Swear to me thou wilt love me even when old, / Gray-haired, and past desire, and in despair,' Tristram refuses, though it would be expedient for him to lie, for to pledge everlasting love would be to violate the only law whose jurisdiction he acknowledges, the law of his own being:

> my soul, we love but while we may:
> And therefore is my love so large for thee,
> Seeing it is not bounded save by love.

Isolt's response shows that she understands Tristram less well than the reader does. She asks him how he would feel if she treated him in the way he is treating her. Tristram does not try to answer her: he simply invites her to partake of the waiting meal of meats and wines which 'comforted the blood ... and satiated their hearts' – a decorous emblem of the satisfaction of their erotic hungers. After this Tristram sings of the winds that bend the briar, bow the grass, and move the mere. He then presents to Isolt the ruby necklace he has won for her and is just bowing to kiss her jewelled throat when Mark steps from the darkness.

It has been argued that Mark's butchery of Tristram should be read as an authorial judgment on the knight's conduct, that 'Tristram's sudden humiliating death cancels any belief that he offers a viable alternative' to Arthur's ideals.[18] But Tristram never claimed to offer a viable alternative to anything; he claimed only to be himself. His death changes and disproves nothing, any more than Arthur's fatal wounding by Modred in *The Passing of Arthur* cancels the King's ideals. If a moral judgment is implied by Tennyson, it is surely of the crudest and most resistible sort. I would myself argue that the very gratuitousness and gruesomeness of Mark's action suggest on Tennyson's part not a moral judgment but a revulsed reflex action away from Tristram's amoral attractiveness. But no matter what we imagine his creator's intention to have been, Tristram's death no more cancels the power of his naturalistic music than the dismemberment of Orpheus did his.

It is easy to overlook the basic differences between the Guinevere group, with its predominantly moral concerns, and the Tristram group, with its predominantly psychological ones. The reasons include the critical rage for order which predisposes one to discover homogeneity not heterogeneity, and the fact that both groups centre on relationships between knights and ladies, are woven of the same stylistic fabrics, and are all part of the same rich tapestry of Tennyson's retelling of the Arthurian legends. There are, however, appreciable differences. Thomas Hardy said: 'I hold that the mission of poetry is to record impressions, not convictions: Wordsworth in his later writings fell into the error or recording the latter. So also did Tennyson.'[19] One does not know precisely to which texts Hardy was referring, but the distinction (which recalls Hallam on poets of sensation versus poets of reflection) between merely recording convictions and the more authentically imaginative task of recording impressions may be usefully applied to the Guinevere and Tristram groups. So may Yeats' famous dictum: 'We make out of the quarrel with others, rhetoric, but out of the quarrel with ourselves, poetry.'[20]

In the idylls of the Holy Grail group there are many powerful impressions but few convictions. The dominant subject of these three idylls is not sexuality but vision: its nature, its loss, and its possible recovery. *The Passing of Arthur*, the last of the *Idylls of the King*, is told from the point of view of Bedivere, 'First made and latest left all the knights.' The story concerns two complementary losses. *The Passing of Arthur* is Bedivere's account, told in 'the white winter of his age, to those / With whom he dwelt, new faces, other minds,' how Arthur and his magical sword passed from the world of human experience. But the present time of the poem – Arthur's last battle, fatal wounding, relinquishing of the sword, and reception by the three Queens – is itself dominated by a sense of loss, a longing for the true life which is now absent and known mainly through contrast with the diminished present. Bedivere says he has lost the 'true old times' of the early days of the Round Table, 'When every morning brought a noble chance, / And every chance brought out a noble knight.' But what he really mourns is more the loss of vision or light than the comradeship of knights of noble ideals and deeds in the days before the Round Table began to decay (days about which *Idylls of the King* tells one very little indeed). Bedivere intimates it is vision more than deed that he laments in the lines following those just quoted: 'Such times have been not since the light that led / The holy Elders with the gift of myrrh.'

To learn more about the vision or light that has vanished, one has to go back to *The Coming of Arthur*, the first of the idylls, and to a very few retrospective passages interpolated into the intervening idylls. One is led to do so because it is precisely these moments of vision which *The Passing of Arthur* recalls. In the first idyll there are two scenes in which vision and an extraordinary light dominate. The first is the crowning of Arthur on 'that high day,' as Bedivere remembers it, 'when, clothed with living light,' the three Queens had stood by Arthur in silence. On that joyous occasion the knights had risen from taking their vows as one who wakes 'Half-blinded at the coming of a light.' Then, according to Bellicent who describes the scene, from eye to eye through all the knights of Arthur flashed 'a momentary likeness of the King.' No lordly music is said to be heard, but Merlin is of course present at the crowning in the city he caused to be built and which in the next idyll he will describe as a city built to a ceaseless music, 'therefore never built at all, / And therefore built for ever.'

Also present is the Lady of the Lake who had given Arthur his sword, Excalibur. In *The Passing of Arthur* Bedivere is reluctant to return this sword to its miraculous maker for several reasons: its splendour – its haft 'twinkled with diamond sparks, / Myriads of topaz-lights, and jacinth-work / Of subtlest jewellery' – recalls the early visionary light; its remaining in the darkened present would suggest the continuity of past and present; and in future times, so Bedivere reflects, it would be a 'relic' aiding 'an old man' (Bedivere himself of course) in silencing 'rumours of a doubt' concerning the vision among the new faces, other minds. But the sword, which says 'Take me' on one side of its blade, says 'Cast me away' on the other; and the 'summer noon' in the past when the sword was given to Arthur has become 'the winter moon' of the present, when the light of Excalibur, 'like a streamer of the northern morn,' must be quenched in the darkness of the mere.

The other moment of vision in *The Coming of Arthur* is the wedding of the King and Guinevere. Again, from the perspective of *The Passing of Arthur*, there is the contrast of past richness and the desolating poverty of the present.

Arthur and his bride were wed in May in the 'stateliest of ... altar-shrines' in Britain; but in the late December of the present, the wounded King is carried to a chapel with a 'broken chancel and a broken cross' which stands 'on a dark strait of barren land.' At the King's wedding, his knighthood had sung a joyous martial song of blowing trumpets, clanging battleaxes, clashing brands, flashing lances, and the mighty sun of May. In *The Passing of Arthur* these sights and sounds are hideously echoed in the King's 'last, dim, weird battle':

> Shocks, and the splintering spear, the hard mail hewn,
> Shield-breakings, and the clash of brands, the crash
> Of battleaxes on shattered helms, and shrieks
> After the Christ ...

In *Merlin and Vivien*, Merlin recalls that this wedding song, the 'glorious roundel' as he calls it, was sung when some of the still young knights rode after the 'beauteous beast,' the hart with golden horns which flashed in the light as they chased it. In *The Passing of Arthur*, this joyous quest for a visionary gleam has also become hideously transformed for the knights who remain to die in Arthur's final battle. In the 'deathwhite mist' friend slays friend, 'not knowing whom he slew'; some of the knights 'had visions out of golden youth' (perhaps of the likeness of the King that flashed on them at his crowning, perhaps of the horns of the fabled hart). Others as they fall to earth 'looked up to heaven' for a light, 'but only saw the mist'; and what they hear on the field of slaughter is neither lordly music nor glorious roundel but

> Oaths, insult, filth, and monstrous blasphemies,
> Sweat, writhings, anguish, labouring of the lungs
> In that close mist, and cryings for the light,
> Moans of the dying, and voices of the dead.

It is not only Bedivere who in *The Passing of Arthur* laments the loss of vision and light. Arthur himself, 'widowed of the power in his eye' that had once made his knights instantly obey him and so baffled and confused that at one point he cries out that he knows 'not what I am, / Nor whence I am,' yearns for the sight and the illumination that were once his. Even his countenance suggests this. In the last idyll the King's face is 'white / And colourless, and like the withered moon,' and parched with dust are his curls that once had 'made his forehead like a rising sun / High from the daïs-throne' (presumably the daïs on which he was crowned in the first idyll while the miraculous light played over the faces of his knights). And in the first idyll, before one of his victorious battles, Arthur had experienced the same moment of vision that Tennyson describes in 'Timbuctoo' (when each sense 'As with a momentary flash of light / Grew thrillingly distinct and keen'). For the young King,

> the world
> Was all so clear about him, that he saw
> The smallest rock far on the faintest hill,
> And even in high day the morning star.

But in *The Passing of Arthur*, the King, enveloped in the 'blind haze,' moans that his vision of the natural world, which in the past gave him assurance of a higher reality, has darkened, and has not been compensated for by his observation of the ways of men:

> I found Him in the shining of the stars,
> I marked Him in the flowering of His fields,
> But in His ways with men I find Him not.

Arthur goes on to ask whether the darkness and horror of the tragic present are owing to the nature of the world; whether they are caused by the inability of men to perceive the world as it really is; or whether things seem as they do because men cannot see into the future:

> O me: for why is all around us here
> As if some lesser god had made the world,
> But had not force to shape it as he would?
> …
> Or else as if the world were wholly fair,
> But that these eyes of men are dense and dim,
> And have not power to see it as it is:
> Perchance, because we see not to the close.

Arthur asks these questions at the beginning of *The Passing of Arthur*, suggesting that the narrative which follows will explore the question of what has happened to the light and whether the enhanced vision of the past is recoverable. One should not, however, expect anything like a clear-cut answer to these questions, for it is a principal strength of the idylls of the Holy Grail group that they are diagnostic not remedial, explore complex questions without attempting simplistic answers, offer impressions not convictions. (The major exception to this is the single weak spot in *The Passing of Arthur*: the King's platitudinous and intrusive convictions concerning the power of prayer, which are capped by the bizarre, and anachronistic, image of the 'whole round earth' being 'every way / Bound by gold chains about the feet of God.') Still, one expects some intimation of whether or not the vision which existed in the past, the radiance which was once so bright, is recoverable in the present or future. In crude terms, is the ending of *Idylls of the King* optimistic or pessimistic?

Commentators have differed widely in their answers to this question. For Ryals, 'Societies may fail and heroes may pass, Tennyson implies, but their passing does not mean that all Godhood is forever withdrawn from the universe. For the hero will come again ... as [Arthur] vanishes into light the sun rises bringing the new year, clearly indicating, I believe, that the hero will come again.'[21] But for James R. Kincaid the ending is 'bitter and entirely pessimistic': 'The death of Arthur confirms no justice, universal or local; the poem ends ... in darkness and uncertainty, without heroism, even without meaning.'[22] The reason for these diametrically opposed readings is that there is some evidence for each in the text of *The Passing of Arthur*. But this means that the correct answer to the question posed above is that the ending of *Idylls of the King* is neither optimistic nor pessimistic; it is indeterminate, offering alternative possibilities.

It is perhaps surprising that this has not been more clearly seen by Tennyson's commentators, for in its indeterminateness and open-endedness the Holy Grail group of idylls is in the central Romantic tradition of spiritual quest in the nineteenth century. 'Was it a vision, or a waking dream?' asks Keats at the end of 'Ode to a Nightingale.' Shelley, a sceptical idealist, speaks of 'doubtful knowledge' in the Preface to *Alastor* and provides 'The Two Spirits – An Allegory' with alternative endings, one saying that the questing spirit died exhausted at the upper limits of the phenomenal world, the other that in night he found day. In *Moby-Dick*, Ishmael survives at least partially because, unlike Ahab, he maintains an open-mindedness and flexibility concerning the illusive 'ungraspable phantom of life' which is 'the key to it all.'[23] And at the end of *Wuthering Heights* one cannot say whether or not in dying Heathcliff called a lovelier life from death (as his creator said she wished to do in one of her poems) and was united with the object of his visionary longing. In the closing two pages of the novel, the shepherd boy may possibly not be wrong in saying that he saw near the Heights the spirits of Catherine and Heathcliff; but Lockwood, so often wrong earlier in the novel, may for once be right when he looks at the lovers' graves and wonders 'how any one could ever imagine unquiet slumbers for the sleepers in that quiet earth.'[24]

At the end of *The Passing of Arthur*, having been received into the dusky barge by the three Queens who minister to him, the King admits that his 'mind is clouded with a doubt' as to whether, as prophesied, he will really be taken to the island valley of Avilion where his grievous wound will be healed. The barge moves off into the deep, and the moans of lamentation from the three Queens grow faint. When they can no longer be heard, Bedivere, 'revolving many memories,' is appalled by the 'stillness of the dead world's winter dawn.' He climbs to a higher position to catch a last glimpse of the barge and cries out that the King has only passed away, not died, and that 'He comes again'; 'but – if he come no more –' Bedivere immediately goes on to say, showing that his mind too is clouded with doubt. Then, from the coming dawn toward which the barge has sailed,

> it seemed there came, but faint
> As from beyond the limit of the world,
> Like the last echo born of a great cry,
> Sounds, as if some fair city were one voice
> Around a king returning from his wars.

The aural impressions of joyous shouts, however faint and far away, mitigate the ghastly quiet of the winter present, recall the glorious springtime roundel of *The Coming of Arthur*, and answer the 'dim cries' heard by Arthur in his sleep at the beginning of the last idyll, cries suggestive of a grimmer passing, 'As of some lonely city sacked by night, / When all is lost, and wife and child with wail / Pass to new lords.' But the tone and movement of the passage, if not elegiac, are hardly triumphant; they are rather dolorously slow moving, as if reluctant to allow the 'last echo' and its verbal representation wholly to fade. And the repeated qualifiers (*seemed, as, like, as if*) insist that strictly speaking Bedivere's hearing is not what Wallace Stevens calls a 'final finding of the ear,'[25] but rather a possibility, a hopeful analogy, not a realized vision. So too in the last lines when, having climbed as high as possible, Bedivere 'saw ... Or thought he saw' what is now to his vision the 'speck' of the barge 'on the deep / Somewhere far off' go from less to less and finally, in a wonderfully suggestive (but not assertive) oxymoron, 'vanish into light.' In the last line of the *Idylls* this dawning light is identified as 'the new sun ... bringing the new year': perhaps a 'mockery of renewal by a cruel and deceptive nature';[26] but perhaps, especially if one remembers the revelatory potentialities of dawn elsewhere in Tennyson, the intimation of the dawn of a new vision.

Thus, at the end of *The Passing of Arthur* the possibility of a recovery of vision and light is neither asserted nor gainsaid; it remains a possibility. But while Tennyson is careful to allow for the possibility, he has nothing to say or show concerning the instrumentality through which the possible vision may be regained. Can it be recovered only apocalyptically, through external agency, as the extraordinary events said to surround Arthur's coming in the first idyll suggest (especially the night 'In which the bounds of heaven and earth were lost')? Or can the vision be recovered in memory and through the cyclic (non-apocalyptic) processes of the natural world, as the 'living spirit' of Hallam (Tennyson's Arthur, just as the King is Bedivere's) was in *In Memoriam* and as the last line of *The Passing of Arthur* allows one to think? Tennyson is characteristically non-specific concerning such questions, for the very good reason that he is not sure. We saw in the previous chapter how in two early poems quite different origins were assigned to the lordly music of the illimitable years; and in the very late lyric 'Far – Far – Away' Tennyson is still uncertain whether that 'vague world-whisper, mystic pain or joy' is

> A whisper from his dawn of life? [or] a breath
> From some fair dawn beyond the doors of death
> > Far – far – away?

That is, does the mystic or lordly music, the aural equivalent of vision, flow out of the past and echo in the memory, or does it flow from the future beyond?

Tennyson not only finds this question unanswerable; at the end of *The Holy Grail*, in Arthur's speech on the sacred dimensions of ordinary human existence, he puts forward a third possibility: that the source of vision is in neither the past nor the future, not far, far away but right here in the present, in the imminent, in simply living as and where we live. Arthur's speech does not have authorial sanction, but then neither do any of the other visions in the *Idylls*; as Culler has noted: 'One would not have thought it possible, but Tennyson has written an entire poem on King Arthur and his knights without one single instance of magic or the supernatural offered on the poet's own authority.'[27] But Arthur's speech does have a powerful simplicity and directness, and Tennyson did call the ending of it 'the (spiritually) central lines of the Idylls.'[28] And the speech is the last and clearly the best word in an idyll that devotes itself to distinguishing different kinds of vision and their sources; and does so with such power and mature psychological insight as to make *The Holy Grail* arguably the richest of the *Idylls*.

There is the nun, Percivale's sister, whose devotion to the Grail is psychosexual in origin. In her earlier maidenhood she had 'glowed' with a

> > fervent flame of human love,
> Which being rudely blunted, glanced and shot
> Only to holy things.

When the Grail does appear to her it seems more erotic than mystical, and even recalls the orgiastic gyrations of the second section of 'The Vision of Sin':

> and then
> Streamed through my cell a cold and silver beam,
> And down the long beam stole the Holy Grail,
> Rose-red with beatings in it, as if alive,
> Till all the white walls of my cell were dyed
> With rosy colours leaping on the wall;
> And then the music faded, and the Grail
> Past, and the beam decayed, and from the walls
> The rosy quiverings died into the night.

There is Gawain, who cares more for pleasure than vision. There is Bors, who though he does not greatly desire to, sees the Grail (if it was not a meteor). But he 'may not speak of it,' is saddened by what he has experienced, and in any event cares more for his beloved cousin, Lancelot. There is Lancelot himself, for whom the Grail becomes the opportunity to cleanse himself of the hidden sin that is tormenting him, the cleansing of which is a precondition of his seeing the Grail. There is Galahad, who alone of the knights seems to have the genuinely other-worldly vocation of the religious visionary who must lose himself to this world to find himself in the higher world. And there is Percivale, whose life is ruined and whose natural, human instincts are corrupted by the pursuit of a higher, but for him disabling and unattainable, vision. When Percivale begins his quest he is 'lifted up in heart' and his sight is enhanced, for never yet 'Had heaven appeared so blue, nor earth so green.' But by the end of his journeys his heart has shrunken and he has come to hate 'mine own self / And even the Holy Quest' and all but the women he has forsaken because of his burning vow to pursue the Grail. But even if he were to see the sacred cup, it would be a projection of what was within him and for that reason 'crumble into dust'; for Percivale's quest is grimly reductive and makes a desert of his consciousness.

Finally, at the end of *The Holy Grail*, there is the visionary alternative of Arthur. The King had not been present at Camelot when thunder and a light 'seven times more clear than day' had struck his hall. His knights, having convinced themselves that this was a veiled apparition of the Grail, had sworn to ride in its quest; but on hearing of it Arthur had immediately recognized that this vision was unlike the circumstantially similar light that had earlier flashed before the knights at his crowning. He had called the cup a 'sign to maim' his order and had rightly predicted that his knights would 'follow wandering fires, / Lost in the quagmire.' As this scene recalled *The Coming of Arthur*, so the final scene of *The Holy Grail* looks forward to *The Passing of Arthur*. For when the knights return from their quest a year later, it is to a Camelot blasted by a fierce gale; and, while he does allow the possibility that the Grail was a vision and not a waking dream, the most that Arthur can say concerning the experiences of his finest knights is so minimal and relativistic as to be only notionally or rhetorically positive:

> But if indeed there came a sign from heaven,
> Blessed are Bors, Lancelot and Percivale,
> For these have seen according to their sight.
> …
> And as ye saw it ye have spoken truth.

Arthur concludes his analysis by bearing witness to the truth and superiority of another kind of vision:

> And some among you held, that if the King
> Had seen the sight he would have sworn the vow:
> Not easily, seeing that the King must guard
> That which he rules, and is but as the hind
> To whom a space of land is given to plow.
> Who may not wander from the allotted field
> Before his work be done; but, being done,
> Let visions of the night or of the day
> Come, as they will; and many a time they come,
> Until this earth he walks on seems not earth,
> This light that strikes his eyeball is not light,
> This air that smites his forehead is not air
> But vision – yea, his very hand and foot –
> In moments when he feels he cannot die,
> And knows himself no vision to himself,
> Nor the high God a vision, nor that One
> Who rose again: ye have seen what ye have seen.

The hind (a farm worker) is anticipated earlier in the idyll by the simple monk Ambrosius, the interrogator of Percivale, who lives 'like an old badger in his earth,' has never known 'the world without,' and rejoices in the quotidian life of his abbey and the little thorpe nearby. As opposite equals, the hind on the one hand and King Arthur on the other are a Tennysonian version of the Carlylean 'Two men I honour and no third' who in *Sartor Resartus* are the peasant toiling for his daily bread and the hero toiling for the bread of life, both of them finding fulfilment in doing the work that lies nearest them.[29] While at the end of his speech King Arthur naturally expresses himself in a Christian idiom, one should not fail to see that the kind of experience he describes is by no means traditionally Christian. It is a version of the great Romantic doctrine of 'natural supernaturalism' (to again use Carlyle's terminology), of living in the present, in the imminent, so fully and so unself-consciously that vision, moments of transcendence and experiential immortality (what Arthur calls moments when man feels he cannot die), come as they will – not as a result of quest, but precisely because they are unsought. Emerson's account of such Romantic moments seems especially close to Arthur's: 'Standing on the bare ground, – my head bathed by the blithe air and uplifted into infinite space, – all mean egotism vanishes. I became a transparent eyeball; I am nothing; I see all; the currents of the Universal Being circulate through me. I am part or parcel of God.'[30]

The content of these visionary moments is simply the natural world and its motions raised in intensity so that they seem to be more than themselves and to give access to a higher realm: what Arthur describes in Christian images, Emerson in the language of idealist philosophy, and what elsewhere, as we have seen, Tennyson calls 'the lordly music of the illimitable years' or 'the deep pulsations of the world.' Despite its Carlylean emphasis on duty, Arthur's speech has little to do with letting the wife known to be false abide and rule the house or with praying night and day for someone's soul (to recall other of the King's speeches). Indeed, it should give one pause to reflect that Arthur's vitalist living-in-the-present vision has more in common with the orphic naturalism of Tristram than with any of the convictions in the Guinevere group of idylls. At the same time, *mutatis mutandis*, it has more in common with certain poems of Tennyson's younger contemporary Swinburne than with most of the Laureate's own post-*In Memoriam* poetry.

5

Swinburne's Internal Centre

Of all the major nineteenth-century English poets, Swinburne's reputation is by far the most equivocal. One reason is that while he has been the subject of a disproportionately large amount of belletristic and crackpot commentary, there has been a paucity of serious critical and scholarly work. During the past thirty years, for example, what has become a flood of scholarly and interpretative work on Tennyson, Browning, Arnold, Hopkins, and Hardy, not to mention the major Romantic poets of the early decades of the century, has in the case of Swinburne remained a trickle.[1] Another reason involves the severely limited range of Swinburne's subject matter, tone, and style and the fact that, as Harold Nicolson long ago observed, his worst poetry 'is so disconcertingly similar to his best.'[2] To speak bluntly, even by the copious standards of Tennyson and Browning, Swinburne, whose *Collected Poetical Works* fill over twenty-two hundred pages, wrote far too much poetry. Large tracts of this corpus are virtually unreadable and recall Swinburne's own description of the Dunwich seacoast: 'Miles, and miles, and miles of desolation! / Leagues on leagues on leagues without a change!'[3]

A third reason for his equivocal reputation is that Swinburne's poetry has on the whole not fared well in the estimation of his peers. On the one hand, there is D.H. Lawrence's extraordinary praise:

he moves me very deeply. The pure realisation in him is something to reverence: he is very like Shelley, full of philosophic spiritual realisation and revelation. He is a great revealer, very great. I put him with Shelley as our greatest poet. He is the last fiery spirit among us. How wicked the world has been, to jeer at his physical appearance etc. There was more powerful rushing flame of life in him than in all the heroes rolled together.[4]

But on the other hand there is George Meredith writing in 1861 at the beginning of Swinburne's career: 'I don't see any internal centre from which springs anything that he does. He will make a great name, but whether he is to distinguish himself solidly as an Artist, I would not willingly prognosticate';[5] there is William Morris saying in 1882:

you know I never could really sympathize with Swinburne's work; it always seemed to me to be founded on literature, not on nature ... in these days the issue between art, that is, the godlike part of man, and mere bestiality, is so momentous, and the surroundings of life are so stern and unplayful, that nothing can take serious hold of people, or should do so, but that which is rooted deepest in reality and is quite at first hand: there is no room for anything which is not forced out of a man of deep feeling, because of its innate strength and vision.[6]

There is Gerard Manley Hopkins on the third series of *Poems and Ballads* of 1889: 'It is all now a "self-drawing web"; a perpetual functioning of genius without truth, feeling, or any adequate matter to be at function on';[7] and finally there is T.S. Eliot in his 1920 'Swinburne as Poet,' a masterpiece of backhanded compliment:

his diffuseness is one of his glories ... in Swinburne meaning and sound are one thing ... he uses the most general word, because his emotion is never particular, never in direct line of vision, never focused; it is emotion reinforced, not by intensification, but by expansion ... The poetry is not morbid, it is not erotic, it is not destructive. These are adjectives which can be applied to the material, the human feelings, which in Swinburne's case do not exist. The morbidity is not of human feeling but of language. Language in a healthy state presents the object, is so close to the object that the two are identified ... Only a man of genius could dwell so exclusively and consistently among words as Swinburne.[8]

Quantitatively speaking, it cannot be denied that there is much truth in these four trenchant observations. Even the most sympathetic reader of Swinburne can only plead *nolo contendere*. But a qualitative point of view is another matter; and if one is interested not in the most, but in the best of Swinburne these comments can be indirectly helpful in locating what is most vital and alive in his poetry. The first chapter of this study suggested that Swinburne's deepest poetic beliefs could be gauged with negative reference to Tennyson, the dominant poet of the previous generation; and in the present chapter)I want to outline the core of naturalistic beliefs (and belief in the poetic vocation) that from first to last are the 'internal centre' of Swinburne's poetry, the personal truths and 'deep feeling' that are 'adequate matter' for his poetic genius, and that are rooted not in literature but in a fiercely independent and stoic vision of human existence in a 'stern and unplayful' world. In the poetry informed by this vital core, there may well be diffuseness or vagueness in the description of external phenomena: Swinburne's eye is seldom on the object in a way that Eliot or T.E. Hulme would applaud. But in Swinburne it is essential to distinguish between diffuseness or vagueness in the description of objects and diffuseness or vagueness in the depiction of mental and spiritual states. If one is looking for it one can find a great deal of the former. There is a regrettably good deal of the latter and it is to be found in the poems that seem automatic: that lack 'adequate matter' and are 'founded on literature.' But in his finest poetry, Swinburne's interests are never in language per se but in language as the expression of his own 'human feelings,' as the articulation of a distinctive vision of human existence, and as the record of his long struggle to move from darkness to some measure of light.

Let us begin with Swinburne's first collection of verse, the *Poems and Ballads* of 1866. Like much of Tennyson's early verse, many of these pieces are conscious experiments with an impressive variety of metres and conventional forms. In Morris' phrase, they are 'founded on literature.' 'Song before Death,' for example, is a translation of a lyric in de Sade's *Aline et Valcour*, 'Love at Sea' an imitation of Gautier's 'Barcarolle.' 'Saint Dorothy' is an imitation of a Canterbury tale, and several dramatic monologues show the influence of Browning. 'A Ballad of Life' and 'A Ballad of Death' are verse paintings in the Pre-Raphaelite manner; several poems are early instances of Swinburne's lifelong interest in the ballad; and there are graceful exercises in a number of other forms: sonnets, aubades, a masque, rondels, and Villonesque ballades. Other pieces – 'Phaedra,' 'Hendecasyllabics,' and 'Sapphics' – are exercises in classical metres. And, according to Whistler, 'Faustine' was written to see how many rhymes to the name Swinburne could find.[9]

But it is not the technical experiments that have made the 1866 *Poems and Ballads* the best known of Swinburne's many volumes. The major reason is its importance to the study of Victorian taste and morality, and its usefulness to literary historians in pointing up the beginnings of art for art's sake in England and the change in later nineteenth-century English poetry from the mastication of social problems and moral and theological dilemmas to a more exotic diet. The publication of *Poems and Ballads* was a cause célèbre. The young Thomas Hardy, who responded to the volume with a 'quick glad surprise,' and read it even while 'walking along the crowded London streets to my imminent risk of being knocked down,' described its effect on literary London to be 'as though a garland of red roses / Had fallen about the hood of some smug nun.'[10] Certainly the subject matter of a number of poems – leprosy, male homosexuality, lesbian love, necrophilia, sadism, and masochism – was unconventional, to say the least. The influence of Baudelaire is apparent, and what Swinburne said about *Les Fleurs du mal* in an 1862 review serves equally well as a description of *Poems and Ballads*: 'Throughout the chief part of this book he had chosen to dwell mainly upon sad and strange things – the weariness of pain and the bitterness of pleasure – the perverse happiness and wayward sorrows of exceptional people. It has the languid, lurid beauty of close and threatening weather – a heavy, heated temperature, with dangerous hothouse scents in it; thick shadow of cloud about it, and fire of molten light.'[11]

It would be idle to attempt to play down the sensational aspects of *Poems and Ballads*: the self-conscious, flaunted decadence; the celebration of strange sexual passions; the attempt to *épater le bourgeois*. These are the qualities which accounted for the volume's notoriety a hundred years ago, and which are still synonymous with it today. But it may be said that these are not the only, and not the most intrinsically important, aspects of *Poems and Ballads*, and that the meaning and distinction of several of the volume's strongest poems have been obscured by its reputation. It is mainly in these poems, not in the conventional exercises or lurid shockers, that the pervasive concerns of Swinburne's most deeply felt and authentic poetry are foreshadowed.

'Itylus' is an example. Through the nightingale's recollection the poem re-tells the ghastly story of Tereus, Procne, Philomela, and the slaying of Itylus. It is a fine exercise in delayed meaning, for only gradually do the full circumstances of the nightingale's appeal to her sister, the swallow, became clear. What the poem basically does is dramatize two different kinds of existence. The sisters have both lived through the same hideous experiences, but they are very different singers, who make mutually exclusive kinds of poetry. All of the adjectives describing the swallow suggest her swiftness and lightness. Her heart is 'full of the spring,' and she annually follows the sun into the south. The nightingale, on the other hand, is a creature belonging to the night. Her heart is an unquenchable 'molten ember' and she is 'fulfilled' not by seasonal renewal but by feeding 'the heart of the night' with the fire of her song. She can neither forget the past nor forgive the 'changing swallow' her forgetfulness: 'Thou hast forgotten, O summer swallow, / But the world shall end when I forget.' The 'heart's division' that separates the sisters is two different responses to a world of gross tragedy and personal violation. Swinburne does not arrange his poem to suggest which of these responses he favours, nor is there any reason why he should do so. One might associate the swallow with the husband in Robert Frost's 'Home Burial,' who is able to assuage his grief over the death of his young child by living in the present, yielding to the rhythms of the natural cycle, and turning to fresh tasks – unlike his wife who, like the nightingale, thinks 'the world's evil' and refuses to be consoled. But one might also reflect that the swallow seems an Edgar Linton type, lacking the passion and stature of Heathcliff, who cannot be reconciled to his loss. In any event, it is not hard to understand what 'Itylus' is doing in the first *Poems and Ballads*. What the sisters have experienced suggests an analogy to the world of these early poems. It is what may be called a *fleurs du mal* world, where vice is stronger than virtue and weakness dominates will. To sing like the nightingale is to make personal trauma the subject matter of poetry, to live locked in the harshness of the past and keep always present 'the grief of the old time.' To sing like the swallow is to be able to naturalize grief, to find something glad 'in thine heart to sing,' and to become renewed through identification with natural process.

'Hymn to Proserpine,' one of Swinburne's most negative statements on the human condition, is another example. The poem's concerns – mutability, mortality, and the ambiguous nature of the poet's privileged insight – Swinburne will repeatedly return to throughout his poetic career, but his treatment of them will seldom be so despairing. The poem is a dramatic soliloquy; its speaker a Roman of the fourth century A.D., a pagan poet who, like Julian the Apostate (whose supposed last words are the poem's epigraph), thinks that Christianity does not represent an advance over the pagan gods. But Swinburne's poem is not really about the reaction of a classical pagan to the new religion of Christ in the way that Browning's 'Cleon' or Pater's *Marius the Epicurean* is. The speaker has no real faith in the pagan gods; for him they are simply metaphors, and he feels that Christianity and the Christian pantheon (the 'New Gods' crowned in the city) are simply another set of metaphors which will also pass away.

The poem's basic tension is between the speaker's desires and his overpowering awareness of mutability, which he calls 'Time' or 'Fate.' The overthrow of the pagan by the Christian gods is simply one instance of mutability's work. For the speaker, the only reality is change, which terrifies him. His only release from this pained awareness comes from sensation, his sensuous pleasure in both natural and human beauty. But since this beauty all too quickly fades, his release is short-lived. The sharper his pleasure, the keener his realization of its transience: 'Laurel is green for a season, and love is sweet for a day; / But love grows bitter with treason, and laurel outlives not May.' This is the situation that Pater would describe a decade later in the famous 'Conclusion' to *The Renaissance*. But the speaker of the 'Hymn to Proserpine' cannot maintain the ecstasy of burning always with a 'hard, gemlike flame'; he is too overwhelmed by his awareness of what Pater called the 'awful brevity' of human life.

His languorous mood and world-weary manner also recall the early Yeats. For him, as for Yeats' Happy Shepherd: 'The woods of Arcady are dead / And over is their antique joy.' But while Yeats' singer is at least able to assert that 'Words alone are certain good,' Swinburne's poet is unable to find certainty or joy in his vocation as a poet: 'I am sick of singing: the bays burn deep and chafe.' Apollo, symbol of poetry and poetic life, is the god who slays his own worshippers: though 'a beautiful god to behold,' he is 'a bitter god to follow.' The speaker's sole utterance has become a chant of oblivion, and it is a measure of his estrangement from natural process that he views death more as an escape from the meaningless flux of life than as a necessary part of it, more as life's extinction than its completion. Only at one moment does he seem to remember what Swinburne in his later poetry will seldom forget, that death is an integral part of the natural world and its cyclic change, and that an individual's life is rooted in this process: 'O daughter of earth, of my mother, her crown and blossom of birth, / I am also, I also, thy brother; I go as I came unto earth.' One may say that the speaker has not yet learned fully to accept death as a condition of life, and to accept the circumstances of his life as tolerable. At least implicitly, there is a connection between this and his inability to fulfil himself as a poet. In later poems of Swinburne, an acceptance of death as the completion of life, beyond which there is nothing else, is closely linked to an affirmation of the value of poetry and the poetic vocation, and to a recognition of the bonds of love and compassion that bind poets (and, by extension, all men) together in their common mortality. But the speaker of the 'Hymn to Proserpine' has not yet learned that although death destroys a man, the idea of death saves him.

'Anactoria' is another dramatic monologue about an unhappy poet. It is not the sadistic effusion it is sometimes taken to be, but a poem about the fate of poets and the nature of poetic vocation. The speaker of 'Anactoria' is Sappho, the lyric poetess of antiquity, for Swinburne 'simply nothing less ... than the greatest poet who ever was at all.'[12] She also appears in 'Sapphics,' another of the first *Poems and Ballads*. There, as the representative of poetry and the poetic life, she is opposed to Aphrodite, the Venus of 'Hymn to Proserpine,' who represents an exclusive devotion to physical love. Sappho's song can make the gods 'wax pale: such a song was that song,' and almost move the 'implacable Aphrodite.' Her song gives her 'a crown forever,' but because she sings to her own devotees, and not to Venus, the goddess of love withdraws her amorous retinue from Lesbos, leaving the island barren. The point of this dream-poem is obscure, but its main theme is clear: the opposition between the erotic life and the influential but isolating gift of poetry. The theme of 'Anactoria' is the same.

'Sapphics' describes the poetess' song as

her visible song, a marvel,
Made of perfect sound and exceeding passion,
Sweetly shapen, terrible, full of thunders,
    Clothed with the wind's wings.

This is a not unfair description of 'Anactoria,' a poem of great technical virtuosity. A mosaic of elaborations of various Sapphic fragments, the poem is flawed by a certain looseness of organization, but one can nevertheless discern a basic conflict and its resolution. The opening line – 'My life is bitter with thy love' – introduces one pole of the poem's tension: Sappho's perverted and sadistic emotions towards her beloved, best epitomized in the chilling line: 'Yea, all thy beauty sickens me with love.' Opposed to this is her awareness of her vocation as a poet and, consequently, of her closeness to the natural world. What happens in the poem is that her initial, almost total, submersion in her compulsive love gradually gives way before an increasingly exultant realization of her poetic powers, so that by the poem's conclusion she is able to chant an extraordinary hymn to the powers of poetry.

Only after she has been speaking for some time does Sappho first mention her poetic gifts, and then in passing – 'Though my voice die not till the whole world die.' Soon after this comes the poem's most unnerving moment – when Sappho desires to exchange her poetic gifts for the fulfilment of her sadistic lust:

Ah that my lips were tuneless lips, but pressed
To the bruised blossom of thy scourged white breast!
Ah that my mouth for Muses' milk were fed
On the sweet blood thy sweet small wounds had bled!

Her most despairing cry comes soon after: 'Yea, though their alien kisses do me wrong, / Sweeter thy lips than mine with all their song.' Swinburne next allows Sappho an extended vituperation against 'God,' a section which is something of an intrusion into the poem.[13] With the end of this tirade, 'Anactoria' abruptly modulates into the sustained brilliance of its closing section, beginning 'Thee too the years shall cover' – lines which Hardy described in a letter to Swinburne as presenting 'the finest *drama* of Death and Oblivion ... in our tongue.'[14] This section grows out of the few lines of a Sapphic fragment: 'When you are dead you will lie unremembered for evermore; for you will have no part in the roses that come from Pieria; nay, obscure here, you will move obscure in the house of Death, and flit to and fro among such of the dead as have no fame.'[15] To have 'the high Pierian flower' is to have the gift of poetry; not to have it is to 'be not anymore at all, / Nor any memory of thee anywhere.' Sappho asserts that, unlike her beloved, she will not wholly perish because her poems will survive, and that with men's perceptions of the natural world memories and metaphors of her 'shall mix.' She goes on to claim for the poetic life an additional consolation, another way in which poets may be said to be immortal. Sappho foresees that, like the apotheosized Keats at the climax of Shelley's 'Adonais,' she will be 'made one with Nature' and become 'a portion of the loveliness' which once she made more lovely through her singing:

> Of me the high God [of death] hath not all his will.
> Blossom of branches, and on each high hill
> Clear air and wind, and under in clamorous vales
> Fierce noises of the fiery nightingales,
> Buds burning in the sudden spring like fire,
> The wan washed sand and the waves' vain desire,
> Sails seen like blown white flowers at sea, and words
> That being tears swiftest, and long notes of birds
> Violently singing till the whole world sings –
> I Sappho shall be one with all these things,
> With all high things forever.

Sappho's assertions of a mixture of natural and creative immortality are so triumphant and unqualified, and so uncharacteristic of Swinburne's vision, as to make one reflect that, however closely the young Swinburne may have identified with its speaker, 'Anactoria' is after all a dramatic poem. For Swinburne seldom if ever makes such claims in his own voice; and in 'Ave atque Vale,' which one might call his definitive statement on the fate of poets, Swinburne will offer a quite different account of poetic immortality, including that of Sappho. And in another dramatic poem from the 1866 *Poems and Ballads*, the triumphant conclusion is of a quite different kind from that of 'Anactoria.'

The speaker of 'Laus Veneris' is Tannhäuser, the knight of medieval legend. Like 'Anactoria,' his poem is rather longer and more rambling than one would wish it to be. But it is wrong to say 'the poem has no logical development; nor ... any emotional development. One simply joins the knight in spirit as he moves through the conflicting emotions which obsess him. There is no escape from them and no hope of bringing them into unity.'[16] On the contrary, there is in the poem a real development and a final emotional unity.

A poem which resembles 'Laus Veneris' in interesting ways is Tennyson's 'Tithonus.' Each has at its centre an immortal goddess and an exhausted human lover who is condemned to live forever. Like Tithonus, Tannhäuser longs for naturalistic fulfilment, to return to the world of 'happy men that have the power to die.' There is a cricial difference between the two poems, however, which underlines a basic aspect of Swinburne's vision. 'Tithonus' ends with an enormously poignant lament for the tears of things, with the speaker's haunting wish one day to be dead. Tannhäuser, on the other hand, comes to resolve his dilemma in a much more affirmative manner.

Unlike most of Swinburne's poems, 'Laus Veneris' relies for its basic situation on a Christian framework – that of sin, repentance, and redemption. In 'Notes on Poems and Reviews' – his apologia for the first *Poems and Ballads* – Swinburne put forward an interpretation of the poem in keeping with its Christian framework, chastely saying: 'Once accept or admit the least admixture of pagan worship, or of modern thought, and the whole story collapses into froth and smoke.'[17] But there is good reason to think that much of the 'Notes' was written with tongue in cheek,[18] and in any event it is clear that Swinburne was being disingenuous in his remarks on 'Laus Veneris,' for Christian belief is hardly what the poem advocates, and it is not against a Christian background that the poem must be viewed if it is to be understood.

Tannhäuser speaks the poem from inside the Horsel with Venus, where he is condemned (so he thinks) to remain until the end of the world. He is exhausted and enervated, his psychological condition mirrored in the oppressive heat and desiccation of the Horsel. in contrast is the freshness and movement of the natural world outside, to which Tannhäuser longs to be united:

> Ah yet would God this flesh of mine might be
> Where air might wash and long leaves cover me,
>   Where tides of grass break into foam of flowers,
> Or where the wind's feet shine along the sea.
>
> Ah yet would God that stems and roots were bred
> Out of my weary body and my head,
>   That sleep were sealed upon me with a seal,
> And I were as the least of all his dead.

It is in the world of nature and natural process that death, the release from the bonds of Venus, is to be found:

> Alas, but surely where the hills grow deep,
> Or where the wild ways of the sea are steep,
>   Or in strange places somewhere there is death.

Simultaneously repelled by and attracted to Venus, Tannhäuser goes on to recount the strength of her bittersweet charms, and to tell the story of his life. Finally comes the poem's astonishing conclusion: it does not end with Christian resignation to the will of God, with Tannhäuser's despair, with a Tithonus-like death wish, or with a hint of eventual redemption (the blossoming of the Pope's staff is not mentioned in the poem). At the end of 'Laus Veneris,' Tannhäuser, with a ringing rhetorical insistence, comes fully to accept his fate:

Ah love, there is no better life that this;
To have known love, how bitter a thing it is,
    And afterwards be cast out of God's sight;
Yea, these that know not, shall they have such bliss

High up in barren heaven before his face
As we twain in the heavy-hearted place,
    Remembering love and all the dead delight,
And all that time was sweet with for a space?

For till the thunder in the trumpet be,
Soul may divide from body, but not we
    One from another; I hold thee with my hand,
I let mine eyes have all their will of thee,

I seal myself upon thee with my might,
Abiding alway out of all men's sight
    Until God loosen over sea and land
The thunder of the trumpets of the night.

Tannhäuser has come to accept what is as good. He realizes that what he possesses inside the Horsel is enough to sustain him and preferable to a 'barren heaven' beyond. This distillation of peace and resignation out of apparent defeat and damnation is sudden and unexpected, and one should not fail to notice just how striking a resolution it is. It is as if the lotos eaters had ended their chant with a fuller self-consciousness than Tennyson grants them, and had decided to remain in contentment in the lotos land simply because there was no longer any other place for them to go. Doubtless, this kind of resolution is morally intolerable to some; and it is certainly in contrast to the ethical vigour and idealizing propensities of much Victorian literature. But as this theme is handled in Swinburne's poetry it does have an impressive dignity which it would be quite unreasonable to despise. For it is one of the major accomplishments of his poetry, as of Yeats', to discover possibilities for joy and assertion in very unpromising materials.

In his later poetry, Swinburne came to develop more fully and more positively the themes of 'Itylus,' 'Hymn to Proserpine,' 'Anactoria,' 'Laus Veneris,' and some other of the first *Poems and Ballads*. These early poems tend to present the poet's deepest concerns in an oblique, even a semi-disguised manner, but they can be nevertheless recognized: a concern with natural process and its relation to man; a preoccupation with death and change; a questioning of poetry's value in a world of mutability and mortality. A fairly consistent contrast runs through these poems: on the one hand, an unhealthy sensuality, a world-weariness, and a sense that the only possible poems are cries of perverted delight or chants of despair; on the other hand, a sense of the healing qualities of the natural world, a realization of the value of poetic vocation, and a determination to accept the circumstances of one's life as tolerable, whatever they happen to be. The former qualities have given *Poems and Ballads* its notoriety; the latter give it much of its distinction.

The major exception to generalizations about the informing themes of Swinburne's poetry are the political poems of *Songs before Sunrise*, published in 1871, five years after the first *Poems and Ballads*. The sunrise is the glorious dawn of the Italian Republic and the songs are public statements, doctrinal hymns, hortatory chants, and cosmic visions of Hugoesque sweep. The 'Prelude' aside, the songs are not personal poems dealing with felt experience and individual beliefs, dilemmas, and aspirations. The voices of *Songs before Sunrise* are disembodied and vatic, and the liberty of which they so relentlessly speak is an abstraction which has little to do with the individual's struggle to move from darkness to light. As A.E. Housman was to put it: 'Liberty is by no means so interesting as Aphrodite [Housman's personification of the first *Poems and Ballads*], and by no means so good a subject for poetry. There is a lack of detail about Liberty, and she has indeed no positive quality at all. Liberty consists in the absence of obstructions; it is merely a preliminary to activities whose character it does not determine; and to write poems about Liberty is very much as if one should write an Ode to Elbow-room or a panegyric on space of three dimensions.'[19] Furthermore, the positivist doctrines promulgated in the *Songs* demand the sacrifice of the individual on the altar of humanity: not men but man is the object of worship. This precludes a personal, reflective kind of poetry, a poetry of meditation and self-discovery. That the concerns of *Songs before Sunrise*, so lacking in convincing personal accent, were abandoned by Swinburne as abruptly as they were taken up suggests that they are not in the main line of his poetic development and not part of his abiding poetic concerns.

'On the Downs' is an example of the volume's characteristics and of the damage that philosophical and political beliefs, however pure, lofty, or suitable to human nature, can do to Swinburne's poetry. The poem is in form a reflective lyric which is crushed by the weight of Positivist doctrine it is forced to carry, by the substitution of imposed beliefs for personal reflection, of massive assertion for hard-won insight, of a quarrel with others for a quarrel with oneself. The poem is of a type that Swinburne often writes: meditation in the presence of a landscape, here, as elsewhere, the waste area between land and sea, a place where sun, wind, and water come to represent the basic realities of existence. In these poems it is implicitly or explicitly hoped that observation of, and reflection on, the natural setting will bring a clarifying insight into life. 'On the Downs' opens with a terse description of the landscape's barrenness, and intimates that a personal need has compelled the speaker to seek for solace in nature. But like himself nature seems 'full of care' and empty: 'Scarce wind enough was on the sea, / Scarce hope enough there moved in me.' The end of the poem's first movement underlines the shared bleakness: 'Life hopeless lies.' But at this point the similarities between 'On the Downs' and Swinburne's more mature poems of landscape meditation end. For the speaker's 'soul' is sent on a seven-stanza journey around the world in order to ascertain that its peoples lie crushed by tyranny: 'And my soul heard the songs and groans / That are about and under thrones.' The natural setting is then suddenly made to yield up its happy message, a chunk of Positivist doctrine which fills some eight stanzas before the poem ends. These lines parade a facile optimism as uncommon in Swinburne as the fact that at the end of 'On the Downs' the natural setting becomes a neon sign switched on just in time for the poem's technicolour finale, as the red, white, and green of the sun, wind, and water flaunt the colours of Republican Italy's flag.

It is instructive to contrast 'On the Downs' with what is up to a point a similar poem of seashore meditation, the very fine 'Neap-Tide,' from the third series of *Poems and Ballads* of 1889. Despite a number of salient characteristics, one hesitates to describe 'Neap-Tide' as a greater Romantic lyric (a genre earlier discussed in connection with section xcv of *In Memoriam*). For in Swinburne's poem there is no epiphany, no revelatory meeting of imagination and the natural world, which in the poem is totally uncongenial and seems capable of revealing only the Hardyesque finality of total darkness and lifelessness:

Full fain would the day be dead
And the stark night reign in his stead:
The sea falls dumb as the sea-fog thickens
And the sunset dies for dread.

A poem about loss for which there is no gain or recompense, 'Neap-Tide' recalls the landscape meditations of Wordsworth less than it anticipates those of Hardy and Robert Frost. For in 'Neap-Tide' Swinburne treats the bleak perceptual given and the diminution of the present in a way that recalls Frost's oven-bird: he knows how 'in singing not to sing,' how to make poetry not out of something evermore about to be but out of 'what to make of a diminished thing.'

Neap-tide is the time of the month when the high-water mark is at its lowest and in Swinburne's poem the time of the month, or the year or the lifetime, when the things of the speaker's spirit are at their lowest. The opening stanzas emphasize the isolation of the setting, its distance from human or natural comforters, the unlikelihood of vision or revelatory 'gleams'; and in the reference to the 'leap of a boy' give the first suggestion of a past-present contrast, of awareness that the glory and freshness of an earlier dream have now departed:

> Far off is the sea, and the land is afar:
>   The low banks reach at the sky,
>   Seen hence, and are heavenward high;
> Though light for the leap of a boy they are,
>   And the far sea late was nigh.
>
> The fair wild fields and the circling downs,
>   The bright sweet marshes and meads
>   All glorious with flowerlike weeds,
> The great grey churches, the sea-washed towns,
>   Recede as a dream recedes.
>
> The world draws back, and the world's light wanes,
>   As a dream dies down and is dead;
>   And the clouds and the gleams overhead
> Change, and change; and the sea remains,
>   A shadow of dreamlike dread.
>
> ...
> The fairest thing that beholds the day
>   Lies haggard and hopeless here.

In the next stanzas the past-present contrast is made explicit:

> The sea-forsaken forlorn deep-wrinkled
>   Salt slanting stretches of sand

That slope to the seaward hand,
Were they fain of the ripples that flashed and twinkled
And laughed as they struck the strand?

As bells on the reins of the fairies ring
The ripples that kissed them rang,
The light from the sundawn sprang,
And the sweetest of songs that the world may sing
Was theirs when the full sea sang.

The 'bells on the reins of the fairies' is a deliberate poetic flourish and functions like the 'ghost of sleigh-bells in a ghost of snow' simile in Frost's 'Hyla Brook.' In that poem Frost had demonstrated his ability to make poetry out of a diminished thing by celebrating the dried-up stream of midsummer, its bed 'a faded paper sheet / Of dead leaves stuck together by the heat,' on which sheet, so to speak, he indites his lyric about the way brooks really are. In 'Neap-Tide,' Swinburne similarly contrasts the 'poetic' past to the forlorn sands of the present: then there were twinkles and flashes and sundawn; but 'Now no light is in heaven.'

In the poem's penultimate stanza the speaker momentarily allows himself to speculate on what might lie beyond, 'Outside of the range of time, whose breath / Is keen as the manslayer's knife,' and even experiences a sort of agnostic twitch: 'Who knows if haply the shadow of death / May be not the light of [a presumably supernatural] life?' This stanza finally makes explicit that what the speaker has sought in his seaside quest was some insight into his mortality, a sign of something outside himself to assuage his isolation and mitigate the barrenness of the present. So deep is the need that Swinburne is brought to the brink of what one might call the Tennysonian moment: when transcendent yearnings might well be ambiguously answered by the sight of a far-off gleam of light – an evening star or rose of dawn, perhaps. The distinctive Swinburnean moment is rather different, however, and at the end of 'Neap-Tide' Swinburne turns away from the brink of transcendence in a way that anticipates Frost's 'There may be little or much beyond the grave, / But the strong are saying nothing until they see' (from 'The Strong Are Saying Nothing'). In the final stanza of 'Neap-Tide' the poet is sustained only by the hope that because he has 'mourned not to-day,' tomorrow he may be able to rejoice 'In the sun and the wind and the sea' of a possibly revivified natural world.

'Neap-Tide' is only one of countless examples of the fact that Swinburne, like other Romantic poets, looks *out there* to the natural world for the possible satisfaction for emotional and spiritual needs which in pre-Romantic periods were more frequently directed *up there* towards God. Unlike either the Christian God of Love or Wordsworth's maternal nature, however, the natural world that is the source of Swinburne's inspiration and the object of his prayerful longings is 'dispassionate.' At times its destructive aspects suggest that the natural world is at best capricious, at worst inimical to man, and even at its most lovely and sympathetic nature usually offers man much less than he would like to have. As Swinburne beautifully says in the elegy on his friend, the painter John William Inchbold:

> Vain, divine and vain,
> The dream that touched with thoughts or tears of ours
> The spirit of sense that lives in sun and rain,
> Sings out in birds, and breathes and fades in flowers.
>
> Not for our joy they live, and for our grief
> They die not. Though thine eye be closed, thine hand
> Powerless as mine to paint them, not a leaf
> In English woods or glades of Switzerland
>
> Falls earlier now, fades faster.

In 'The Sundew,' a lyric from the first *Poems and Ballads*, the subject of the distance between man and the natural world is handled with an unusual terseness and concreteness. At one level the poem is an unpretentious piece of natural description, charmingly ended with the shared secret of the beloved's name bringing speaker and flower into intimate communication. At a deeper level – this is another example of Swinburne's indirection in his first volume of poems – 'The Sundew' is about the stark fact of man's mortality and his separation from nature. The crucial stanzas are these:

> The deep scent of the heather burns
> About it; breathless though it be,
> Bow down and worship; more than we
> Is the least flower whose life returns,
> Least weed renascent in the sea.
>
> We are vexed and cumbered in earth's sight
> With wants, with many memories;
> These see their mother what she is,
> Glad-growing, till August leave more bright
> The apple-coloured cranberries.

Wind blows and bleaches the strong grass,
Blown all one way to shelter it
From trample of strayed kine, with feet
Felt heavier than the moorhen was,
Strayed up past patches of wild wheat.

You call it sundew: how it grows,
If with its colour it have breath,
If life taste sweet to it, if death
Pain its soft petal, no man knows:
Man has no sight or sense that saith.

Nature is reborn annually, and in this sense does not share in an individual man's mortality. Sufficient to itself, untroubled by wants or memories, the flower can enjoy its life span and without remorse observe the cranberries, whose August redness reminds the sundew of its own seasonal end. Man can name the flower but he cannot understand it or fully enter into its purely natural life. He is apart from the natural world and can do nothing himself to heal the wound of separation.

At times the anguishing isolation of the human condition and the weight of mortality prompt Swinburne to a longing to have his separateness, his human individuality, obliterated through absorption in nature, as in 'To a Seamew,' which expresses the wish to exchange his human identity for that of the free, graceful, and self-fulfilled bird, 'by time untarnished,' who reminds the poet of his own vanished youth:

Our dreams have wings that falter,
    Our hearts bear hopes that die;
For thee no dream could better
A life no fears may fetter,
A pride no care can alter,
    That wots not whence or why
Our dreams have wings that falter,
    Our hearts bear hopes that die.
...
Ah, well were I for ever,
    Wouldst thou change lives with me.

But much more characteristic of Swinburne's poetry is an acceptance of human limitations and of man's separation from nature, and a determination to make the best of this situation. The opposite of his desire to sink to the level of a natural object is his positive attempt, in poems like 'By the North Sea' and 'A Nympholept,' to become united with natural process while retaining his individuality, something quite different from the attempt to heal the wound of selfhood and of separation from the natural world through the obliteration of the self.

Swinburne's reading of human life presupposes the rejection of the consolations of religion, as well as those of Wordsworthian nature, and insists on the necessity to accept life's harshness and the inevitability of human suffering, and to endure them without the comforts of illusion. One of the best expositions of his thought on this matter is found in his early epistolary novel, *Love's Cross-Currents* (also known as *A Year's Letters*), which was written in the 1860s and first published pseudonymously in 1877. In this work, the closest thing in English to Laclos' *Les Liaisons dangereuses*, on which it is modelled, Lady Midhurst, the eminence grise of the story, writes to her granddaughter a letter of consolation on the sudden death of her husband. In her letter, so different in tone and substance from the novel's other epistles, Lady Midhurst can offer only a 'pagan consolation.' She reminds her correspondent that 'Stoicism is not an exploded system of faith' and urges her to 'Bear what you have to bear steadily, with locked teeth as it were'; 'Time will help us; there is no other certain help'; 'those who cannot support themselves cannot be supported'; 'The world will dispense with us some day; but it shall not, while we can hold out.'

Lady Midhurst leaves no doubt as to what things sap the spirit's strength. Her view of life rejects the consolations of religion and insists that the free spirit must be upheld by its own strength and vitality: 'any one who is utterly without self-reliance *will* collapse. There *can* be nothing capable of helping the helpless.' She further insists that the 'endurance of things that are' must not degenerate into 'a sacrifice of Christian resignation.' To allow this to happen

is the unhealthy side of patience; the fortitude of the feeble. Be content to endure without pluming yourself on a sense of submission. For indeed submission without compulsion can never be anything but the vicious virtue of sluggards. We submit because we must, and had better not flatter ourselves with the fancy that we submit out of goodness ... It is a child's game to play at making a virtue of necessity. I say that if we could rebel against what happens to us, we would rebel. Christian or heathen, no man would really submit to sorrow if he could help it ... Courage, taking the word how you will, I have always put at the head of the virtues. Any sort of faith or humility that interferes with it or impairs its working power, I have no belief in ...

We are beaten upon by necessity every day of our lives; we cannot get quit of circumstances; we cannot better the capacities born with us ... I would have you endure as much as you can; repent of as little as you can, and hope for as little as you can. All wise and sober courage ends in that ... try to keep free of false hopes and feeble fears. Face things as they are; think for yourself when you think of life and death, joy and sorrow, right and wrong. These things are dark by the nature of them; it is useless saying they can be lit up by a candle held in your eyes. You are only the blinder; they are none the clearer. What liberty to act and think is left us, let us keep fast hold of; what we cannot have, let us agree to live without.[20]

But although Swinburne was assured that man's life was a being-unto-death, the fact of which must be faced alone and without exterior solace, he did not at all times adopt a purely negative position with regard to the possibility of some kind of life beyond the grave. This is not because he was afflicted with the doubt and vacillation he insisted were not proper subjects for poetry, or that he ever came close to embracing a Christian view of live. But there are traces in his work, as at the end of 'Neap-Tide,' of a kind of residual scepticism, a reluctance entirely to dismiss the possibility of some kind of life after death:

> If any place for any soul there be,
> Disrobed and disentrammelled;
> ...
> The life, the spirit and the work were one
> That here – ah, who shall say, that here are done?
> ...
> For if, beyond the shadow and the sleep,
>   A place there be for souls without a stain;
> ...
> If light of life outlive the set of sun
>   That men call death and end of all things;
> ...
> If that be yet a living soul which here
>   Seemed brighter for the growth of numbered springs.[21]

After Gabriel Rossetti died in April 1882, Swinburne sent a mutual friend a copy of his sonnet 'A Death on Easter Day' with this comment: 'You know, I am sure, that I am incapable of dealing at such a time and on such a topic in poetical insincerity or sentimental rhetoric: so perhaps I need hardly add that I do now – on the whole – strongly incline to believe in the survival of life – individual and conscious life – after the dissolution of the body. Otherwise, I would not on any account have affected a hope or conviction I did not feel.'[22] Cecil Lang's comments on this important passage are telling:

On the question of immortality Swinburne seems to have been at odds with is own instincts. He remained skeptical, but in his letters one seems to perceive a yearning for a kind of commitment that intellectually he could not allow, and every single allusion to the problem leaves one with an impression of cautious fingers searching among broken glass ... But a strong inclination is not actual belief. The occasion being, in a way, a double crisis, the death of the most intimate friend he had ever known occurring on Easter Day, the emotional pull of the latent symbolism perhaps allured him into assenting poetically to a doctrine that his intellect rejected. For it is a fact that Swinburne never again made such a statement. [23]

But in order to understand fully Swinburne's occasional flirtations with the idea of an afterlife, it is necessary to say more than this and to note that conditional statements like the above are usually made in the context of his lamenting the death of a fellow poet and/or his pondering the meaning and value of poetic vocation. It is especially when considering the future of poets that Swinburne is unwilling to accept the fact that death means total extinction.

The reason for this is that for Swinburne there is something about the vocation of a poet that strongly suggests a kind of religious calling, and about poetry and the visionary company of poets a kind of sacred aura, a dimension of meaning and significance which Swinburne often describes in terms and symbols appropriated from the language of religious worship, just as he more than once speaks of poetic tradition as a sacred line of inspiration, a kind of apostolic succession. It is because Swinburne invests the poetic life with such dignity and importance that he is often unwilling to accept the death of a poet as the final end, especially when such survival may be taken as a sign of the value of his own work. As he says to the spirits of Marlowe and Shelley, whom he tries to summon up in 'In the Bay': 'O well-beloved, our brethren, if ye be, / Then we are not forsaken.' In his memorial verses on Inchbold, in which there are no fewer than four 'if' clauses, Swinburne is at his most self-conscious (and his most disarming) concerning his tendency to allow himself to speculate on possibilities which at other times he insistently dismisses:

> Peace, rest, and sleep are all we know of death,
>   And all we dream of comfort: yet for thee,
> Whose breath of life was bright and strenuous breath,
>   We think the change is other than we see.

Despite the loveliness of this, it is hard not to feel that those poems of Swinburne's which dismiss any thought of a future existence ring truer than those which do not. It can certainly be said that in some of his poetry's finest and most triumphant moments Swinburne rejects all thoughts of a future state, and, accepting the naked fact that nothing abides, is nevertheless able to affirm the sufficiency of mortal life and the value of poetic vocation. And in other poems, the possibility of immortality is not so much denied as rendered meaningless by the awareness that man's life on earth can provide a joy and a fulfilment that more than compensates for the inevitability of death and oblivion. It is not only Swinburne's intellect that rejects immortality, but also his whole emotional and perceptual being. At moments of full response to nature, as he says in 'A Nympholept,' 'Heaven is as earth, and as heaven to me / Earth.' And in 'The Lake of Gaube' he insists that it is only fear of freedom and of the full expansion and enjoyment of human powers that makes man yearn for eternal life.

Most of the mythological personages who figure in Swinburne's poetry – Apollo, Hertha, Venus, Proserpine, Hesperia, Pan – relate either positively or negatively to his conception of the imagination, the poetic life, and man's relationship to the natural world. By far the most important of them is Apollo. 'The Last Oracle,' the poem which opens the second series of *Poems and Ballads* of 1878, is a Swinburnean version of the Romantic myth of the fall in which Apollo is worshipped as the only possible redeemer of a fallen humanity corrupted by Christianity. Swinburne called 'The Last Oracle' 'one of my most important lyric works,'[24] and, most unusually, provided several of his correspondents with a précis of the poem. The fullest of them is as follows:

Starting from the answer brought back from Delphi to Julian by his envoy (a.d. 361) [that Apollo is dead], I go on to reinvoke Apollo to reappear in these days when the Galilean too is conquered and Christ has followed Pan to death, not as they called him [i.e. Apollo] in Greece, merely son of Zeus the son of Chronos, but older than Time or any God born of Time, the Light and Word incarnate in man, of whom comes the inner sunlight of human thought or imagination and the gift of speech and song whence all Gods or ideas of Gods possible to man take form and fashion – conceived of thought and imagination and born of speech or song. Of this I take the sun-god and the singing-god of the Greeks to be the most perfect type attained, or attainable; and as such I call on him to return and reappear over the graves of intervening Gods.[25]

In the poem, Apollo is described as nothing less than the creative imagination itself, not a being separate from man, but a power dwelling, at least latently, within him. 'The light and the Word incarnate in man' is his imagination, his power to create even the gods he chooses to serve. The speaker of 'The Last Oracle' insists that Christianity has crippled poetry with its 'hymns of wrath and wrong,' replacing paeans with psalms and chants with wails. In contrast to earlier pagan poets who had worshipped in Apollo their own poetic powers, the Christian, or anyone professing belief in a power higher than the imagination, delimits the power of poetry. But what the religious person does not realize is that it is man's own imaginative activity – 'the song within the silent soul' – that creates the gods he worships. As Wallace Stevens was to put it: 'the gods of China are always Chinese.'[26] 'The Last Oracle' insists that the recovery of imaginative power, of man's 'divine' capabilities, is the prime condition of humanistic awareness ('Till the blind mute soul get speech again and eyesight, / Man may worship not the light of life within') and ends with an incantatory insistence that the power of imagination (the 'kingdom' of Apollo) is still capable of sustaining man:

> For thy kingdom is past not away,
>   Nor thy power from the place thereof hurled;
> Out of heaven they shall cast not the day,
>   They shall cast not out song from the world.

Apollo is the sun god as well as the god of poetry; as such he symbolizes Swinburne's belief that poetic inspiration is analogous to, if not identical with, natural process. The sun nourishes and sustains the natural world as Apollo nourishes and sustains poets. In 'Thalassius,' and allegory of poetic growth in the manner of Shelley's 'Alastor' or Keats's 'Endymion,' an elder poet, a surrogate of Apollo, instils through his 'high song' a sense of the young poet's high destiny. This song is not a disembodied message coming from a noumenal realm, for through simile and metaphor it is repeatedly stressed that the song is identical with the music and motions of natural process. The high song also insists that poetry, the imaginative faculty, can reconcile life and death, just as in the natural world light and darkness die into each other.

In another poem, 'Off Shore,' when Swinburne calls the sun 'the slayer and the stayer and the harper, the light of us all and our Lord,' he attributes to it powers identical with those of Apollo. Like Apollo, the sun is a replacement for the Christian God, the naturalistic equivalent of a creator and redeemer, who propagates, brings to fruition, and recalls to life the natural world. 'Off Shore' worships the sun as 'the father of song,' whose cosmic music finds an echo in the songs of earthly poets. For Swinburne, it is the sun who is God, and his kingdom is of this world.

The function of poets in relation to the rest of mankind is to mediate between nature and man, between Apollo's realm and the human world. This is the subject of the short lyric, 'The Interpreters.' The natural world at moments contains a fullness that renders the function of the poet unnecessary, when, as Wallace Stevens puts it, 'consciousness takes the place of imagination':[27]

Days dawn on us that make amends for many
    Sometimes,
When heaven and earth seem sweeter even than any
    Man's rhymes.

But without the song of the poet nature is often a dead blankness, its moments of splendour mocked by their very transience:

Dead air, dead fire, dead shapes and shadows, telling
    Time nought;
Man gives them sense and soul by song, and dwelling
    In thought.

In human thought their being endures, their power
    Abides:
Else were their life a thing that each light hour
    Derides.

Without the poet, 'Our days / Laugh, lower, and lighten past, and find no station that stays.'

That the sun is a 'slayer' as well as a 'stayer' points to another major aspect of Swinburne's Apollo, and consequently of his conception of the poetic life. For Apollo is the god who torments his own votaries, the poets. In 'Ave atque Vale,' his elegy on Baudelaire, Swinburne says of the French poet that 'Thy lips indeed he [Apollo] touched with bitter wine / And nourished them indeed with bitter bread.' Echoing this allusion to the crucifixion, one may say that Apollo's crowns are not only of laurel; they are also of thorns; and that for Swinburne, as for the early Tennyson, suffering is an inalienable part of the poetic vocation. The children of Apollo, who wear his crowns, are the historical figures of poets who abound in Swinburne's poetry. They include Villon, Rudel, Marlowe, Shelley, Gautier, Hugo, Landor, and such lesser figures as Swinburne's friends Inchbold and 'Barry Cornwall.' But it is Sappho and Baudelaire who are Swinburne's chief archetypes of the lyric poet, and the figures with whom he most closely identifies himself. (They are much more qualitatively important in his poetry than Victor Hugo, his favorite poetic superstar and the subject of some intolerable panegyrics.)

Sappho figures importantly in 'On the Cliffs,' a long meditative poem written in 1879, which is Swinburne's most sustained reflection on 'Song, and the secrets of it, and their might, / What blessings curse it and what curses bless.' In the evening, by the seashore, the poem's speaker, 'With sick heavy spirit, [and] unmanned with strife,' longs for some insight into the abiding affliction and unfulfilment of his life. He first listens to the sea, but, as in Whitman's 'Out of the Cradle Endlessly Rocking,' the sea has only one unchangeable word, which is death. But only at the beginning of his career was the thought of extinction delicious or soothing to Swinburne or his personae; and in 'On the Cliffs' the speaker turns from the sea to the song of the nightingale, which is complexly bird, Sappho, and Apollo in one, to gain insight into what makes bearable 'This gift, this doom' of poetic vocation, which has set him apart from other men:

>   yet can no memory say
> How many a night and day
> My heart has been as thy heart, and my life
> As thy life is, a sleepless hidden thing,
> Full of the thirst and hunger of winter and spring,
> That seeks its food not in such love or strife
> As fill men's hearts with passionate hours and rest.
> From no loved lips and on no loving breast
> Have I sought ever for such gifts as bring
> Comfort, to stay the secret soul with sleep.
> The joys, the loves, the labours, whence men reap
> Rathe fruit of hopes and fears,
> I have made not mine; the best of all my days
> Have been as those fair fruitless summer strays,
> Those water-waifs that but the sea-wind steers,
> Flakes of glad foam or flowers on footless ways
> That take the wind in season and the sun,
> And when the wind wills is their season done.

This lament, perhaps the most simply affecting lines in all of Swinburne, is answered by a passage Yeatsian in its tone and complexity. Together with the memory of loss and deprivation, poets are also said to retain

> A memory mastering pleasure and all pain,
> A spirit within the sense of ear and eye,
> A soul behind the soul, that seeks and sings
> And makes our life move only with its wings
> And feed but from its lips, that in return
> Feed of our hearts wherein the old fires that burn
> Have strength not to consume
> Nor glory enough to exalt us past our doom.

The poet's vocation has no reward exterior to it; it is self-fulfilling and self-sustaining. Poets are ennobled by a fiery creative core ('a spirit within the sense' or 'soul behind the soul') that continues to burn only because it continues to be fed by the lacerating fires of the poet's own being: in Yeats' similar image, 'Whatever flames upon the night / Man's own resinous heart has fed' (from 'Two Songs from a Play').

Sappho is also mentioned in 'Ave atque Vale,' the Baudelaire elegy, a poem which sums up most of what this chapter has been saying about Swinburne's naturalism, his acceptance of mortality, rejection of the comforts of religion, and conception of the poetic life and the fate of poets. In a writer as voluminous as Swinburne it is not easy to pick out a single cumulative and synthesizing poem. But in terms of his poetic development up to the second series of *Poems and Ballads* of 1878, 'Ave atque Vale,' written in 1868 and collected in that volume ten years later, may be so considered.[28]

Compared with the other great English elegies, with 'Lycidas,' 'Adonais,' *In Memoriam*, and 'Thyrsis,' Swinburne's elegy is marked by its wholly naturalistic and unflinching acceptance of death as the final, irremissive end. There are of course no Miltonic blest kingdoms meek of joy and love to receive Baudelaire's spirit; there is only the lower world of an indifferent nature – of the hurled bones, the gory visage, the weltering to the parching wind. Nor does Swinburne try to read into nature the traces of a still existent spirit. In 'Anactoria,' Swinburne's Sappho had made such claims for herself in a way that recalled the pantheistic rapture of the end of Shelley's elegy on Keats. But when the Lesbian poetess is recalled in the second stanza of 'Ave atque Vale,' she is no longer said to be apotheosized through being made one with the recurrent music of nature; her suicide is recalled, but all that is subsequently said of her is that her bones, like Edward King's, are hurled 'Hither and thither' by the wild sea and green gulfs, 'blind gods that cannot spare.' And while in their elegies Tennyson and even Arnold found consolation and renewal through memory and the ministrations of the natural world, Swinburne is not able to do so in 'Ave atque Vale,' his elegy standing in something of the same relation to *In Memoriam* as Hardy's novels to George Eliot's, or Frost's poems to Wordsworth's.

In 'Ave atque Vale' the dead Baudelaire's non-existence is from the first accepted; all that remains of him is the 'shut scroll' of his poems. Thus, while Swinburne's poem retains many of the conventions of pastoral elegy, it does not have the characteristic pattern of loss, dejection, and troubled questioning culminating in recompense, apotheosis, and joyful celebration. There is no apotheosis because there is no immortality for Baudelaire, and the rapturous closing sections of Milton's, Shelley's, and Tennyson's elegies are replaced by a primordial sombreness that recalls the poem that gives Swinburne his title: the elegy that the pagan Catullus wrote at his brother's grave, of which Tennyson said: no 'modern elegy, so long as men retain the least hope in the after-life of those whom they loved, [can] equal in pathos the desolation of that everlasting farewell.'[29] All that Catullus can say to the dead one is 'Ave atque Vale' ('Hail and Farewell'), and it is this same desolating realization that informs Swinburne's poem.

For several reasons Baudelaire is an appropriate poet for Swinburne to lament. Unlike King, Keats, or Hallam, the French poet was not a bright-eyed youth of morn figure, whose premature demise, with early promise unfulfilled, provokes questioning of life's meaning and of the forces that govern the universe. There is no attack on the age in 'Ave atque Vale' and no troubling deaf heaven with the bootless cries of confusion and doubt. Like Swinburne, Baudelaire was untroubled by the hopes and fears of Christianity, the 'gnatstings and fleabites of belief and unbelief.'[30] And the French poet's *fleurs du mal*, his 'half-faded fiery blossoms,' also describe the first *Poems and Ballads*, to several of which Swinburne deliberately alludes in 'Ave atque Vale.' Baudelaire's symbolic figure of 'La Géante,' for example, the 'pale Titan-woman' as Swinburne calls her, becomes one with the 'obscure Venus of the hollow hill,' the goddess of 'Laus Veneris.'

'Ave atque Vale' opens with the traditional choice of flowers. Those selected are, like Tannhäuser's Horsel, 'pale with heat / And full of bitter summer.' In the second stanza the death of Sappho, 'the supreme head of song' and a poet of passion like Baudelaire and the early Swinburne, is recalled in order to pose one of the poem's main questions: what happens to a dead poet? The third stanza stresses Baudelaire's 'subtler eye,' his privileged insight into the fallen world of 'Sin without shape and pleasure without speech.' Gazing on the world of 'stricken spirits' he sees on each face the shadow of its future extinction. He knows (as does Paul in Galatians 6:7) that 'as men sow men reap,' but here this implies only the inevitability of death and decay. The next stanza, insisting that Baudelaire is totally dead, 'Spirit and body and all the springs of song,' asks another question: is not death a happy state, a welcome release from life? Is not to be freed from the pains of life enough to give savour to oblivion?

> Is it well now where love can do no wrong,
> Where stingless pleasure has no foam or fang
>   Behind the unopening closure of her lips?
> Is it not well where soul from body slips
> And flesh from bone divides without a pang
>   As dew from flower-bell drips?

The fifth stanza simply answers that 'It is enough,' the couplet at its centre encapsulating both the release offered by death and its essential emptiness: 'No triumph and no labour and no lust, / Only dead yew leaves and a little dust.'

Stanzas 6 and 7 ask a third question: is there anything in death analogous to life? Is the land of the dead like the natural world?

> Hast thou found any likeness for thy vision?
>   O gardener of strange flowers, what bud, what bloom
>   Hast thou found sown, what gathered in the gloom?
> What of despair, of rapture, of derision,
>   What of life is there, what of ill or good?
>   Are the fruits grey like dust or bright like blood?
> Does the dim ground grow any seed of ours,
>   The faint fields quicken any terrene root,
>   In low lands where the sun and moon are mute
> And all the stars keep silence? Are there flowers
>   At all, or any fruit?

As the ironic, faintly mocking tone suggests, these questions are rhetorical. The answer they presuppose is: No, death is not at all like life and if it were (so the tone insinuates) it would be distastefully stale and insipid. Swinburne's point is George Santayana's:

When ... it is clearly seen that another life, to supplement this one, must closely resemble it, does not the magic of immortality altogether vanish? Is such a reduplication of earthly society at all credible? And the prospect of awakening again among houses and trees, among children and dotards, among wars and rumours of wars, still fettered to one personality and one accidental past, still uncertain of the future, is not this prospect wearisome and deeply repulsive? Having passed through these things once and bequeathed them to posterity, is it not time for each soul to rest?[31]

The next two stanzas insist on the impossibility of contacting the dead. 'Anactoria' notwithstanding, the visible or auditory world contains no vestige of the dead. The 'hearkening spirit' hears only murmurs: 'Some dim derision of mysterious laughter ... Some little sound of unregarded tears ... some cadence of dead sighs.' Nor can the dead be imaginatively apprehended: section ciii of *In Memoriam* notwithstanding, 'Our dreams pursue our dead and do not find.' Nor are there any Tennysonian gleams or glimmerings to kindle hope in a beyond:

> the thin flame flies,
> The low light fails us in elusive skies,
> Still the foiled earnest ear is deaf, and blind
> Are still the eluded eyes.

In the teeth of these insistences, stanza 10 is able to affirm that even though the poet dies, there is something of him that survives:

> Not thee, O never thee, in all time's changes
> Not thee, but this the sound of thy sad soul,
> The shadow of thy swift spirit, this shut scroll
> I lay my hand on, and not death estranges
> My spirit from communion of thy song.

This is the climactic moment of 'Ave atque Vale,' the muted equivalent of the sudden turn which in other elegies brings release and affirmation. 'All time's changes' will not bring back the man; but in his poetry, his spirit is preserved. All that survives of Baudelaire are his poems, and this is enough to give a sense of continuity and the illusion of contact: 'These I salute, these touch, these clasp and fold / As though a hand were in my hand to hold.'

The ensuing procession of mourners past the coffin of the dead includes Apollo. The 'lord of light' had nourished the dead poet with bitter wine and bitter bread; and at his flame was lighted 'The fire that scarred thy spirit.' But it is Apollo's laurel alone that saves Baudelaire's dust 'from blame and from forgetting.' The procession concludes in stanza 16 with a terse insistence on the need to accept the unchangeable harshness of life and a frank admission of the limitations even of poetry, of its inability fully to comprehend, and hence assuage, the fact of death (an admission which, one must note, qualifies the claims made for poetry's power in 'The Last Oracle'):

> There is no help for these things; none to mend
> And none to mar; not all our songs, O friend,
> Will make death clear or make life durable.

The penultimate stanza quietly urges the acceptance of life as it is, regardless of its content, and closes with a final rhetorical question, a reminder of the common mortality in which all men share: 'Shall death not bring us all as thee one day / Among the days departed?' In the beautifully balanced final stanza the poet lays down his offering to the dead – the 'garland' of his poem – and the poem ends. The 'solemn earth, a fatal mother' becomes the figure of 'La Géante' ready to receive the dead poet: 'And in the hollow of her breasts a tomb.' And the silence and darkness of the essential natural elements of wind, sun, and water (a diminished substitute for the traditional natural consolations of pastoral elegy) suggest the final silence of death:

> Content thee, howsoe'er, whose days are done;
>> There lies not any troublous thing before,
>> Nor sight nor sound to war against thee more,
> For whom all winds are quiet as the sun,
>> All waters as the shore.

'A Vision of Spring in Winter' was one of the poems collected with 'Ave atque Vale' in the second series of *Poems and Ballads* of 1878. It is a rather less sombre poem than the Baudelaire elegy and even implies a less austere and bleak vision of human existence, though the difference is one of degree, not of kind. This is well worth noting, for the poems of Swinburne that are best known – 'Hymn to Proserpine,' 'The Garden of Proserpine,' 'The Forsaken Garden,' 'Ave atque Vale' – tend to be ones touching the nadir of his vision. And even such excellent commentators as McGann and Rosenberg have perhaps tended to make Swinburne out to be a rather more negative and tragic poet than he always is. This can be seen if the above-named poems are compared with the four discussed in the following chapter, which in different ways comprise the apogee of Swinburne's vision, and to which 'A Vision of Spring in Winter' may be regarded as a prelude.

Like the 1871 'Prelude' to *Songs before Sunrise*, the poem is both a summing up of what has gone before and a prevision of what the poet hopes will follow in the years before him. But compared with the assured, declamatory, and at times strident tenor of the 'Prelude,' the tone of 'A Vision of Spring in Winter' is tentative, reticent, supplicatory. One is tempted to think of it as a mid-life crisis poem, though there are no *crise de quarante* agonizings and recantations, but rather the quiet acceptance of a lost lustre, a rejection of the comforts of memory (of studying the nostalgias), and a quiet appeal to the natural world not for vision or succour but simply for the flowers, winds, and 'hours of ease' that it annually bestows.

At the end of winter, the poet thirsts for an indication of the coming of spring, and, stretching his 'spirit forth to the fair hours,' begins to see in his vision the 'fair face that art not' yet and to feel the 'maiden breath' that will soon 'fill the fields and fire the woods.' One would tend to expect in a poem of this sort (as in sections lxxxiii and cxv of *In Memoriam*) that the poet would associate the return of spring with his own renewal and regeneration. The second half of the fifth stanza does seem to intimate such a correspondence in its transferred epithets of nature's 'cold heart' and softening 'Tears joyfuller than mirth.' But at the end of the stanza Swinburne explicitly refuses to associate natural renewal with his own, for the flowers of his 'fair first years' are said to 'revive not with thy flowers on earth.' And not only is the Wordsworthian reciprocity of self and nature gainsaid; in the next stanza the Wordsworthian and Tennysonian myth of the restorative power of memory is also rejected, as well as the Tennysonian intimations of the dawn – for in the lines quoted below it is hard not to think that Swinburne is alluding to Tennyson, for example to the coming of 'The dawn, the dawn' at the end of the section xcv of *In Memoriam*, just as he was in his comments in the 'Prelude' on misuse of 'the lights of even and morn':

> I would not bid thee, though I might, give back
>   One good thing youth has given and borne away;
>   I crave not any comfort of the day
> That is not; ...
> ...
> Nor light nor love that has been, nor the breath
>   That comes with morning from the sun to be
>   And sets light hope on fire.

The last stanza of 'A Vision of Spring in Winter' is balanced between past and future:

> The morning song beneath the stars that fled
>   With twilight through the moonless mountain air,
>   While youth with burning lips and wreathless hair
> Sang toward the sun that was to crown his head,
> Rising; the hopes that triumphed and fell dead,
>   The sweet swift eyes and songs of hours that were;
> These may'st thou not give back for ever; these,
>   As at the sea's heart all her wrecks lie waste,
>   Lie deeper than the sea;
> But flowers thou may'st, and winds, and hours of ease,
>   And all its April to the world thou may'st
>   Give back, and half my April back to me.

The youth with burning lips and wreathless hair is the bard of the first *Poems and Ballads* and the opening of the 'Prelude' to *Songs before Sunrise*, just as 'the hopes that triumphed and fell dead' are the latter volume's Positivist and Republican chants. These are gone 'for ever'; what remains is what the 'Prelude' called the 'actual earth's equalities,' which are thought to be enough, even though the poem ends with the recognition that half of the poet's Aprils are behind him and that what remains unexpired is the diminished – the falling not the rising – half. It is to some of the major imaginative creations of Swinburne's remaining Aprils, the most mature and positive statements of his reading of human life, that we may now turn.

6

Swinburne after 1878: Four Readings

In the summer of 1879, a year after the publication of the second series of *Poems and Ballads*, Theodore Watts (later Watts-Dunton) took the care of Swinburne into his own hands. The poet was persuaded to leave London, and went to live at Watts' suburban villa in Putney. There Swinburne put behind him the dissipations which would soon have brought him to a premature end (with Swinburne a little dissipation went a long way) and lived quietly and temperately until his death in 1909. The enormous body of poetry he published during these thirty years is almost totally neglected today. It is not hard to understand why. The widespread assumptions that 'both as a person and as a poet [Swinburne] never grew up' and that the was 'at the height of his powers' during the 1860s imply the conclusion that his ripest fruits were his first and that after *Atalanta in Calydon* (1865), the first *Poems and Ballads* (1866), and *Songs before Sunrise* (1871) a long, uninterrupted decline set in.[1] And, while it is possible to find a certain coherence and a pattern of development in Swinburne's poetry up to the second *Poems and Ballads*, it is not possible to do so for the torrential outpouring of verse during the following three decades. Roundels, parodies, a sonnet series on the English dramatic poets, verses celebrating various parts of the English countryside and seashore, a long retelling of the Balen and Balan story, political pieces (in which at times a jingoistic patriotism replaces Swinburne's earlier revolutionary ardour), memorial verses occasioned by the deaths of friends and various eminent Victorians, celebrations of infants (described by Hopkins as '*rot* about babies, a blethery bathos ... his babies make a Herodian of me'):[2] poems of these and other kinds flowed from Swinburne's pen with great facility and in seemingly endless numbers.

Among the exceptions to the general quality of the post-1878 work are four major poems which are among the finest things Swinburne produced. While each of the four is formally and generically different from the others, all have 'adequate matter,' for all are concerned with Swinburne's fundamental poetic themes: man's relation to the natural world; the strictures and satisfactions of poetic vocation; the necessity of rejecting all supernatural beliefs in favour of a purely naturalistic vision of life that accepts death as the final end; and the concomitant necessity to accept what is as sufficient. 'By the North Sea' (1880), *Tristram of Lyonesse* (1882), 'A Nympholept' (1894), and 'The Lake of Gaube' (1904) are all complex and difficult texts demanding sustained attention. Because these accomplished poems have suffered critical neglect for so long, what is most needed at present are straightforward readings of them. In this chapter I have attempted to provide clear and accurate accounts of these poems, with special emphasis on thematic development.

I

Like many of Swinburne's poems, 'By the North Sea' is a meditation in the presence of a landscape; as in a number of other poems, the specific setting is the seashore.[3] One reason for Swinburne's fondness for shoreline settings is his aesthetic preference for the more sweeping, fluid, and primeval aspects of the natural world. He likes to paint on a large canvas striking natural contrasts and swiftly moving natural elements, and to capture 'the moment when one thing shades off into its opposite, or when contraries fuse.'[4] For these interests, the meeting place of sea, land, sky, and wind makes a splendid subject. More important, the contrasts of land and sea are often used by Swinburne to bring into focus a contrast or a conflict within himself. These conflicts turn on the difference between the actual and the possible, between what Swinburne has and what he would like to have, or (to borrow the terms of Wallace Stevens) between a 'naked Alpha' and a possible 'hierophant Omega.'[5] The specific forms of these contrasts often are a sterile imprisonment in self versus a sense of individual freedom and vitality; terror in the face of nature's indifference and cruelty versus joyful reciprocity between consciousness and the natural world; the difficulty of singing versus creative fulfilment. In these poems, the meeting place of land and sea comes to suggest the possibility of a resolution of these conflicts, or at least of a momentary stay against the confusion that they cause. To put it another way, in these poems Swinburne, at the edge of the known, peers expectantly into the unknown expanse of sky and sea, the place from where – if from anywhere – revelation, or at least some clarifying insight into life, is likely to come.[6] For Swinburne, as for Robert Frost (in 'Neither Out Far nor In Deep'):

The land may vary more;
But wherever the truth may be –
The water comes ashore,
And the people look at the sea.

The barren coastal wilderness near Dunwich, in Suffolk, is the locale of 'By the North Sea.' In no other poem of Swinburne's, not even 'Neap-Tide,' is the natural setting so unrelievedly desolate and inimical to man, and the cruel destructiveness of the elements so insistently underlined. Swinburne's prose description of this setting is of value in clearing up some initially obscure points in 'By the North Sea,' and in reminding one that several of the poem's more arresting features are neither fantastic nor surrealistic:

Le poème ['By the North Sea'], ou bien l'étude de paysagiste autant que de poète qui termine ce recueil [*Studies in Song*], essaye de faire la peinture ou bien l'esquisse d'une étrange et lente ruine, sans catastrophe actuelle ni coups de théâtre; la ville de Dunwich, en Suffolk, autrefois métropole de province ayant six grandes églises dont une cathédrale, n'est plus qu'un petit village qui ne sera probablement plus rien en moins d'un siècle. La mer a mangé tout le reste; elle ronge encore les ruines. Un débris de la grande église se tient encore debout sur la dune auprès des restes d'un grand monastère hospitalier où l'on recueillait les pauvres infirmes. J'ai monté la tour croulante [sic] et j'ai vu du côté de la plage les ossements des morts qui trouaient les sables de la dune-cimitière qui s'élève en haut des marais salés – vastes landes qui n'appartiennent ni à la terre ni à la mer et qui s'émiettent littéralement dans les flots de la mer toujours croissante.[7]

'By the North Sea' is prefaced by an epigraph from Landor – 'We are what suns and winds and waters make us' – and a dedicatory sonnet to Watts. The epigraph lays down the ground rules, so to speak, for the poem, stating that at least for the poem's speaker, human life, its determining factors and possible satisfactions, are defined by these basic natural elements. In the sonnet, Swinburne expands this remark:

Sea, wind, and sun, with light and sound and breath
    The spirit of man fulfilling – these create
    That joy wherewith man's life grown passionate
Gains heart to hear and sense to read and faith
To know the secret word our Mother saith
    In silence, and to see, though doubt wax great,

> Death as the shadow cast by life and fate,
> Passing, whose shade we call the shadow of death.
> Brother, to whom our Mother as to me
>   Is dearer than all dreams of days undone,
> This song I give you of the sovereign three
>   That are as life and sleep and death are, one:
> A song the sea-wind give me from the sea,
>   Where nought of man's endures before the sun.

The sun, wind, and sea fulfil man's spirit; they make his life passionate and give him joy. Because they have this power, it is not inappropriate to describe them, as the sestet does, as a kind of trinity, the naturalistic godhead of a man's life. 'Our Mother' the sea is 'dearer than all dreams of days undone': that is, more to be cherished than the hope of an existence which survives death and never ends. This anticipates the answer to one of the principal questions pondered in 'By the North Sea': in the absence of belief in any kind of immortality, what can sustain and console a man in a world where his days are all too soon done? Appropriately, this introductory sonnet is not fully understandable in itself. It does not tell what 'The secret word our Mother saith' is, nor does it explain what is meant by 'doubt.' One must pass from the sonnet to the poem itself in order to discover the full meaning of these terms.

The first of the poem's seven sections is a prolonged and dirge-like description, unrelieved by any hint of beauty, of the desolate shore. The land is 'lonelier than ruin' and the sea 'stranger than death.' The earth 'lies exhausted,' and even the winds 'lack breath.' Two lords – 'Death's self and the sea' – preside over the shore and pledge mutual devotion, finding in their murderous appetites a happy reciprocity. Their pledge culminates in a description of a perpetually renewed cycle of destructiveness and carnage:

> And year upon year dawns living,
>   And age upon age drops dead:
> And his hand is not weary of giving,
>   And the thirst of her heart is not fed.

The only possible solace in the face of this horror is said to be the numbness of death. If anything of those buried in the seaside cemetery survives, it is their envied 'sense' that they can no longer suffer; for them 'the wind is divested of danger / And scatheless the sea.' Like the inert void of the dead in 'The Garden of Proserpine' and the torpor and lassitude of the Horsel in 'Laus Veneris' (to recall two of the 1866 *Poems and Ballads* to which Swinburne alludes in this section),[8] The Dunwich shore seems the negation of anything life-giving or healthy. So dominant is the setting's oppressiveness that only once in the section is there any indication of an 'I' in the poem, a speaker who perceives and responds to the scene. By the end of 'By the North Sea' the speaker's perception of the setting, and consequently his emotional state, will have greatly changed. What happens between the opening and the close of the poem is that, through continued meditation on the scene he confronts, Swinburne eventually comes to realize that in what had initially seemed so hostile there is enough to sustain him, and to provide 'All solace ... for the spirit.' The stages by which this transformation occurs are detailed in the intervening sections of the poem.

Section 2, like section 5, is a short, lyrical intermezzo. The contrast in each of these sections between the destructive and the attractive aspects of the natural setting parallels a contrast in the speaker's mind between his awareness of the cruelty and ferocity of nature's elements when they are considered in the immediate context, and his apprehension of their loveliness and freedom when they are viewed in a more inclusive and disinterested manner. This contrast is developed in the opening stanzas of section 2:

> For the heart of the waters is cruel,
>   And the kisses are dire of their lips,
> And their waves are as fire is to fuel
>   To the strength of the sea-faring ships,
> Though the sea's eye gleam as a jewel
>   To the sun's eye back as he dips.
>
> Though the sun's eye flash to the sea's
>   Live light of delight and of laughter
> And her lips breathe back to the breeze
>   The kiss that the wind's lips waft her
> From the sun that subsides, and sees
>   No gleam of the storm's dawn after.

Considered in relation to man – from the point of view of human endeavour (the sea-faring ships) – the sea is cruel and perilous. But when the sea is considered in relation to the sun and the wind, these elements are seen to radiate a loveliness and harmony. In the early sections of 'By the North Sea,' it is the former relation that almost entirely dominates the speaker's awareness; and section 2 ends with a reiteration of nature's endless cycle of destruction: 'The lists are set from of old, / And the warfare endureth for ever.'

In section iii, which opens with a repetition of the funereal chant of section i, we are for the first time allowed inside the mind of the speaker:

Slowly, gladly, full of peace and wonder
  Grows his heart who journeys here alone.
Earth and all its thoughts of earth sink under
  Deep as deep in water sinks a stone.
Hardly knows it if the rollers thunder,
  Hardly whence the lonely wind is blown.

It is at first surprising to hear that the heart of the solitary journeyer grows 'full of peace and wonder,' for one would not have expected the desolate setting to inspire these emotions. One gradually comes to see, however, that he has become content precisely because the scene's starkness and desolation have fully entered into him. He can 'hardly' (only with difficulty) realize what is happening around him, and is content solely because he seems to have reached a totally inert and passive spiritual state, like that of the denizens of Proserpine's garden.

His eye perceives 'Clear grey steeples' which 'cleave the low grey sky,' and he reflects that they are the only part of the scene which do not fear nature's cycle and the force of her elements. These steeples are the remains of those edifices which had once dominated the landscape, 'un débris de la grande église' and the 'restes d'un grand monastère hospitalier.' Later in the poem these ruins will be used as emblems of the permanent decline of the Christian religion; here they serve primarily as emblems of the spiritual condition of the speaker. Like them, he too is a burnt-out case, no longer filled with 'change of cares' or concerned with 'how the wild world frets and fares.' In this state of unfeeling emptiness, he is untroubled by the 'Doubt and death' which pervade the landscape. The dedicatory sonnet to 'By the North Sea' had stated that doubt and death were what the sun, wind, and sea could teach man how to master; but at this point in the poem it is wrong to think that the speaker has mastered them. In becoming numb to the force of the elements, and unaware of the natural world surrounding him, he has not triumphed over doubt and death, only repressed them.

Section 3 now explains what has brought the speaker into the poem's wasted landscape. He has come because here he 'might end his quest.' This quest centres on an answer to the question that now for the first time in the poem is directly asked: 'What sign of life or death survives?' The speaker feels he has arrived at the 'goal' of his journey, the place where, if anywhere, it is possible to communicate with the spirits of the dead: 'Here is Hades, manifest, beholden, /

Surely, surely here, if aught be sure!' The experiences of Odysseus in the underworld (as described in book 11 of the *Odyssey*) are now recalled. By going to Hades, Odysseus had met the shades of his dead comrades, seen his beloved mother Anticleia, and, most important, acquired knowledge about himself and his destiny. The love of Odysseus and his mother is described as a force 'more strong than death and all things fated' even though the son had found that he was physically separated from his mother, unable to touch her. We are of course meant to contrast this journey to the underworld with the speaker's journey to the desolate shore. If Odysseus was not able to be fully reunited with his mother, he was at least able to make some contact with the dead, and to find out things unknown to the living. For the poem's speaker, however, such a possibility no longer exists: 'all dispeopled here of visions / Lies, forlorn of shadows even, the shore.' The Hades of the speaker is 'Ghostless': it holds no message for him and no sign of any transcendent reality capable of transforming the poverty and oppressiveness of the purely naturalistic world of the shore. Because this is so, the speaker's quest comes to nothing, and his only relation to the scene from which he had expected so much is found in his being equally desolate. At the end of section 3, he is left with no more than what he possessed at the poem's opening: simply the oppressive awareness of the bleak scene: 'Sky, and shore, and cloud, and waste, and sea.'

In section 4, the speaker's meditation finally moves forward, as he begins to see the Dunwich coast, and consequently his own predicament, in a different way. This change is signalled in the section's opening stanza:

> But aloft and afront of me faring
>   Far forward as folk in a dream
> That strive, between doubting and daring,
>   Right on till the goal for them gleam,
> Full forth till their goal on them lighten,
>   The harbour where fain they would be,
> What headlands there darken and brighten?
>   What change in the sea?

The speaker has turned his attention from his immediate surroundings outward to the larger scene of which the shore is only a part. One may say that he has begun to move outside himself towards a new and more proper goal – not contact with the dead but simply a fuller and more objective perception of the natural world. Now for the first time he notices on one side of him green lawns, bright fields, and pine woods – something quite different from the 'miles of desolation.' The heart of these verdant places is 'alive' and 'the sense of their spirit is free.' Their heart and spirit are not his, however, and it is an index of the speaker's progression that he can realize this and know that they are not the places where he can turn to find peace and fulfilment. His gaze returns to the shore where 'the grasp of the sea is as iron / Laid hard on the land.'

The poem's turning point is now at hand. The fifth stanza of section 4 begins with a deliberate echo of the opening lines of the first section, recalling the speaker's earlier obsession with the landscape's destructive qualities. But suddenly, he is able to move beyond his earlier inertia and hopelessness and to assert that the cruel, desolate setting contains enough to solace him:

> A land that is thirstier than ruin;
>   A sea that is hungrier than death;
> Heaped hills that a tree never grew in;
>   Wide sands where the wave draws breath;
> All solace is here for the spirit
>   That ever for ever may be
> For the soul of thy son to inherit,
>   My mother, my sea.

This startling reversal is a distinctively Swinburnean moment. It is reminiscent of Tannhäuser's triumphant assertion at the end of 'Laus Veneris,' and of the insistence in 'Ave atque Vale' that no matter how dark and perverse the circumstances of Baudelaire's life, they were 'enough.' Like Coleridge's Ancient Mariner blessing the water snakes, the speaker has a decisive change come upon him unaware: he makes no deliberate choice, nor has he consciously willed anything to happen. He has simply come to accept the scene he confronts – the way things are for him – as the place where he has to be, and as a place which can sustain him. Because he has been released from the strictures of his mistaken quest and from the trance-like condition that had earlier rooted his attention to the shore's desolation, he is now free to accept what formerly he had been forced to submit to. No longer does he wish the shore to be any different from what it is, or attempt to find there the materials for transcendence.

The speaker's tone now shifts from funereal lament to an impassioned celebration of the wind which lasts until the section's end. In the wind, which had previously seemed to 'lack breath,' he now discovers a perpetual, vibrant movement, and a delight 'but in living.' At the close of section 4, the reason for the speaker's celebration of the wind becomes clear. As in many Romantic poems, the wind is identified with the force which inspires the poet, blesses him and sets him free. Among men it is poets who are most like the wind: never satisfied, finding delight 'but in living,' immortal in the sense that their poems survive their bodies. The final stanzas of section 4 go on to speak more fully of the correspondence between poets and the wind:

> For these have the toil and the guerdon
>   That the wind has eternally: these
> Have part of the boon and the burden
>   Of the sleepless unsatisfied breeze,
> That finds not, but seeking rejoices
>   That possession can work him no wrong:
> And the voice at the heart of their voice is
>   The sense of his song.

> For the wind's is their doom and their blessing;
>   To desire, and have always above
> A possession beyond their possessing,
>   A love beyond reach of their love.
> Green earth has her sons and her daughters,
>   And these have their guerdons; but we
> Are the wind's and the sun's and the water's
>   Elect of the sea.

The oppositions of 'toil' and 'guerdon,' 'boon' and 'burden,' 'doom' and 'blessing' all point to what is for Swinburne the central fact of poetic vocation: that pain and suffering are necessarily involved in creative experience, as they are in all human existence. Like the west wind in Shelley's ode, the wind here described is both 'destroyer and preserver.' It had been the destructive aspects of the wind – as of the sea – that dominated the poet's awareness in the opening sections of the poem. From now until the end of 'By the North Sea' this is balanced by a corresponding awareness of the beneficent, life-giving part of natural process.

This change is emphasized in section 5, the second of the lyrical intermezzos. Like section 2, it develops the contrast between the beauty and grandeur of the elements seen in the fullness of an expansive vision and their fierce destructiveness seen from the limited viewpoint of the shore. But where the earlier section had ended with a reiteration of the continual warfare between the land and the sea, section 5 (this is another index of the speaker's progression, a sign that something has happened in the poem) ends with a picture of the beauty and purity of the mingled elements of sea and sun:

But afar where pollution is none,
  Nor ensign of strife nor endeavour,
Where her heart and the sun's are one,
  And the soil of her sin comes never,
She is pure as the wind and the sun,
  And her sweetness endureth for ever.

In section 6, the poet returns to a consideration of nature's cycle of destruction and of man's mortality, for these realities have hardly been negated or made to vanish by the affirmations of 4 and 5. This section opens with a repetition of the dirge-like rhythm of the earlier sections and again chants a litany of desolation:

Death, and change, and darkness everlasting ...
These, above the washing tides and wasting,
Reign, and rule this land of utter death.

Two opposing godheads are now described, and implicitly compared to the naturalistic trinity of sun, wind, and sea mentioned in the dedicatory sonnet. One of them is the Christian God, for whom Swinburne intones a requiem. This God's temples have been destroyed by the more powerful and lasting force of Time, the other deity. Time is not a god who casts out fear, but a primitive and implacable force worshipped because of fear. His most appalling devastation is described in one of the most spectacular moments in all of Swinburne's poetry. In the first section of 'By the North Sea,' the speaker had derived some comfort from the thought that to be dead was to be free from nature's cruel assaults. This assumption is now revealed to have been mistaken:

Now displaced, devoured and desecrated,
  Now by Time's hands darkly disinterred,
These poor dead that sleeping here awaited
  Long the archangel's re-creating word,
Closed about with roofs and walls high-gated
  Till the blast of judgement should be heard,

Naked, shamed, cast out of consecration,
  Corpse and coffin, yea the very graves,
Scoffed at, scattered, shaken from their station,
  Spurned and scourged of wind and sea like slaves,
Desolate beyond man's desolation,
  Shrink and sink into the waste of waves.

Tombs, with bare white piteous bones protruded,
   Shroudless, down the loose collapsing banks,
Crumble, from their constant place detruded,
   That the sea devours and gives not thanks.
Graves where hope and prayer and sorrow brooded
   Gape and slide and perish, ranks on ranks.

Those buried near the shore – 'They that thought for all time through to be' –
are not left to rest in peace. They suffer a sea change, but not into something
rich and strange; they rather become fodder for the sea's destructive appetite.
We are reminded by this ghastly mockery of the Christian belief in the
resurrection of the body that there is nothing cosy about a naturalistic acceptance of death as the final end. We are not to think that after burial we shall be
absorbed into and become part of the living and verdant natural world, and
survive as part of the perpetually renewed cycle of the seasons. This condition
would perhaps be appropriate to the sons of the 'green earth' mentioned in
section 4, and would be like the eternal sleep of Merlin in Broceliande that
Swinburne describes in *Tristram of Lyonesse*. Swinburne himself is not a son of
the green earth but of the harsher elements of sun, wind, and sea. Instead of
Merlin, we should rather think of Tristram himself, whose burial place was
shattered by the sea, and whose remains the sea devoured. It is with this
disturbing reminder of the harsh culmination of human existence that the
speaker is left at the end of section 6.

The closing section of 'By the North Sea' joyfully proclaims the sufficiency
of man's purely naturalistic condition. In its contrast with section 6, the earlier
contrast of 2 and 5 is writ large. At the opening of 7, the speaker for the last
time turns his gaze from the 'grim field' of the shore, whose god is Time,
outward to the expanse of sky and sea where another god rules:

But afar on the headland exalted,
   But beyond in the curl of the bay,
From the depth of him dome deep-vaulted
   Our father is lord of the day.

As the lyrical interludes of sections 2 and 5 had celebrated 'our mother' the sea,
and as 4 had celebrated the wind, so the poem's closing section celebrates the
apex of this trinity, the sun, who is 'Our father, the God.' This is of course
Apollo, god both of poetry and of the natural world to which he brings life and
light.

The sun is asked to behold 'the place of the sepulchres,' which is 'the shadow
of this death.' This is the shadow mentioned in the dedicatory sonnet, where it

was said to pass, giving way to the fulfilment possible when man has learned to put aside his fear and to give himself fully and freely to the natural world. For the sun can be father only to 'the soul that is free,' free from a merely enforced submission to nature's domination and free from the futile quest to go beyond the données of a man's life, however bleak. 'By the North Sea' closes with a celebration of the gladness that all nature, including the speaker, has for the force that sustains it in life. The poet gives thanks for the song of natural forces, of which his own song is a part, but which had been silent in him until he had realized the sustaining power of even the most unadorned and seemingly comfortless setting.

One is now in a position to understand fully what the dedicatory sonnet meant by 'doubt' and by the sea's 'secret word.' Doubt in the speaker's mind was connected with his inability to believe that the harsh natural forces surrounding him could have a value and significance beyond their manifest destructiveness and indifference. Doubt also referred to the speaker's reluctance to accept death as the final end. It was the pressure of this doubt that had sustained his misdirected quest for contact with the dead. Only when this doubt had been put aside was it possible for him to move beyond the spiritual impasse described in the poem's opening three sections. What worked against and finally triumphed over the poet's doubt was the 'secret word' of the sea. One meaning of its utterance, as the poem graphically showed, was that death was the final end, absolute and without memorial, and that consequently man must learn to accept the circumstances of his life – symbolized by the bleak landscape – as sufficient to sustain and fulfil him. Second, the 'secret word' had to do with the song of natural forces. The word is the logos of poetic inspiration which is made flesh and given voice by the poet, who shares with these elements, when he has fully given himself to them, the secret of their song.

II

Tristram of Lyonesse, published two years after 'By the North Sea,' was Swinburne's attempt to write a long poem of epic dimensions, comparable to Tennyson's *Idylls of the King* and Browning's *The Ring and the Book*, which would embody his mature reflections on human life and human destiny and present in a spacious narrative framework insights and beliefs usually articulated through more subjective lyric and meditative forms. The challenge Swinburne set himself was perhaps over-ambitious for a poet of primarily lyrical gifts. None would want to suggest that *Tristram of Lyonesse* is a flawless or even consistently engaging work, and none, as Johnson said of *Paradise Lost*, ever wished it longer. Matthew Arnold was referring to the poem – 165 pages of rhyming iambic pentameter – when he made his notorious remark about Swinburne's 'fatal habit' of using a hundred words where one would suffice.[9] But the prolixity of *Tristram of Lyonesse* should not be allowed to obscure the poem's powerful thematic thrust, masterly architectonics, and splendid flashes of episodical illumination.

The major theme of *Tristram of Lyonesse*, to which everything in the poem is subordinated, is the dignity and grandeur of a wholly naturalistic vision of human existence. The major devices that Swinburne uses in organizing his poem and orchestrating its themes are parallelism and contrast. One example is his having the poem's Prelude and its final book open with matching invocations – one to Love, the other to Fate – in which for forty-four lines the same rhyming words are employed. This may seem as pointless a tour de force as Dylan Thomas' rhyming the first line of his 102-line 'Author's Prologue' with the last, the second with the penultimate, and so on. But there are understandable thematic reasons for Swinburne's procedure. It is essential to his purpose that the similarity between Love and Fate be underlined, just as it is important to the pattern of his poem that these invocations be followed by parallel speculations on death and the possibility of immortality.

During the poem, Tristram and Iseult are allowed only two brief periods in which to enjoy their love. These periods (in books 2 and 4) balance the rising and falling halves of the poem. More important, this patterning invites the reader to notice the differences between the two episodes, and consequently to realize how decidedly the lovers' attitudes to each other and to nature have changed and matured. Similarly, the contrast between Iseult of Ireland's vigil in book 5, when she prays for Tristram's safety, and the vigil of the other Iseult in book 7, during which she demands of God that Tristram be damned eternally, is designed to lead the reader to a sympathetic acceptance of the poem's naturalistic values. Finally, twice during the poem Tristram dives from a great height into the sea, first to escape death at the hands of King Mark's men, later to recapture his early joy in the natural world and his sense of oneness with it. Both plunges suggest a pattern of death and rebirth; but something very different is suggested by Tristram's final return to the sea in the poem's closing lines.

Love and Fate are the twin forces which dominate *Tristram of Lyonesse*. In the Prelude, Love is described as the active, generative force which enlivens and sustains all things, a power reminiscent of the life-giving Venus of Lucretius. It is 'first and last of all things made' and is spoken of as a 'light' and a 'spirit.' It is the principle of order and harmony in the universe which keeps 'the choir of lives in chime'; the force that strikes the twin chords of life and death, keeping them in tune with the 'day and night of things alternative'; and the 'root and fruit of terrene things.' The characteristics of Fate, described in book 9, are virtually identical to those of Love: it is a vital principle existing before 'spirit and flesh were made,' a 'fire' and a 'power,' a force which strikes the 'chord of change unchanging.' It teaches man how to accept his mortality since it makes 'life no discord in the tune with death,' and shows man that life and death are like the 'pulse and lapse of tides alternative.' In the words of Dylan Thomas, it shows men that, like light and dark, life and death are 'no enemies / But one companion.'[10] In the words of section cxxi of *In Memoriam*, it shows man that Hesper and Phosphor are a 'double name / For what is one.'

There is nothing in the notion of Fate in *Tristram of Lyonesse* to remind one of Hardy's 'Hap,' Housman's 'Whatever brute or blackguard made the world,' or the malign providence of 'The supreme evil, God' of Swinburne's youthful *Atalanta in Calydon*. In *Tristram of Lyonesse*, Fate is not the haphazardness of a mechanical universe, a moral nemesis, or the iron whims of an indifferent deity. In book 9, Tristram, on his deathbed, attacks the conception of a 'miscreant God': 'That sovereign shadow cast of souls that dwell / In darkness and the prison-house of hell.' For him this God is the product of the imagination of those who fear the power and grandeur of a naturalistic vision of life. He insists that man does not have to interpret his destiny as the working out of God's wrath (what the chorus of *Atalanta in Calydon* called Fate). For Tristram this God can be cast out by a realization of the creative and sustaining forces of the natural world (what *Tristram of Lyonesse* calls Love-and-Fate):

> That ghost whose core of life is very death
> And all its light of heaven a shadow of hell,
> Fades, falls, wanes, withers by none other spell
> But theirs whose eyes and ears have seen and heard
> Not the face naked, not the perfect word,
> But the bright sound and feature felt from far
> Of life which feeds the spirit and the star,
> Thrills the live light of all the suns that roll,
> And stirs the still sealed springs of every soul.

If Love and Fate are so similar, what is the difference between them? Fate and Love are two names for the same process: Love describes this process from the point of view of its active, generative, and cosmic force; Fate from the point of view of an individual man's life, which is inevitably from the viewpoint of death and perpetual change. Fate is Love seen *sub specie mortalitatis*. Fate is simply the way things are, of which the circumstances of a man's life are a part. Because it is nothing more than this, because it is not something other than man, it is meaningless for man to fight against or attempt to change it. For 'How should it turn from its great way to give / Man that must die a clearer space to live?'

It is in this light that the love potion, which plays such a large role in the destiny of Tristram and Iseult, must be understood. Their accidental drinking of this potion determines the course of their lives, bringing them two brief intervals of intense joy, but much unhappiness, sorrow, and pain. Yet the potion must not be seen as something extraneous to the lovers, some capricious and absurd accident, or as punishment for a previous or future transgression of some universal law. Whatever its meaning in other versions of the Tristram legend, in Swinburne's poem the love potion is simply a symbol of the circumstances of a man's life, over which he has no control. It represents the way things are, which a man must learn to understand and to accept. It is not unlike Swinburne's own physical peculiarities, like the sudden death which prompts Lady Midhurst's letter of consolation in *Love's Cross-Currents*, like the Pope's judgment of Tannhäuser in 'Laus Veneris,' or like the facts of Baudelaire's 'bitter' life.

The moment when the lovers drink the love potion is described by Swinburne in a way which recalls Adam and Eve's eating of the forbidden fruit in the ninth book of *Paradise Lost*:

And all their life changed in them, for they quaffed
Death; if it be death so to drink, and fare
As men who change and are what these twain were.
And shuddering with eyes full of fear and fire
And heart-stung with a serpentine desire
He turned and saw the terror in her eyes
That yearned upon him shining ...

Swinburne underplays the dramatic moment in somewhat the same way Milton does. That Tristram and Iseult 'quaffed Death' echoes Eve's 'eating Death.' A few lines further on Swinburne says of the lovers: 'and they saw dark.' One is reminded of Milton's lowering sky. Finally, there seems no reason for Swinburne's speaking of 'serpentine desire' unless he wants his reader to think of *Paradise Lost*. It is doubtless because he wished to invest this moment of his poem with a gravity and a resonance that Swinburne alludes to the Miltonic description of the fall. But a comparison of the two situations suggests no theological or ethical similarities. In this regard the phrase 'serpentine desire' is unfortunate; for Swinburne – as the rest of his poem manifests – hardly means to suggest that Tristram and Iseult become creatures of sin and evil, or lose their place in the scheme of creation and descend to a bestial level. There is no suggestion in the poem that they are guilty of anything, or that they have fallen at all. Neither must they learn to submit to and obey any deity. Their fate is not, as in Milton, what God wills, but simply the données of their life.

What Swinburne does mean to suggest by the parallel may be put in the following way. Before drinking the love potion, the lovers, as the imagery describing them suggests, are innocent and seem to exist in a state of beautiful simplicity, of unself-conscious absorption in the natural world. After they have drunk they come gradually to lose this innocence, in the sense that they become committed to a course of life which forces them to examine closely the nature and meaning of their existence and which finally leads them through much suffering to death. Through the love potion they enter a world of experience in which they first become aware of the force of Fate. The most certain fact in a man's life is the inevitability of his death, and in *Tristram of Lyonesse* Swinburne makes it clear that ultimately man's Fate is simply to be a creature who must die. It is precisely this that Tristram eventually comes to realize is the meaning of the love potion:

> Fate and Love with darkling hands commixt
> Poured [the potion], and no power to part them came betwixt,
> But either's will, howbeit they seem at strife,
> Was toward us one, as death itself and life
> Are one sole doom toward all men, nor may one
> Behold not darkness, who beholds the sun.

Fate and Love are not supernatural forces or transcendent realities: they are firmly rooted in Swinburne's wholly naturalistic vision of man and nature, parts of the one process of life and death.

For Tristram and Iseult to be fulfilled they must completely give themselves to the forces of Love and Fate, even at the cost of personal unhappiness, and even though to do so violates accepted social and moral values. Swinburne does not invite the reader to judge the lovers in any way except by measuring the fullness of their response to each other and to the natural world. This is the index of their virtue and their greatness. An important phrase that Swinburne uses in this poem (as elsewhere in his poetry) to describe the character of the lovers' perception of each other and of nature is 'the spirit of sense' or some variation of it. Leone Vivante's comments on these terms are helpful:

Swinburne's use of the word 'sense' ... deserves special consideration. 'Soul within sense,' 'spirit in sense,' ... 'spirit within sense,' 'one soul of sense,' and other similar expressions which frequently occur, do not oppose 'spirit' to 'sense'; on the contrary, they are intended to point out 'sense' in its full significance, in its deepest nature. The expression 'spirit and sense' is also very frequently used, and these words, generally, are not opposed: they are meant to signify one and the same reality and indeed to integrate each other, as if each in itself were not sufficient to convey the full meaning.[11]

'Spirit of sense' is Swinburne's phrase for man's most spiritual faculty, which is nevertheless something inseparable from his perception of other human beings and of the external world. Without sense, spirit cannot exist; without spirit, sense perceives merely a drab otherness.

During their time at Joyous Gard in book 6, Tristram and Iseult are unusually responsive to the visible world:

> many a noon
> The took the moorland's or the bright sea's boon
> With all their hearts into their spirit of sense,
> Rejoicing, where the sudden dells grew dense
> With sharp thick flight of hillside birds, or where
> On some strait rock's ledge in the intense mute air
> Erect against the cliff's sheer sunlit white
> Blue as the clear north heaven, clothed warm with light,
> Stood neck to bended neck and wing to wing
> With heads fast hidden under, close as cling
> Flowers on one flowering almond-branch in spring,
> Three herons deep asleep against the sun,
> Each with one bright foot downward poised, and one
> Wing-hidden hard by the bright head, and all
> Still as fair shapes fixed on some wondrous wall
> Of minster-aisle or cloister-close or hall
> To take even time's eye prisoner with delight.

What the lovers perceive is no hazy transcendent vista, no gleams or glimmerings of higher things. Their spirit of sense shows them simply the clear, sharply etched, and particularized world of nature. They have no need of anything more than this.

The fullest description of a person completely filled by his 'spirit of sense' is found late in the poem, in 'The Last Pilgrimage.' The pilgrimage is Tristram's final journey, before his fatal wounding, into the holy shrine of the natural world. He comes to the seashore which 'strikes rapture through the spirit of sense.' He feels his perception of the natural world 'sink through his spirit and purge all sense away / Save of the glorious gladness of his hour.' Just after this, Tristram dives into the sea, and in his momentary suspension between land and water Swinburne finds a splendid metaphor for the sense of wholeness and of oneness with nature that full perceptual awareness brings:

> and his heart
> Sent forth a shout that bade his lips not part,
> But triumphed in him silent: no man's voice,
> No song, no sound of clarions that rejoice,
> Can set that glory forth which fills with fire
> The body and soul that have their whole desire
> Silent, and freer than birds or dreams are free
> Take all their will of all the encountering sea.

It is the capacity of Tristram and Iseult to experience these moments that sets them apart from the other characters in the poem. In terms of the poem's naturalistic ethos it is these moments which give to their lives meaning and to the poem as a whole its centre of value. It is not in terms of Victorian moral standards or medieval Christian ethics that one must judge the lovers, but in terms of how fully they give themselves to the terrestrial forces of Love and Fate. For Swinburne, it is only the weak and the wicked who must rely on moral conventions and on what they interpret as God's law in order to support themselves.

Iseult of the White Hands, the other Iseult, Tristram's lawful wife, is such a person. Admittedly, she suffers greatly because of the love of Tristram and his Iseult. The reader first views her with considerable sympathy, but the degeneration of her character into an obsession with punishment, destructiveness, and hate eventually makes her repellent. Swinburne does not sentimentalize Iseult's situation, as Arnold perhaps did in his version of the Tristram story, nor does he allow the reader to regard her as the wronged woman of melodrama. Iseult of the White Hands has allowed her mind to become 'like a field of graves'; for her the natural world exists only to mirror her obsession: she thinks 'The fires of sunset [are] like the fires of hell' waiting to devour Tristram. The key to her character is that she is a strict moralist with all the fervour of a Jeremiah. She is self-righteous and assured of her own virtue: 'For is it I, perchance, I that have sinned?' Astonished that God has yet to reveal a judgement of the lovers as harsh as her own, she rebukes His leniency and longs to be transformed into the engine of His vengeance:

make mine hand
As lightning, or my tongue a fiery brand,
To burn or smite them with thy wrath: behold,
I have nought on earth save thee for hope or hold,
Fail me not thou.

The vigil of Iseult of the White Hands manifests her ugly corrupting reliance on a higher power. In the poem's other vigil in book 5, Tristram's Iseult meditates on her destiny and on what God's judgment of her will be. She beseeches God, with violent shifts of consciousness, to grant her mercy and relief from suffering; to save Tristram from eternal pain even at the price of her own damnation; to have Tristram return to her for a renewal of their physical passion; and finally to allow them to be reunited somewhere after death. This section of the poem, one suspects, may well owe something to Pope's 'Eloise to Abelard.' In Pope's poem the speaker, like Iseult, is separated from her beloved, and, addressing herself to God, asks for His mercy and for union with Him, while at the same time struggling with a persistent revival of her earthly passion for Abelard, which colours all her attempts a single-minded worship. As Eloise says: 'All is not Heav'n's while Abelard has part, / Still rebel nature holds out half my heart.' There is a basic difference between these two situations, however. 'Eloise to Abelard' dramatizes a perennial Christian dilemma: the obstinate tug of the flesh on the spirit, the inability of human nature fully to put aside the things of this world and to become a pure instrument of God's will. A gloss for Pope's poem might well be Paul's 'For the good that I would I do not: but the evil which I would not, that I do' (Romans 7:19). Iseult's situation, on the other hand, is only in a superficial way like the dilemma described by Pope and Paul. Like Tannhäuser's in 'Laus Veneris,' Iseult's situation is placed in the Christian framework of sin and repentance. But, like Tannhäuser, she resolves her situation humanistically and naturalistically.

Iseult admits that she can bring herself to love God only slightly, with a fraction of the intensity that informs her love for Tristram. She considers herself none the less 'blest,' not because she has tried, however unsuccessfully, to follow God's will, but because she has been faithful to her love for Tristram, though this entails no promise of future reward:

Shall I repent, Lord God? shall I repent?
Nay, though thou slay me! for herein I am blest,
That as I loved him yet I love him best –
More than mine own soul or thy love or thee,
Though thy love save and my love save not me.

Later on, in book 6, she says simply that the greatest joys are those of this earth: 'heaven above / Hath not more heavenly holiness of love / Than earth beneath.' Iseult's meditation ends with her yearning for reunion with her lover, if not on earth, then either in hell or in heaven. As long as the lovers are together, she considers herself blest, and it matters not at all to her what form God's judgment takes. Iseult thus embodies characteristics that Swinburne in his poetry repeatedly insists on as the prerequisites for a fully human existence: strength of character, self-reliance, the necessity of accepting the conditions of one's life and of fulfilling oneself in this world and not in a possible future one.

Another way in which Swinburne provides his reader with a means of correctly judging his lovers is through the interpolation of the story of the love of King Arthur for his half-sister. Tristram tells this story to Iseult early in book 1, before they have drunk the love potion. It has been thought that this episode is extraneous and indelicate, a failure in decorum on Swinburne's part, perhaps prompted by his eagerness to make a spiteful flick at Tennyson's 'blameless King.'[12] But there is another way of viewing the episode, which makes it not a superfluous addition but an integral part of *Tristram of Lyonesse*. In the story of Arthur and Queen Morgause of Orkney Swinburne provides an analogue to the story of Tristram and Iseult. In showing the way in which his lovers judge Arthur's illicit love, Swinburne shows the reader how he should later judge the love of Tristram and Iseult. Arthur experiences only one brief interval of union with his half-sister. He is ignorant of the fact of their relationship, of 'The bitter bond of blood between them two, / Twain fathers but one mother.' Like the drinking of the love potion, Arthur's love for his half-sister is something over which he has no control, but which nevertheless determines the course of his life. Realizing this, Tristram and Iseult consider the King no less great and noble. In spite of what conventional moral judgment (of the kind that Tennyson's Arthur dispenses in the 'Guinevere' idyll) would regard as adultery and incest followed by a just nemesis, Arthur is no less to be revered, no less the embodiment of an ideal: 'His name shall be one name with knightliness, / His fame one light with sunlight.' In an uncharacteristic moment, Tristram suggests that Arthur's kingdom was destroyed because 'God shall not suffer scorn.' Iseult quickly picks him up on this, delivering a judgment similar to what the reader's judgment of her and Tristram should come to be. She completely rejects the notion that the providence of any possible God has any possible meaning in a naturalistic vision of the universe:

What good is it to God that such should die?
Shall the sun's light grow sunnier in the sky
Because their light of spirit is clean put out?

Tristram of Lyonesse's most sustained instance of parallelism-with-a-dif-
ference occurs in the contrast between the lovers' two brief interludes of
happiness and joy. During the first of these, in book 2, Tristram and Iseult
inhabit a bower in the depths of a forest for the three summer months. During
this time they seem completely satisfied and happy:

> and here
> More sweet it seemed, while this might be, to dwell
> And take of all world's weariness farewell
> Than reign of all world's lordship queen and king.
> ... Sweet earth
> Fostered them like her babes of eldest birth.

Though Tristram and Iseult have already drunk the love potion, they have yet
to realize that they 'quaffed Death.' In these lines there is certainly more than a
hint that there remains in them something innocent and childlike. This impression is deepened by the repeated emphasis on the fact that the lovers are so
absorbed with each other that they are oblivious of the natural world whose
beauty surrounds them. At one point Iseult 'knew not if night or light were in
the skies,' and it is said of both lovers that they do not know

> If cloud or light changed colour as it grew,
> If star or moon beheld them; if above
> The heaven of night waxed fiery with their love,
> Or earth beneath were moved at heart and root
> To burn as they.

More important, the lovers are unconscious of, and seem unable to believe
in, the reality of change and death:

> But like a babbling tale of barren breath
> Seemed all report and rumour held of death,
> And a false bruit the legend tear-impearled
> That such a thing as change was in the world.
> And each bright song upon his lips that came,
> Mocking the powers of change and death by name,
> Blasphemed their bitter godhead, and defied
> Time.

Iseult, feeling she has experienced the most intense possible moment of their
love – 'That one pure hour all golden' which never can be repeated – comes to

wish for death and asks Tristram to slay her with his sword. One is doubtless meant to feel a certain frisson at this, but seen in the light of their later meeting (and of the poem as a whole) her wish, it is clear, is naive and unnatural. Implicitly, there is a connection between her arbitrary wish to die and the lovers' complete unawareness of nature and natural process.

In book 2, then, the lovers are presented as immature and as not having fully realized what it means to live in terms of the powers of Love and Fate. By the time of their second and last meeting, in book 6, they have realized this, and in comparing the two situations the reader comes to understand better the nature of their love and the gravity and dignity of the view of life which informs it. The lovers' final meeting has as its setting something quite different from the verdant depths of a forest. At Joyous Gard they spend their time in a more characteristically Swinburnean setting, on the 'utmost margin of the loud long sea,' between 'the wild sea and the broad wild lands.' In contrast to their earlier meeting, the lovers now have a clear, passionate apprehension of the natural world even though the nature they perceive is rather more bleak. Far from being unaware of death and change, the lovers speak openly of these inevitabilities. They speculate on the possibility of some kind of continued existence after death, but they reach no conclusions. Unlike their earlier selves in book 2, Tristram and Iseult have come to understand that death is a part of life, something that when accepted detracts nothing from life: 'Nor loved they life or love for death's sake less, / Nor feared they death for love's or life's sake more.'

To a greater extent than almost any other poem of Swinburne, *Tristram of Lyonesse* ponders the question of what happens after death, especially to the two lovers who seem to represent something that should not pass wholly away. There are several instances of this concern in the poem: the allusions to Merlin's eternal 'sleep' in Broceliande, the gropings towards something that is eternal that follow the invocations of books 1 and 9, and the way that the lovers turn more than once to this question. This probing does not negate or run counter to the deeply naturalistic values which permeate the poem. The dual impulse detected at moments in *Tristram of Lyonesse* is described very well by a remark of Graham Hough, made with reference to D.H. Lawrence's *Last Poems*. Hough speaks of 'what must always be for man the inescapable paradox – the necessity to accept death as absolute darkness, and the impossibility of accepting the darkness as absolute.'[13] In many of his poems Swinburne is open enough to allow this paradox to remain visible. But its presence no more detracts from the strength and dignity of his naturalistic vision of life than the hint of rebirth at the climax of his great death poem, 'The Ship of Death,' does from Lawrence's similar vision.

The last page of *Tristram of Lyonesse* suggests, however, a resolution of this question more decisive and unequivocal than anything else in the poem. After their death the lovers are buried in the chapel 'bright like spring,' and, like Merlin in his 'sleep,' they remain close to, and in this sense a part of, the perpetually renewed natural world. But even this sense of natural immortality does not abide. For the sea comes and 'swallows' the chapel, and the 'coffined bones' of the lovers come to rest at the bottom of the ocean. The lovers are thus returned to the most primal and permanent of elements, and like Baudelaire at the end of 'Ave atque Vale' they find quiet in the silent void of death:

> But peace they have that none may gain who live,
> And rest about them that no love can give,
> And over them, while death and life shall be,
> The light and sound and darkness of the sea.

III

At a crucial moment in 'By the North Sea' the poem's speaker turned his attention from the desolate shore. Inland he saw

> Fields brighten and pine-woods blacken,
>   And the heat of their heart is alive;
> They blossom and warble and murmur,
>   For the sense of their spirit is free.

It was an index of his psychological progression that he realized his spirit was not like their spirit, and that the pine-woods were not the place where he should turn for solace and fulfilment. Something very like these woods, however, is the setting of 'A Nympholept' and of the first section of 'The Lake of Gaube,' poems very different from 'By the North Sea' and from the majority of Swinburne's landscape meditations. 'A Nympholept' is set in the middle of a forest in the full radiance of the summer sun: 'Summer, and noon, and a splendour of silence' as the poem's opening announces. It is not a time when nature is desolate but when 'the world is good.' It is explicitly stated near the poem's opening that this particular time and place are quite distinct from the more common settings of Swinburne's poems, and that they contain possibilities for joy and fulfilment which the natural world seldom offers:

> The passing noon that beholds not a cloudlet weep
> Imbues and impregnates life with delight more deep
> Than dawn or sunset or moonrise on lawns or glades
>   Can shed from the skies that receive it and may not keep.

The skies may hold not the splendour of sundown fast;
   It wanes into twilight as dawn dies down into day.
And the moon, triumphant when twilight is overpast,
   Takes pride but awhile in the hours of her stately sway.
   But the might of the noon, though the light of it pass away,
Leaves earth fulfilled of desires and of dreams that last.

In 'A Nympholept,' while there is full awareness of nature's destructive aspects, the emphasis falls on the natural world's 'extraordinary actuality,'[14] on its power at this certain moment in time, this 'perfect hour,' to satisfy completely human desire. It is a moment which offers what Browning's Cleon describes as 'a world of capability / For joy, spread round about us, meant for us, / Inviting us.' The poem is not so much a meditation as a movement from excited anticipation to rhapsodic acceptance and fulfilment. The speaker's difficulty is not how to go on living in a bleak and comfortless world, but how to summon the strength to surrender himself to one of nature's perfect moments, while retaining the knowledge that it is a moment that will pass.

To describe 'A Nympholept' as a unique poem in Swinburne's canon, however, is not to suggest that the poem is a lusus naturae. Paull F. Baum is wrong in saying that 'it is not what one ever expected' of the poet.[15] In this poem, as in 'The Lake of Gaube,' Swinburne is preoccupied with his fundamental and abiding poetic concerns: naturalism, transience, mortality, and poetic vocation. Far from being outside of the main current of Swinburne's poetry, 'A Nympholept' occupies a major place within it. It is one of his few poems which describe an important phase of man's relation to nature – what may be called the summer vision. In the three lovely hawthorn poems from A Channel Passage and Other Poems Swinburne describes three different seasons in terms of their effect on man. Spring is the time when the rebirth of nature signals the rebirth of hope and desire in man. Summer is the time of stasis, of full contentment and peace. In autumn, the seasonal death of nature leaves man desolate, with his thoughts turning to death. 'Ave atque Vale,' 'By the North Sea,' and many other poems belong to the autumn vision. 'A Vision of Spring in Winter,' as its title suggests, intimates the renewal of April, while the movement of Tristram of Lyonesse is from the springtime world of the Prelude and book 1, through the high summer of the lovers' fulfilment, into the autumnal world of their separation and death. What 'A Nympholept' does is to describe in detail the summer vision, when nature's abundance and completeness suggest a moment when all yearnings can be put aside and all desires satisfied.

An analogous way of describing this poem is to say that it occupies in Swinburne's poetry the same place that 'Credences of Summer' does in the poetry of Wallace Stevens. Stevens' poem celebrates the time when nature is 'too ripe for enigmas, too serene,' when 'the mind lays by its trouble.' It is the time when nature is at its most luxuriant – 'green's green apogee'; when the poet's awareness is focused completely on the brilliant immediacy of the scene; when everything in nature is actual and nothing has to be imagined. Stevens' ambition in this poem, like Swinburne's in 'A Nympholept,' is to apprehend the 'secret,' the essence, of this 'extraordinary actuality':

> Let's see the very thing and nothing else.
> Let's see it with the hottest fire of sight.
> Burn everything not part of it to ash. [16]

In confronting this natural setting, Swinburne refuses to assume a religious posture in his desire to possess nature's 'secret':

> I seek not heaven with submission of lips and knees,
> With worship and prayer for a sign till it leap to light:
> I gaze on the gods about me, and call on these.

The spirit which impregnates nature and quickens the speaker's response to it is no supernatural force, not the logos of Saint John, but

> the word that quickened at first into flame, and ran,
> Creative and subtle and fierce with invasive power,
> Through darkness and cloud, from the breath of the one God, Pan.

Pan, who is spoken of more than once in the poem, is for Swinburne the god of the earth, who personifies the beauty, power, and terror of nature. He deals 'shafts' of anger as well as of love, inspires both 'love' and 'dread,' and can change quickly from a beneficent deity into a terrifying one. [17] Swinburne devotes two poems to a description of this god. 'The Palace of Pan,' from the same volume as 'A Nympholept,' describes the pine forest which is the god's palace and, as the poem's imagery invites one to say, his temple and cathedral as well. 'Pan and Thalassius,' from the third series of *Poems and Ballads* (1889), is a dialogue, in a light, half-jocular vein, between Thalassius, who owes his allegiance to 'the human soul, the stars, Urania and the sea,' and Pan, who is 'lord of the mystery of earth, and immortal godhead of – or in – the terrene All.' [18] This contrast between Thalassius and Pan is analogous to that between Swinburne's seashore poems and 'A Nympholept,' and to that between what I have called the autumn vision and the summer vision. In his final remarks, Pan, speaking in the poem's awkward metres, invites his interlocutor to come from the world of meditation into the fullness and brightness of the summer world:

> Call
> No more on the starry presence
> Whose light through the long dark swam:
> Hold fast to the green world's pleasance:
> For I that am lord of it am
> All.

The dialogue between the two is left unresolved, and it may be said that 'A Nympholept' begins where 'Pan and Thalassius' ends, with the Thalassius-like speaker preparing to cast off those things which keep him from wholly surrendering himself to the world of Pan.

The opening stanza of 'A Nympholept' intimates the poem's major concerns:

> Summer, and noon, and a splendour of silence, felt,
>   Seen, and heard of the spirit within the sense.
> Soft through the frondage the shades of the sunbeams melt,
>   Sharp through the foliage the shafts of them, keen and dense,
>   Cleave, as discharged from the string of the God's bow, tense
> As a war-steed's girth, and bright as a warrior's belt.
>   Ah, why should an hour that is heaven for an hour pass hence?

In 'A Nympholept,' the term 'spirit' is used to refer both to the life-giving force of natural process and to the faculty within the speaker that responds to and is quickened by this force. The description of the sunbeams suggests something of nature's destructiveness and of the terror which this inspires. The closing line states simply and directly the poem's preoccupation: the mutability of nature, the fact that its moments of serenity all too quickly pass, giving way to something frightening and inimical to man. This is the first indication of a constant tension in the poem, only resolved at its climax, between awareness of the moment and awareness that the moment will pass. 'A Nympholept' takes place in 'the perfect hour,' but from another and equally correct point of view, it takes place during 'the passing noon.'

What 'the perfect hour' makes possible for man is, in a phrase from 'The Lake of Gaube,' a 'sense of unison,' the ecstatic experience of being made one with the visible universe. But together with this possibility is the awareness of the inevitability of change. Pan, the god of nature, is 'the God who has change to wife.' In the poem it is clear that the speaker's continual brooding on nature's latent ferocity is intimately connected with his preoccupation with change. This aspect of nature is imaged in the poem in a number of different ways: by the snake that creeps from the breath of noon but returns at nightfall; by the eruptions of Mount Etna; by the wolves howling for their prey; and by 'the sea's wild will / That shifts and grinds [men] as grain in the storm-wind's mill.'

It is in terms of the speaker's awareness of this ambivalence in nature that the key words of both this poem and 'The Lake of Gaube' must be understood. 'Desire' (like 'hope') is the wish to possess nature – not just an aspect of it, but its totality, both its splendour and its terror, and to possess it without changing it. 'Secret' and 'mystery' are terms which denote what is at the heart of nature, the essence which the speaker wants revealed to him. 'Dreams' are illusory substitutes for this 'secret.' They are not real and are something quite distinct from the naked apprehension of nature. 'Heaven,' when the term is used pejoratively, means the heaven of the Christian or something that is the product of a 'dream.' When used positively the word describes that moment when man and nature are rapturously united – when 'heaven is about me here.' 'Fear' and 'dread' are negative and unhealthy reactions to nature's power, ones which inhibit man and keep him from accepting his purely naturalistic condition.

For approximately the first half of the poem the fear of nature's power and the difficulty of apprehending its 'secret' are foremost in the speaker's mind. He knows that man moves toward union with nature at his peril: 'For if any there be' that have sight of fulfilled desires and 'dreams that last'

> His lips shall straiten and close as a dead man's must,
>   His heart shall be sealed as the voice of a frostbound stream.
>   For the deep mid mystery of light and of heat that seem
> To clasp and pierce dark earth, and enkindle dust,
>   Shall a man's faith say what it is? or a man's guess deem?

A direct confrontation with nature, it is said, may well leave man speechless: that is, imaginatively dead, without the power of creating poetry. There is no guarantee that 'the deep mid mystery' will be beneficial to man or that man will survive such an encounter with all his faculties intact. But the speaker does not allow these thoughts to turn him from his desire for revelation from nature. He is encouraged by the peacefulness and beauty of the world at this particular moment:

> Ah, what should darkness do in a world so fair?
> The bent-grass heaves not, the couch-grass quails not or cowers;
>   The wind's kiss frets not the rowan's or aspen's hair.

The next several stanzas describe the tension between 'hope' and 'fear' and analogous sets of opposites: 'love' and 'dread,' 'mercy' and 'wrath,' the 'God of life' and the 'God of ravin.' While the speaker's desire for revelation grows increasingly stronger, he is still not certain that the scene he confronts will bring him joy. The 'strong sun's imminent might ... Pervades, invades' but also 'appals' him. The tension between desire and fear and the speaker's concern to resolve this tension are the subject of the following stanza:

> Is it rapture or terror that circles me round, and invades
>   Each vein of my life with hope – if it be not fear?
> Each pulse that awakens my blood into rapture fades,
>   Each pulse that subsides into dread of a strange thing near
>   Requickens with sense of a terror less dread than dear.
> Is peace not one with light in the deep green glades
>   Where summer at noonday slumbers? Is peace not here?

Midway through the poem comes its turning point, when the speaker's vacillation between desire and fear gives way to his first unequivocal affirmation:

> The skies that scorn us are less in thy sight than we,
> Whose souls have strength to conceive and perceive thee, Pan,
>   With sense more subtle than senses that hear and see.
>
> Yet may not it say, though it seek thee and think to find
>   One soul of sense in the fire and the frost-bound clod,
> What heart is this, what spirit alive or blind,
>   That moves thee: only we know that the ways we trod
>   We tread, with hands unguided, with feet unshod,
> With eyes unlightened: and yet, if with steadfast mind,
>   Perchance may we find thee and know thee at last for God.

In tones which recall the 1871 'Preface' to *Songs before Sunrise*, the speaker affirms that while man shares the helplessness of all things in the presence of nature's power and grandeur, his human consciousness – his uniqueness as a human being – makes him of more worth than animals or inanimate objects.[19] There is no indication here, or in any other part of Swinburne's poem, that man's individuality – his self-awareness and his awareness of his separateness from nature – is in any way negated or put aside as a condition of union with nature. It is rather the case that a realization of these truths must form the basis for union.

After this point in the poem the speaker's utterance changes from eager anticipation mixed with fear to unreserved acceptance and delight. What is now emphasized is not the tension between hope and fear but the conviction that hope can absorb fear, if only nature will reveal enough of its 'secret.' Nature's essence, its 'spirit of sense,' now begins to open itself to the speaker. The fear that had previously almost overwhelmed him is not negated or shown to be delusory; it is transformed into something positive. Fear now changes 'to desire, and desire to delight.' Those things which had made the speaker afraid are now accepted and celebrated as part of the totality of the natural world. The hour of 'breathless rapture' that the speaker had waited upon is now at hand. He is not united to nature in a trance-like condition or a swoon, in which the outlines of the natural world become hazy and indistinct. He does not give himself to a 'dream.' What his 'vision' consists of is simply his clear and 'steadfast' perception of the world around him:

> I sleep not: sleep would die of a dream so strange;
>   A dream so sweet would die as a rainbow dies,
> As a sunbow laughs and is lost on the waves that range
>   And reck not of light that flickers or spray that flies.
>   But the sun withdraws not, the woodland shrinks not or sighs,
> No sweet thing sickens with sense or with fear of change;
>   Light wounds not, darkness blinds not, my steadfast eyes.

Now, for a moment, with full awareness that the moment is transitory, the speaker is fulfilled and sings a rapturous hymn to the joy of being what Stevens calls 'completely physical in a physical world':[20]

> And here is my sense fulfilled of the joys of earth,
>   Light, silence, bloom, shade, murmur of leaves that meet.
>
> Bloom, fervour, and perfume of grasses and flowers aglow,
>   Breathe and brighten about me: the darkness gleams,
> The sweet light shivers and laughs on the slopes below,
>   Made soft by leaves that lighten and change like dreams;
>   The silence thrills with the whisper of secret streams
> That well from the heart of the woodland: these I know:
>   Earth bore them, heaven sustained them with showers and beams.
>
> I lean my face to the heather, and drink the sun
>   Whose flame-lit odour satiates the flowers: mine eyes
> Close, and the goal of delight and of life is one:

No more I crave of earth or her kindred skies.
No more? But the joy that springs from them smiles and flies:
The sweet work wrought of them surely, the good work done,
If the mind and the face of the season be loveless, dies.

This the most radiantly joyous moment in all of Swinburne's poetry, the triumphant culmination of his constant absorption in the question of man's relation to the natural world and of the need to live in the present. None of the awareness of human limitations and of nature's separateness from man that had been described in 'The Sundew,' 'Ave atque Vale,' 'By the North Sea,' and many other poems is forgotten or negated. The limitations are accepted and transformed in a moment of natural ecstasy. From this high point of satisfaction the other, less satisfying moments of nature's cycle are not excluded; for Swinburne goes on to celebrate the very mutability that had previously appalled him:

Thee, therefore, thee would I come to, cleave to, cling,
    If haply thy heart be kind and thy gifts be good,
Unknown sweet spirit, whose vesture is soft in spring,
    In summer splendid, in autumn pale as the wood
    That shudders and wanes and shrinks as a shamed thing should,
In winter bright as the mail of a war-worn king
    Who stands where foes fled far from the face of him stood.

The doubt and terror that had earlier seized the speaker vanish at the moment he realizes the actual world and the ideal world are one:

The terror that whispers in darkness and flames in light,
    The doubt that speaks in the silence of earth and sea,
The sense, more fearful at noon than in midmost night,
    Of wrath scarce hushed and of imminent ill to be,
    Where are they? Heaven is as earth, and as heaven to me
Earth.

While there is nothing in 'A Nympholept' to suggest that Swinburne had forgotten or deliberately put aside the awareness of death – the fact that his own mortality was a part of nature's cycle of change – it is true that the poem lacks a final or cumulative statement of the place of death in a fully naturalistic view of life. It is to 'The Lake of Gaube' – explicitly a death poem – that one must turn for such a statement.

IV

The title poem of *A Channel Passage and Other Poems* (1904), which opens the volume, is a description of the hazardous crossing between Ostend and Dover that Swinburne made in the summer of 1855. In the following poem, 'The Lake of Gaube,' Swinburne celebrates another memorable experience of his youth: swimming in the Lac de Gaube in the Pyrenees during a stay at Cauteretz in the spring of 1862, when he was twenty-five. That Swinburne returns to an incident of his youth to give shape to what is primarily a meditation on death suggests he is attempting to sum up, to make a final statement about, his entire life.

In several of his poems, most memorably in book 8 of *Tristram of Lyonesse* and 'In the Water' from *A Midsummer Holiday and Other Poems*, a swimmer's plunge into water was associated with freedom, psychic release, and heightened perceptual awareness. 'The Lake of Gaube' is unique in also associating the plunge with the swimmer's death. For it is not the sea, with its suggestions of life-giving power, which receives the diver, but rather 'the fathomless night of the water' of a cold inland lake. A prose piece by Swinburne, one of his 'Notes of Travel,' contains a helpful description of the lake and its surroundings:

The fiery exuberance of flowers among which the salamanders glide like creeping flames, radiant and vivid, up to the very skirt of the tragic little pine-wood at whose heart the fathomless little lake lies silent, with a dark dull gleam on it as of half-tarnished steel; the deliciously keen and exquisite shock of a first plunge under its tempting and threatening surface, more icy cold in spring than the sea in winter; the ineffable and breathless purity of the clasping water ...; the sport of catching and taming a salamander till it became the pleasantest as well as the quaintest of dumb four-footed friends; the beauty of its purple-black coat of scaled armour inlaid with patches of dead-leaf gold, its shining eyes and its flashing tongue ...[21]

'The Lake of Gaube' is divided into three short parts, each written in a sharply different metre. The centre of the poem is its second section, which describes the actual plunge. Section 1, a description of the lake and its surroundings, leads up to the dive and intimates some of the issues which it is the poem's concern to resolve. Section 3 is a passage of reflection and generalization, the sombreness of which contrasts with the bright landscape of 1 and the excited joy of 2. To understand what the poem is about, and how its parts fit together, it is necessary to realize that the poem turns on the seeming paradox made most fully apparent in section 2: the speaker's plunge into the dark water is both a metaphor for his descent to death and extinction, and a superb image for the freedom and joy of poetic creation and of man's union with nature. The lake is both the abode of death and 'the likeness of infinite heaven' (this last word having the same meaning as it does in 'A Nympholept').

The opening stanza of the first section describes a scene that in several respects – the majesty of the sun, the silence of nature, the presence of an unseen bliss, the 'sense of unison' – is identical with that of 'A Nympholept': 'The sun is lord and god, sublime, serene, / And sovereign on the mountains'; 'The lawns, the gorges, and the peaks are one / Glad glory.' The second and third stanzas describe the brightly coloured salamanders: these 'living things of light' are cold-blooded amphibians who brave their opposite element – the heat of the noontime sun – and whose fear of the human element in the scene gives way to a 'kindly trust in man,' which in turn gladdens the speaker and makes possible his brief experience of contact with their 'harmless little life.' The first lines of the section's last stanza describe a possible human reaction to the salamanders: a fear that holds 'the bright thing hateful' – the same fear that makes man view as hateful *his* opposite element, the dark cold water of the lake:

> Fear held the bright thing hateful, even as fear,
> Whose name is one with hate and horror, saith
> That heaven, the dark deep heaven of water near,
> Is deadly deep as hell and dark as death.

This fear is complementary to the fear of nature's destructiveness described in 'A Nympholept': in the words of D.H. Lawrence's 'Phoenix,' it is the fear of being 'sponged out, erased, cancelled, made nothing ... dipped into oblivion.' It is also synonymous with the fear of freedom, of the full expansion of human faculties. This fear builds a Hell in Heaven's despite, saying that 'the dark deep heaven of water near, / Is deadly deep as hell.' For the person who lacks confidence in the sufficiency of his own powers, who cannot put aside his fear of himself, the plunge into the water would slay 'the soul alive.' But the human who is able to naturalize himself, respond fully to the primitive splendour of the natural setting and its denizens, and sense a sympathetic correspondence between himself and the salamanders (the visual epiphany of nature's 'secret') is also able to accept the inevitability of descent into the dark water of extinction and consequently to experience the 'rapturous plunge that quickens blood and breath.'

This plunge is celebrated in the anapestic couplets of the second section of 'The Lake of Gaube.' The downward passage of the speaker is an active embracing of mortality, not a passive acceptance of the inevitable. Fear of death, the result of fear of life, it put aside, its place being taken by the inclusive moment in which the swimmer is 'free utterly now' and his surroundings become 'heaven':

As the bright salamander in fire of the noonshine exults and is glad of his day,
The spirit that quickens my body rejoices to pass from the sunlight away,
To pass from the glow of the mountainous flowerage, the high multitudinous bloom,
Far down through the fathomless night of the water, the gladness of silence and
    gloom.
Death-dark and delicious as death in the dream of a lover and dreamer may be,
It clasps and encompasses body and soul with delight to be living and free:
Free utterly now, though the freedom endure but the space of a perilous breath,
And living, though girdled about with the darkness and coldness and strangeness of
    death:
Each limb and each pulse of the body rejoicing, each nerve of the spirit at rest,
All sense of the soul's life rapture, a passionate peace in its blindness blest.
   ...
As a sea-mew's love of the sea-wind breasted and ridden for rapture's sake
Is the love of his body and soul for the darkling delight of the soundless lake:
   ...
Might life be as this is and death be as life that casts off time as a robe,
The likeness of infinite heaven were a symbol revealed of the Lake of Gaube.

The passage of man's spirit from light to darkness is equated with the brief but glorious life of the salamander, and the driver rejoices even in the presence of death because it offers him a final moment of rapturous fulfilment. If this passage is compared with the early 'Hymn to Proserpine,' it becomes clear that Swinburne's attitude to death has greatly changed and matured. Death is no more a longed-for oblivion, a release from meaningless imprisonment in mutability. It is rather something intimately a part of man's relation to nature; a culmination, not an escape.

'The Lake of Gaube' concludes with an austere admission of the limits of human vision, of all that man does not know about death and about the possibilities of some kind of life beyond the grave, some way in which the joyous moment during which time is 'cast off' may perhaps be eternalized:

Whose thought has fathomed and measured
    The darkness of life and of death,
The secret within them treasured,
    The spirit that is not breath?
Whose vision has yet beholden
    The splendour of death and of life?
Though sunset as dawn be golden,
    Is the word of them peace, not strife?
Deep silence answers: the glory

We dream of may be but a dream,
And the sun of the soul wax hoary
　　As ashes that show not a gleam.
But well shall it be with us ever
　　Who drive through the darkness here,
If the soul that we live by never,
　　For aught that a lie saith, fear.

This 'lie' is a refusal to believe in man's power and dignity, the same lie that earlier in the poem said the dark water held only death. Who can know completely the 'secret' of life and death? Who can be certain whether it is peace and not strife which is at the heart of nature and a naturalistic view of life? To these questions no answer can be given. But while man cannot be other than sceptical concerning the possibility of a phoenix-like renewal of life, all shall be well with him as long as he fulfils his great destiny in merely being a man, a free man living in the present and sustained by no power but his own. This is the same belief that informed the 'Prelude' to *Songs before Sunrise*, that turning point of Swinburne's early career, and that now sustains the aging poet meditating on his own inevitable death.

7

Tennyson and Swinburne

In 1861, the year before Swinburne visited the area and swam in the Lac de Gaube, Tennyson returned to the valley of Cauteretz after an absence of over thirty years, having first visited the Pyrenees in the summer of 1830 in the company of Arthur Hallam.[1] Just as Swinburne was long to remember his youthful visit and many years later to re-create part of the experience in 'The Lake of Gaube' in giving shape to a profound meditation on life and death, so too in the summer of 1861 Tennyson was borne back into his past and led to reflect on the continuity of life and death. The result was 'In the Valley of Cauteretz,' one of his superlative lyrics and one of the few personal poems he wrote during the 1860s:

> All along the valley, stream that flashest white,
> Deepening thy voice with the deepening of the night,
> All along the valley, where thy waters flow,
> I walked with one I loved two and thirty years ago.
> All along the valley, while I walked today,
> The two and thirty years were a mist that rolls away;
> For all along the valley, down thy rocky bed,
> Thy living voice to me was as the voice of the dead,
> And all along the valley, by rock and cave and tree,
> The voice of the dead was a living voice to me.

'The Lake of Gaube' and Tennyson's poem have more in common than the Pyrenees setting, the vivid remembrance of a youthful experience, and a concern with life and death. Both poems are the work of Romantic naturalists: they hinge upon an intimate sympathetic correspondence between speaker and natural setting and their common subject is the sense of a life in natural things and of man's life as a part of nature (to recall Pater's description of the active principle of Wordsworth's poetry). It is precisely this fusion of setting and subject that gives each poem its power and authority. At the same time there are manifest differences between the poems; none is more important or indicative than the fact that while one poem is about the necessity of living in the present the other is about the power of the past and its determining relation to the present. Over and over again in his poetry Swinburne insists, in the words of one of his characters, that 'now is more than then'; while over and over in his poetry, as in 'In the Valley of Cauteretz,' Tennyson illustrates Emily Dickinson's axiom: 'It is the Past's supreme italic / Makes this Present mean' (No. 1498).

There is another poem of Tennyson's which describes the scenery of the Cauteretz region. But while the landscape of the early 'Oenone' (1832) is opulent, gorgeously detailed with a Keatsian richness of imagery and diction, and largely incidental to the poem's thematic concerns, that of 'In the Valley of Cauteretz' is of unadorned, primordial simplicity – rocks, caves, trees, the stream, and 'the deepening of the night.' This last, the key time in Tennyson for vision or revelation (as we have seen in earlier chapters), ensures that the natural objects in the poem will be perceived only in their elemental generic outlines. But the deeper reason, the psychological reason, for the sombreness of the landscape of 'In the Valley of Cauteretz' may be said to be the death of Hallam in 1833; its sober colouring is taken from the eye of a poet who has kept watch on his own mortality and pondered that of his beloved friend for almost three decades. Similarly, the reason the poem's landscape is not ornamental but an essential constituent of its meaning is that in 1861 Tennyson saw the Pyrenees, as he could not have done in 1830, not only through his eyes but also through his memory.

As the visual element in the landscape becomes recessive with the deepening of the night, its auditory element – the 'voice' of the stream falling over its rocky bed – becomes dominant, its sound being wonderfully imitated by the poem's complex metrical and verbal patterns.[2] At the same time the darkness clarifies and simplifies the speaker's vision, and makes possible that magically charged Tennysonian moment when a white glimmer – here the flashing whiteness of the stream – is seen against a dark background. One recalls the 'gleaming shape' of the white-robed Lady of Shalott floating down her river at 'the closing of the day'; Hallam's burial tablet glowing in the dark church at Clevedon in section lxvii of *In Memoriam*; and the white kine glimmering in the dark field in the climactic ninety-fifth section of the same poem, in which through memory and intimate sympathy with the natural world the 'living spirit' of the dead Hallam is 'flashed' on Tennyson. Exactly the same pattern of loss and gain is repeated in the ten lines of 'In the Valley of Cauteretz,' as 'the living voice' of the flashing white stream becomes associated with the voice of the dead Hallam and, in a moment of imaginative fusion during which the mist of temporal duration rolls away, becomes the living voice of the dead loved one.

In Arthur Hallam's own terms, 'In the Valley of Cauteretz' is wholly the work of 'the delicate sense of fitness' of a 'poet of sensation.' There is nothing in the poem to suggest a 'poet of reflection'; indeed, the poem owes part of its authority and power to being untouched by ideas, abstractions, or assertions concerning a transcendent future realm. The same may be said of Tennyson's other consummate short lyrics, such as 'Tears, Idle Tears,' 'Far – Far – Away,' 'Now sleeps the crimson petal,' and the sections of *In Memoriam* which were analysed in chapter 3. But the same cannot be said of all Tennyson's meditative lyrics, several of which are marred by their creator's succumbing to his habitual temptation to go beyond the boundaries of Romantic naturalism and replace felt emotion with transcendental speculation and assertion.

One example is the famous 'Crossing the Bar':

Sunset and evening star,
   And one clear call for me!
And may there be no moaning of the bar,
   When I put out to sea,

But such a tide as moving seems asleep,
   Too full for sound and foam,
When that which drew from out the boundless deep
   Turns again home.

Twilight and evening bell
   And after that the dark!
And may there be no sadness of farewell,
   When I embark;

For though from out our bourne of Time and Place
   The flood may bear me far,
I hope to see my Pilot face to face
   When I have crost the bar.

Concerning the poem and its obtrusive final stanza, one can do no better than quote Culler's analysis:

The first three stanzas of the poem render death, not fearful and horrible, but beautiful and awesome, purely in naturalistic terms. There is, in the first place, the imagery of the voyage with its sense of a beginning ('embark') rather than an ending and of water as a source of life. Then, there is the beauty of the natural scene – the sunset, the evening star, the twilight bell, and the one 'clear' call. Even the dark is rendered mysterious! Finally, there is the serenity achieved through a balance of opposing qualities: the tide which 'moving seems asleep, / Too full for sound and foam,' and the paradox that to move out into the 'boundless deep' is to turn again 'home.' All these images of plenitude and power, of fullness without terror or doubt, make death acceptable simply as a natural process, so that there is no need for the supernatural apologetic which follows. Yet the fourth stanza offers such an apologetic, and in terms entirely incompatible with the rest of the poem. For whereas the first three stanzas have been conducted entirely in terms of the natural scene and in pure natural language, now we have the capital letters of Pilot, Time, and Place, which take us into the world of moral abstractions, and 'bourne', which takes us into the poetic diction of *Hamlet*. A poem which seemed absolutely authentic in the first three stanzas has somehow lost that quality in the fourth.[3]

Another fine poem similarly blemished by a concluding assertion of supernatural belief is 'The splendour falls,' one of the songs from *The Princess*:

> The splendour falls on castle walls
>   And snowy summits old in story:
> The long light shakes across the lakes,
>   And the wild cataract leaps in glory.
> Blow, bugle, blow, set the wild echoes flying,
> Blow, bugle; answer, echoes, dying, dying, dying.
>
> O hark, O hear! how thin and clear,
>   And thinner, clearer, farther going!
> O sweet and far from cliff and scar
>   The horns of Elfland faintly blowing!
> Blow, let us hear the purple glens replying:
> Blow, bugle; answer, echoes, dying, dying, dying.
>
> O love, they die in yon rich sky,
>   They faint on hill or field or river:
> Our echoes roll from soul to soul,
>   And grow for ever and for ever.
> Blow, bugle, blow, set the wild echoes flying,
> And answer, echoes, answer, dying, dying, dying.

The subject of this poem is the enormously poignant sense of loss as the present gradually recedes into the past. The recompense for loss is the enhanced experience of the moment that its vanishing paradoxically makes possible. In Emily Dickinson's formulation: 'By a departing light / We see acuter, quite, / Than by a wick that stays' (No. 1714). As the 'long light' of late afternoon falls across the landscape it gives a splendour to walls and snowy summits, vivifies the lakes, and seems to make the cataract leap in glory. The dying fall of the bugle's echoed song also serves to intensify the moment. Its sounds, enhanced by the romantic associations of castle walls and summits 'old in story,' evoke for a moment the sense of Elfland, of a world of the heart's desire somewhere beyond, just as does 'the mellow lin-lan-lone of evening bells' in 'Far – Far – Away.'

In the last stanza of 'The splendour falls,' however, the natural magic of felt loss and simultaneous recompense through intimate sympathy with the natural world is shattered; for the ravishing music of the dying fall is interrupted by the strident accents of a spiritual Rotarian. The light and the echoes of the world of nature may fade and die; but for himself and his beloved the voice asserts transcendent gain and everlasting spiritual growth: 'Our echoes roll from soul to soul, / And grow for ever and for ever.' Do they indeed! If so, one can only feel sorry for this voice, for such idealizing propensities could only blunt the ability to sense the bittersweet beauty of the natural music of transience, which is so exquisitely evoked in the first two stanzas of the poem, and which returns in its final two lines to muffle the grotesque auditory image of the ever-growing supernatural echoes, with which Tennyson's poem has nothing really to do.

'Now is more than then.' This un-Tennysonian assertion is uttered by the title character of Swinburne's 1896 lyrical narrative, The Tale of Balen, the last of his creative works intended as a deliberate contrast to a poem of Tennyson's. In Balin and Balan (1885), the last of the Idylls of the King to be published, Tennyson had retold Malory's Balin, or the Knight of the Two Swords with only a very limited fidelity to his source. Swinburne by contrast set himself the task of retelling Malory's 'old tale of chivalry ... in all its incidents, with but few additions or variations: so it is only for the treatment of it that any credit – or discredit – is due to me.'⁴ He certainly realized his intention, for 'it is possible to trace almost every narrative stanza to its source in Malory,' and at times, as David Staines has shown, the retelling 'remains so faithful to the source that it becomes a close paraphrase.'⁵ In addition, in order to underline the contrast with Tennyson, Swinburne chose to cast his verse retelling of the Balen story in the stanzaic form of 'The Lady of Shalott.'

Swinburne's implied criticism of Tennyson's poem and his declared artistic intentions in writing *The Tale of Balen* are peculiar, to say the least. In chapter 1 we saw that Swinburne had a solid critical point when he complained in the 1872 *Under the Microscope* that Tennyson's making Arthur 'the noble and perfect symbol of an ideal man' had unhinged 'the whole legend of the Round Table.' We also saw that his strictures on Tennyson's treatment of his Arthurian sources had less to do with fidelity to source per se than with questions of decorum and internal consistency. But one can hardly argue that Tennyson has done something artistically improper in *Balin and Balan* in pursuing an artistic goal other than that of literal fidelity to Malory's version. Moreover, it is hard to regard Swinburne's employment of the stanzaic form of 'The Lady of Shalott' in his version as other than a pointless exercise in technical ingenuity. The refrain and the shorter line at the end of each of Tennyson's stanzas, together with each stanza's demanding quadruple and triple rhymes, serve to slow up the movement of 'The Lady of Shalott,' to enhance its pictorial, tableau-like quality, and to stylize its incidents in a way that emphasizes their emblematic and parabolic quality. But since *The Tale of Balen* is a fast-paced narrative, full of incident, Swinburne is forced to undermine the raison d'être of Tennyson's stanzaic form: he makes no attempt to create a refrain, adds an extra syllable to the last line of each stanza to speed things up, and greatly de-emphasizes the function of the rhymes by making as few lines as possible end-stopped. The result is that the stanzaic form of *The Tale of Balen* does not sound anything like that of 'The Lady of Shalott' and necessarily eschews that form's distinctive qualities.

What Swinburne would seem to have produced in *The Tale of Balen* is, then, a poem which answers to the negative criticisms of his work made by his creative peers (which were surveyed at the beginning of chapter 5). For the poem's strict fidelity to its source must mean that it is largely 'founded on literature, not on nature' (William Morris' complaint); and its technical virtuosity with a complex stanzaic form related only arbitrarily to its subject matter recalls Hopkins' comment concerning Swinburne's 'perpetual functioning of genius ... without any adequate matter to be at function on.' Parts of *The Tale of Balen* do answer to these descriptions. It is not a consistently interesting work, and it does illustrate something of the results of Swinburne's succumbing to his habitual temptation: to found his work on something other than his own vision of life and to pursue technical virtuosity for its own sake – to dwell exclusively among words, as T.S. Eliot put it. When Swinburne commits his besetting poetic sin the result for the reader is often the ennui of which Tennyson himself complained at a dinner party in 1877: 'He spoke a good deal about Swinburne, "with his marvellous facility". He begged us not to repeat this, which he found it impossible to explain, namely that he always began Swinburne with enthusiasm, but became bored directly and almost always failed to finish a poem.'[6]

There is nevertheless a certain amount of poetic interest and excitement in *The Tale of Balen*, especially if one holds at bay the worm of boredom and succeeds in reaching the poem's impressive closing section. What holds one's attention is the same thing that engages the reader of Tennyson's *Balin and Balan*: not the relation of the poem to its source materials but what in the narrative has been transformed by the intensity of each poet's personal vision – by their exploration of man's relationship to the natural world and to the forces that shape his destiny. So considered, *The Tale of Balen* may be seen as a work of real if intermittent intensity; and the story of its central character may even be regarded as the transposition into a different key of the story of Swinburne that is told in the works examined in preceding chapters – in the poems which are not founded on literature or technically brilliant in vacuo, but which are informed by his naturalistic vision.

The poem opens with the youthful Balen leaving his native Northumberland and journeying to southern England in order to become one of Arthur's knights. It soon becomes clear that his journey involves a passage from innocence to experience, from the 'timeless' world of childhood, in which 'time and death' seem merely a dreamer's words, to the fallen adult world. As soon as he arrives in Camelot the violence, deception, infidelity, false-seeming, and evil of the southern world begin to become apparent. There is the churlish envy of the royal knight whom Balen slays on his first day in Arthur's court, and the corrupt pride and envy of Launceor, whom he dispatches some time later. There are the references to Queen Morgeuse of Orkney, whose incestuous coupling with King Arthur will ultimately lead to the 'darkling doom' of Camelot; and there is Garlon, the murderer who is 'invisible as the spirit of night' and as such the personification of the invisible but pervasive evil found in every corner of Arthur's kingdom.

There are a number of references throughout Swinburne's poem to the Fate or doom which awaits Balen. These references were added by Swinburne to Malory's version, but as the story of Balen is retold by the Victorian poet one comes to see that these references do not really introduce into the narrative an extraneous element. For if we ask in what Balen's fate consists, the literal answer would be that he is fated to kill the one he loves best with the sword that has brought him his first fame, and at the same time to die himself. The more penetrating answer is that Balen's fate is simply that he is necessarily a part of the fallen world in which he must live and move and have his being. However noble-minded, however pure in thought and loyal in conduct, he is none-the-less implicated in the violences and ambiguities of the world around him, and powerless to mitigate them.

Balen gains his second sword early in the poem when he alone of Arthur's knights is able to set free from it 'a maiden clad with grief and shame.' The sword, however, brings with it 'the gifts of fame and fate in one,' for when Balen refuses to return it to the maiden, she is enraged and utters a malediction, prophesying the form his doom will take. To ask if Balen should have returned the sword and was wrong not to do so is an idle question. What is important is to notice that later in the poem the maiden is revealed to be 'the falsest damosel ... That works men ill on earth,' a sorceress who had only wanted the charmed sword so that she could use it to murder the brother who had killed her paramour. This brother may be saved because of Balen's refusal to relinquish the sword, but the quantity of evil in the world of *The Tale of Balen* remains constant. It is Balen's brother Balan, not the brother of the false-seeming maiden, who will be slain with the sword.

A number of other episodes also suggest Balen's complicity in the world's corruption. At one point Merlin points out that he could have saved a maiden from suicide, and later two knights seem to die as much from proximity to Balen as from Garlon's 'invisible evil.' In addition, Balen's killing of Garlon necessi-tates the killing of his brother Pellam with the spear said to have pierced Christ's side. This sacrilege brings some kind of plague on the surrounding land, and as Balen rides from the site of his good deeds he passes through the bodies of dead men and the voices of live folk cursing him. Finally, in the seventh and last part of his poem, Balen meets the distraught and suicidal Garnysshe, who is sorrow-ing over the faithlessness of his beloved. Balen offers to help the knight, visits the beloved's castle, and finds her in a 'sweet small garden' lying with 'love-dishevelled hair' in the arms of a paramour. Balen returns to Garnysshe, brings him to the garden and watches as the knight becomes enraged and beheads his beloved and her lover. Garnysshe's next action is to turn to Balen and announce: 'Thou hast done this deed ... I had lived my sorrow down, hadst thou / Not shown me what I saw but now.' Balen replies that he was interested only in the truth and did what he did to hearten the knight. It is true that before taking his own life Garnysshe reveals himself to be the worst kind of sen-timental idealizer: 'I have slain what most I loved,' he emotes, 'I have shed / The blood most near my heart ...' And he is even called 'a woeful weakling' by the poem's narrator. Still, Balen's actions have once again left death in their wake, and not for nothing does he reflect on leaving the garden that if he stayed 'folk would say he had slain / Those three.'

Even early in the poem, Balen wonders if death is not preferable to life; and in its final section (after the episode with Garnysshe) he seems pleased when an 'old hoar man' (strikingly reminiscent of the 'hoary cripple' at the beginning of Browning's 'Childe Roland to the Dark Tower Came') ambiguously directs him towards a place where it seems likely he might be able to get his life over with. Indeed, so thoroughly do evil and death rule the adult world of *The Tale of Balen* one is led to ask what of positive value may be found in the poem. One positive value dramatized in *The Tale of Balen* is the familiar Swinburnean stoicism: the insistence on not looking before and after and pining for what is not but on living in the present. On the one hand, for Balen to live in the shadow of the Fate or doom that is repeatedly predicted for him would be to become fatalistic and to live in the future rather than in the present. This he explicitly refuses to do on several occasions, even though he is unable to perform any unambiguously efficacious deed. On the other hand, before his climactic fight with his beloved brother (necessitated by the 'evil custom' that all passing knights must fight the resident knight guarding an island, and if successful assume his position and perpetuate the evil by trying to slay the succeeding knights who offer challenge) Balen is tempted to rue the day he ever came to the south of England; but he rallies and refuses to long for what he has put behind him:

> it repenteth me, though shame
> May tax me not with base men's blame,
> That ever, hap what will, I came
>   Within this country; yet being come,
> For shame I may not turn again
> Now, that myself and nobler men
> May scorn me: now is more than then,
>   And faith bids fear be dumb.

The other positive note in *The Tale of Balen* is struck at the beginning of several of the parts of the poem: the descriptions of different seasons, which keep the reader aware throughout of nature's great cyclic processes, of which the cycle of Balen's life is shown to be a part. The poem opens in hawthorn time, when the world is sweet and the heart grows light. But even as the heather kindles and the whin flames one is reminded that discord as well as concord is part of the world of nature, for the poet cannot say if it be for strife or for love that the falcon quickens. At the beginning of the poem's fourth part the acceptance of mutability and transience as essential parts of a fully naturalistic vision of human existence is underlined:

Each day that slays its hours and dies
Weeps, laughs, and lightens on our eyes,
And sees and hears not: smiles and sighs
As flowers ephemeral fall and rise
    About its birth, about its way,
And pass as love and sorrow pass,
As shadows flashing down a glass,
As dew-flowers blowing in flowerless grass,
    As hope from yesterday.

The end of *The Tale of Balen* is wrenching: while in the castle towers nearby the 'blithe and fair' ladies who help to perpetuate the evil custom look on, the two brothers mortally wound each other. They then come to learn who it is that each has slain and to recognize that their doom has been accomplished. As Balen says, in human existence

Light is as darkness, hope as fear,
And love as hate: and none draws near
    Save toward a mortal goal.

The Tale of Balen does not end on this grim Sophoclean note, however. There are two separate recompenses for Balen's loss of his brother, and of his own life, that are suggested at the poem's conclusion. One is the intimation that through the brothers' death the world's evil has been somewhat lessened, for the death of both combatants ends the perpetuation of the 'evil custom.' The other recompense is found in one of the most unexpected moments in Swinburne's poetry: for in the long hours before he dies Balen is granted an unprecedented and unsought vision as he is through memory borne back into the past, to the northern childhood he left behind him at the beginning of his poem. *Then* becomes the redemption of *now* in the Wordsworthian and Tennysonian moment in which Balen fully recovers his past and with it his sense of a life in natural things and of his own life as a part of nature's:

And there low lying, as hour on hour
Fled, all his life in all its flower
Came back as in a sunlit shower
Of dreams, when sweet-souled sleep has power
    On life less sweet and glad to be.
He drank the draught of life's first wine
Again: he saw the moorland shine,

The rioting rapids of the Tyne,
   The woods, the cliffs, the sea.

The joy that lives at heart and home,
The joy to rest, the joy to roam,
The joy of crags and scaurs he clomb,
The rapture of the encountering foam
   Embraced and breasted of the boy,
The first good steed his knees bestrode,
The first wild sound of songs that flowed
Through ears that thrilled and heart that glowed,
   Fulfilled his death with joy.

Notes

PREFACE

1 *The Renaissance: Studies in Art and Poetry* (New York: Macmillan 1909) xii–xiii
2 *Victorian Poetry* 9, 1–2 (1971) [ix]
3 *Victorian Poetry* 8,1 (1970) 89–90
4 'On Sincerity' *Encounter* (October 1968) 64
5 *Romantic Image* (London: Routledge & Kegan Paul 1957) vii, 2
6 *The Poetry of Experience* (New York: Norton 1957) 35
7 *Natural Supernaturalism* (New York: Norton 1971) 14
8 *A Study of English Romanticism* (New York: Random House 1968) 14
9 See J. Hillis Miller *The Disappearance of God: Five Nineteenth-Century Writers* (Cambridge, Mass.: Belknap Press of Harvard Univ. Press 1963).
10 Abrams p 13
11 25 March 1818 verse letter to J.H. Reynolds. *The Letters of John Keats* ed Hyder Edward Rollins (Cambridge, Mass.: Harvard Univ. Press 1958) I, 262

CHAPTER 1: SWINBURNE'S TENNYSON

1 'Tennyson and Musset' (1881), *The Complete Works of Algernon Charles Swinburne* Bonchurch Edition, ed Edmund Gosse and Thomas James Wise (London: Heinemann 1925–7) XIV, 303 (cited hereafter as *Bonchurch*); 'Notes on Poems and Reviews' (1866), *Bonchurch* XVI, 371; 'Tennyson and Musset,' *Bonchurch* XIV, 303; letter of 31 March 1864 (*The Swinburne Letters* ed Cecil Y. Lang [New Haven: Yale Univ. Press 1959–62] I, 97); *Under the Microscope* (1872), *Bonchurch* XVI, 410; *Letters* VI, 21
2 Charles Tennyson *Alfred Tennyson* (London: Macmillan 1949) 514
3 Harold Bloom *The Anxiety of Influence: A Theory of Poetry* (New York: Oxford

Univ. Press 1973). In *Swinburne's Literary Career and Fame* (Durham, N.C.: Duke Univ. Press 1933), Clyde K. Hyder wrote (p 85) that 'Swinburne's relations with the chief of his elder contemporaries, Tennyson, are so complex that they might be the subject of a more extended discourse' than it was his concern to provide.

4 Hallam Tennyson *Alfred Lord Tennyson: A Memoir* (London: Macmillan 1897) I, 496; II, 285 (cited hereafter as *Memoir*)

5 Charles Tennyson p 359

6 *Letters* I, 192

7 Charles Tennyson p 390

8 Charles Tennyson p 374

9 'Swinburne and Tennyson' *Victorian Poetry* 9, 1–2 (1971) 222

10 Quoted in Hyder *Swinburne's Literary Career and Fame* 86

11 *Letters* I, 297

12 *Three Philosophical Poets* (Cambridge, Mass.: Harvard Univ. Press 1922) 19

13 One example of Tennyson's many pronouncements on this subject is particularly apposite to his views on Swinburne. In December of 1864 John Addington Symonds joined the end of a dinner party that included Tennyson and Gladstone. Shortly thereafter he sent his sister an account of what transpired. Here is part of his description of Tennyson's contribution to the conversation (*The Letters of John Addington Symonds* ed Herbert M. Schueller and Robert L. Peters [Detroit: Wayne State Univ. Press 1967] I, 595): 'Then of morality: "I cannot but think morality is the crown of man. But what is it without immortality? Let us eat & drink for tomorrow we die. If I knew the world were coming to an end in 6 hours, sd I give my money to a starving beggar? No. If I did not believe myself immortal. I have sometimes thought men of sin might destroy their immortality. The eternity of punishment is quite incredible. Xt's words were parables to suit the sense of the times." Further of morality: "There are some young men who try to do away with morality. They say, we won't be moral. Comte, I believe, & perhaps Mr Grote too deny that Immortality has anything to do with being moral." Then from material to moral difficulties: "Why do mosquitoes exist? I believe that after God had made his world the devil began & added something." (Cat & Mouse. Leopards) (My father raised moral evil. Morbid art.) The conversation turned on Swinburne for the moment & then dropped.'

14 'Epigrams 1868–1874' vii and xvii (Ricks pp 1226, 1229). The latter ('Art for Art's sake! Hail, truest Lord of Hell!') is discussed below.

15 *Letters* I, 97–8

16 *Memoir* II, 364

17 *Mythology and the Romantic Tradition in English Poetry* (New York: Pageant 1957) 205–6

18 Clyde K. Hyder, ed *Swinburne as Critic* (London: Routledge & Kegan Paul 1972) 54

19 *Bonchurch* xv, 66

20 For the French critic's remarks (*Bonchurch* xv, 67–71) I have used the translation in *Swinburne as Critic* 59–61

21 'In Memoriam' *Selected Essays* (New York: Harcourt Brace 1950) 294

22 'Introduction' to *The Oxford Book of Modern Verse* (Oxford: Clarendon Press 1936) ix

23 *Bonchurch* xiv, 327, 328–9

24 'A Double Frame for Tennyson's Demeter?' *Victorian Studies* 1, 4 (1958) 356–62

25 *The Necessary Angel: Essays on Reality and the Imagination* (London: Faber & Faber 1960) 175

26 *Selected Essays* 338

27 Keats *Letters* ed Hyder Edward Rollins (Cambridge, Mass.: Harvard Univ. Press 1958) ii, 212

28 *Letters* ii, 73

29 Samuel Chew *Swinburne* (Boston: Little, Brown 1929) 166

30 *Bonchurch* xiv, 329

31 *Bonchurch* xiv, 332–3

32 *Bonchurch* xvi, 404, 407

33 *Bonchurch* xiv, 333

34 *Bonchurch* xiv, 331

35 John Dixon Hunt ('The Poetry of Distance: Tennyson's *Idylls of the King*' *Victorian Poetry* eds Malcolm Bradbury and David Palmer, Stratford-Upon-Avon Studies 15 [London: Edward Arnold 1972] 103–4) argues that the King's speech 'seems priggish because the human element proceeds awkwardly from one who has already been established with the ideality of art.' That is to say, the speech is an indecorous break with the iconic presentation of Arthur elsewhere in the poem.

36 *Bonchurch* xvi, 404

37 27 February 1879 letter to Richard Watson Dixon; in *The Correspondence of Gerard Manley Hopkins and Richard Watson Dixon* ed Claude Colleer Abbott (London: Oxford Univ. Press 1935) 24

38 *Bonchurch* xvi, 405, 409

39 *Bonchurch* xvi, 403

40 *Bonchurch* xvi, 406

41 *King Arthur's Laureate: A Study of Tennyson's 'Idylls of the King'* (New York: New York Univ. Press 1971)

42 *The Fall of Camelot: A Study of Tennyson's 'Idylls of the King'* (Cambridge, Mass.: Harvard Univ. Press 1973) 131

43 Tennyson said this in 'To the Queen,' the epilogue to the *Idylls*. Since this was first published in 1873, however, it could only have confirmed, not caused, the opinions voiced in *Under the Microscope*.

44 In his *La Jeunesse de Swinburne* (Paris: Publications de la Faculté des Lettres de l'Université de Strasbourg 1929) I, 163, Georges Lafourcade prints two stanzas of an early satirical poem, written in the form used by Arnold for Empedocles' long tirade in *Empedocles on Etna*, which foreshadow Swinburne's mature Tennyson parodies:

> Thus runs our wise men's song:
> Being dark, it must be light;
> And most things are so wrong
> That all things must be right;
> God must mean well, he works so ill by this world's laws.

> This, when our souls are drowning,
> Falls on them like a benison;
> This satisfied our Browning
> And this delights our Tennyson:
> And soothed Britannia simpers in serene applause.

45 Dahl p 358

46 It is interesting to note that the Victorian critic R.H. Hutton suggested that had it been chronologically possible Tennyson 'might have been supposed' to be referring to Swinburne when in section xxxiv of *In Memoriam* he described the 'wild poet' who works 'without a conscience or an aim' (*Tennyson: The Critical Heritage* ed John D. Jump [London: Routledge & Kegan Paul 1967] 372).

47 This poem is not in the *Collected Poetical Works*. I have used the text in *Bonchurch* VI, 387–91

48 *Letters* II, 86

49 *Bonchurch* XIV, 334–5

50 Clyde K. Hyder 'Swinburne: "Changes of Aspect" and "Short Notes"' *PMLA* 58 (1943) 232–3. First published by Hyder, 'Changes of Aspect' is also included in *New Writings by Swinburne* ed Cecil Y. Lang (Syracuse, N.Y.: Syracuse Univ. Press 1964) 67–8.

51 *Bonchurch* XIII 244

52 *All in Due Time* (London: Rupert Hart-Davis 1955), 125

53 *Tennyson: The Critical Heritage* 37–8

54 *Works* (New York: Scribner's 1909–12) XXVIII, 55

55 *Letters* I, 160

CHAPTER 2: TENNYSON'S POETRY 1830 TO 1842

1 *Memoirs of Shelley and Other Essays and Reviews* ed Howard Mills (London: Rupert Hart-Davis 1970) 128–30

2 *Critical and Historical Essays* (London: Longmans, Green 1874) 3–5. For a discussion of Peacock and Macaulay's strictures in connection with 'issues raised by Tennyson's early poetry' see Isobel Armstrong's introduction to her edition of *Victorian Scrutinies: Reviews of Poetry 1830–1870* (London: Athlone Press 1972) 14ff.

3 *Tennyson: The Critical Heritage* 35–41

4 See A. Dwight Culler's droll analysis of the poem, which he calls grotesque, in *The Poetry of Tennyson* (New Haven: Yale Univ. Press 1977) 61–2

5 Keats *Letters* I, 281

6 D.J. Palmer 'Tennyson's Romantic Heritage' in Palmer, ed *Tennyson: Writers and their Background* (London: Bell 1973) 31, 23

7 'Preface to First Edition of Poems (1853),' *The Poems of Matthew Arnold* ed Kenneth Allott (London: Longmans 1965) 590

8 John D. Rosenberg 'Tennyson and the Landscape of Consciousness' *Victorian Poetry* 12, 4 (1974) 304

9 Sir Charles Tennyson and Hope Dyson *The Tennysons: Background to Genius* (London: Macmillan 1974) 80, 181. Christopher Ricks' *Tennyson* (New York: Macmillan 1972) also contains a full account of the Tennyson family life at Somersby.

10 *Robert Browning: A Collection of Critical Essays* ed Philip Drew (London: Methuen 1966) 176

11 *Tennyson and the Reviewers: A Study of his Literary Reputation and of the Influence of the Critics upon his Poetry 1827–1851* (Cambridge, Mass.: Harvard Univ. Press 1952) 164–5

12 'Preface' to *Philip van Artevelde: A Dramatic Romance* (London: Moxon 1852) xii

13 *Robert Browning and Alfred Domett* ed Frederic G. Kenyon (London: Smith, Elder 1906) 85–6

14 *The Boundaries of Fiction: Carlyle, Macaulay, Newman* (Princeton: Princeton Univ. Press 1968) 68–9

15 Jerome Hamilton Buckley *The Victorian Temper: A Study in Literary Culture* (rept London: Frank Cass 1966). Chapter 2 of Buckley's study is called 'The Anti-Romantics'; chapter 4, 'Tennyson: The Two Voices,' is followed by chapter 5, 'The Pattern of Conversion.' One example of Buckley's influence is John R. Reed's *Perception and Design in Tennyson's 'Idylls of the King'* (Athens, Ohio: Ohio Univ. Press 1969). Reed's thesis (p 3) is that there is 'a moral design in Tennyson's poetry which resembles the pattern of conversion described by Professor J.H. Buckley in *The Victorian Temper.'* In his *The Divided Self: A Perspective on the Literature of the Victorians* (New York: New York Univ. Press 1969) Masao Miyoshi begins his chapter on the situation of the imaginative artist in 1830 as follows: 'Victorian writers started life with the knowledge of the Romantic failure in self-discovery. How they lived with it is the story of their art. To their own great fear of Romantic

indeterminacy, they responded with what is often called the "Victorian conversion", which, defining a moral view of art as of life, tries to put the divided self together and make it work ... This will to cement the disparate parts of life by moral commitment is most noticeable in the works of the early Victorians, the young Tennyson and Browning, and in those of Carlyle' (p 107).

16 For a full discussion of the influence of Carlyle (especially of book 2 of *Sartor Resartus*) on 'Locksley Hall' see William D. Templeman 'Tennyson's "Locksley Hall" and Thomas Carlyle' *Booker Memorial Studies: Eight Essays on Victorian Literature* (rept New York: Russell & Russell 1969) 34–59. In an 1846 poem of Tennyson's, 'The Golden Year,' Carlyle appears in the guise of 'old James,' who admonishes his juniors not to lament that the golden year lies in the unrecoverable past, for

> well I know
> That unto him who works, and feels he works,
> The same grand year is ever at the door.

17 I do not of course mean to suggest that all or even most of Tennyson's revisions answer to this description. The subject of his revisions is complex; but none will agree with Browning's comments on the 1842 *Poems*: 'The alterations are insane. *Whatever* is touched is spoiled. There is some woeful mental infirmity in the man' (13 July 1842 letter to Domett, *Robert Browning and Alfred Domett* 40). Many of these poems were enormously improved by Tennyson's revisions: 'Mariana in the South,' 'The Lady of Shalott,' and 'The Lotos Eaters,' all first published in 1832 and republished with substantial revisions in 1842, are unquestionably examples. It is equally clear that Tennyson's reasons for revising at least these three poems were intrinsic, i.e. to improve them, and not, as Browning thought, extrinsic: i.e., because Tennyson was 'miserably thin-skinned, sensitive to criticism (foolish criticism), [and] wishes to see no notices that contain the least possible depreciatory expressions' (pp 40–1). F.E.L. Priestley's *Language and Structure in Tennyson's Poetry* (London: Deutsch 1973) has some good pages on the subject of Tennyson's revisions of his early poems and the improvements they effected.

18 *Tennyson: Aspects of his Life, Character and Poetry* (London: Constable 1923) 27–8

19 *Mythology and the Romantic Tradition* 199

20 Quoted in James Pope-Hennessy *Monckton Milnes: The Flight of Youth 1851–1885* (London: Constable 1951) 59. Cited in Ricks *Tennyson* 49

21 *Tennyson: The Critical Heritage* 42

22 *Tennyson: The Critical Heritage* 86

23 *The Mill on the Floss* ed Gordon S. Haight (Oxford: Clarendon Press 1980), 193–4

24 *Tess of the D'Urbervilles* The New Wessex Edition (London: Macmillan 1975) 114

25 *Memoir* I, 500
26 *The Finer Optic: The Aesthetic of Particularity in Victorian Poetry* (New Haven: Yale Univ. Press 1975) 21
27 On the helmet and helmet-feather see Culler p 45.
28 One of the best analyses of 'The Lady of Shalott' is James L. Hill's 'Tennyson's "The Lady of Shalott": The Ambiguity of Commitment' *Centennial Review* 12 (1968) 415–29. But some of Hill's commentary is excessively conjectural and uninformed by the context of Tennyson poems on cognate subjects.
29 'Tennyson's Garden of Art: A Study of "The Hesperides"' in John Killham, ed *Critical Essays on the Poetry of Tennyson* (London: Routledge & Kegan Paul 1960) 100, 101
30 Culler p 74
31 *The Renaissance* 250–2
32 *Memoirs of Mark Pattison* introduction Jo Manton (Fontwell: Centaur Press 1969) xix
33 Browning *Poetical Works 1833–1864* ed Ian Jack (London: Oxford Univ. Press 1970) 3
34 *Tennyson: The Critical Heritage* 46
35 Comparison of Tennyson's tableau with an early Victorian story-painting is instructive. The left-hand section of Richard Redgrave's *Sunday Morning, the Walk from the Church,* 1846 (Maas Gallery, London) so resembles Tennyson's verbal picture at the end of 'The Two Voices' that it is difficult not to imagine an indebtedness. The painting exemplifies the same Victorian middle-class pieties and sentimentality as Tennyson's picture. Against a background of medieval church, peacefully grazing sheep, and vicar bowed to by rustics, a well-dressed young couple are walking with their child in front of them. The prudent wife is gazing pensively at the earth, her countenance echoed in her equally musing child's, while the husband firmly clasps his wife's arm and gazes at her attentively, sharing the solemnity of her thought. As the viewer's eye moves to the right to take in the rest of Redgrave's canvas, it encounters two alternative versions of this group. In the middle are an elderly couple – the wife with a cane – whose costume and attitudes are so similar to those of the younger couple at left as to make it clear we are being given a prevision of the latter's mutually supportive and loving future years. The alternative at the right of the picture, however, is much more sombre and helps to explain the serious musings of the healthy young couple: a young widow in black, a twin of the wife at left, walks with downcast eyes as do the two children who flank her. Even the shepherd boy with crook and prayer book at the far right seems struck, as the viewer is invited to be, by the solemnity of the scene before him.
36 'The Poetry of Sorrow' *The Times* 28 November 1851; reprinted in John Dixon Hunt, ed *Tennyson 'In Memoriam': A Casebook* (London: Macmillan 1970) 102–3

37 Ricks cites the analogue (*The Poems of Tennyson* 540n). In *Theme and Symbol in Tennyson's Poems to 1850* (Philadelphia: Univ. of Pennsylvania Press 1964) 120–1, Clyde de L. Ryals emphasizes the similarities between the two moments and goes on to discuss other of the 'many resemblances' between Tennyson's poem and 'The Rime of the Ancient Mariner.'

38 Quoted in Ricks, ed *The Poems of Tennyson* 718

39 *Language and Structure in Tennyson's Poetry* 63, 59

40 See Ricks 'Tennyson: Three Notes' *Modern Philology* 62 (1964) 140. These lines were included in the poem only in an 1864 selection; but, says Ricks, Palgrave's 1863 note 'makes it clear that [the lines] had early been a part of the poem and were not a late addition.'

41 *Mythology and the Romantic Tradition* 202

42 *Tennyson* 129

43 *Troilus and Cressida* III.iii.172–4

44 *The Complete Poems of D.H. Lawrence* ed Vivian de Sola Pinto and Warren Roberts (New York: Viking 1964) II, 716. In Lawrence's passionate advocacy of 'Poetry of the Present' (*Complete Poems* I, 182), it is hard not to think he has Tennyson's poem in mind when he insists: 'If you tell me about the lotus, tell me of nothing changeless or eternal. Tell me of the mystery of the inexhaustible, forever-unfolding creative spark. Tell me of the incarnate disclosure of the flux, mutation in blossom, laughter and decay perfectly open in their transit, nude in their movement before us.'

CHAPTER 3: THE NATURAL MAGIC OF *IN MEMORIAM*

1 *The Mill on the Floss* 37–8, 135

2 *Memoir* I, 196

3 *Tennyson: The Critical Heritage* 188. And see Ian Jack's 1967 Warton Lecture on English Poetry, 'Robert Browning,' *Proceedings of the British Academy* 53 (1968) 232: 'Although it is written in blank verse, in the form of a monologue or soliloquy, "Ulysses" is essentially lyrical or elegiac in its inspiration. As Ulysses urges his men forwards to new adventure, the subversive vowels seem to be tempting them back towards the Sirens from whom they have escaped.'

4 K.W. Gransden *Tennyson: In Memoriam* (London: Edward Arnold 1964) says that 'nature in Tennyson is linked emotively to human experience in various ways, but does not open into any new insight or unifying of experience' (p 35). In *The Poems of Tennyson*, Ricks speaks of 'the beautiful but ineffective consolations of Nature which form a recurring theme of *In Memoriam*' (p 557).

5 'Maurice de Guérin,' *Lectures and Essays in Criticism* ed R.H. Super; vol 3 of *The Complete Prose Works of Matthew Arnold* ed Super (Ann Arbor: Univ. of Michigan Press 1962) 12–13, 33, 34

6 *The Poetry of Tennyson* 34–5

7 See Jerome Buckley *Tennyson: The Growth of a Poet* (Cambridge, Mass.: Harvard Univ. Press 1960) 115–16 for a fuller discussion of Tennyson's 'deliberate use of pastoral motifs' in *In Memoriam*. And see Ian H.C. Kennedy '*In Memoriam* and the Tradition of Pastoral Elegy' *Victorian Poetry* 15, 4 (1977) 351–66.

8 There is a striking allusion to the close of Catullus' elegy on his brother in the last stanza of lvii; Melpomene, for Tennyson the muse of elegy rather than tragedy, who addresses the poet in xxxvii, seems to have been taken over from the pastoral lament in the November eclogue of Spenser's *Shepherd's Calendar*; and there are several echoes of Milton's 'Lycidas' and Shelley's 'Adonais.'

9 '*In Memoriam* and *Lycidas*' *PMLA* 82 (1967) 438

10 See John D. Rosenberg 'The Two Kingdoms of *In Memoriam*' *JEGP* 58 (1959) 228–40 for a discussion of Tennyson's effort to unite evolutionary science and Christian faith.

11 'The American Scholar' *The Complete Works of Ralph Waldo Emerson*, Centenary Edition (Boston: Houghton Mifflin 1903) I, 98

12 *The Language of Tennyson's 'In Memoriam'* (Oxford: Basil Blackwell 1971) 136

13 *A Commentary on Tennyson's 'In Memoriam'* 2nd ed (London: Macmillan 1902) 29

14 Bradley p 179; Sinfield p 63

15 'Structure and Style in the Greater Romantic Lyric' *From Sensibility to Romanticism* ed Frederick W. Hilles and Harold Bloom (New York: Oxford Univ. Press 1965) 527–8. Examples I cite are also noted by Abrams. Robert Langbaum, in discussing 'The Dynamic Unity of *In Memoriam*' in his *The Modern Spirit* (New York: Oxford Univ. Press 1970), does observe that xcv 'is constructed like a Wordsworthian dramatic lyric, in that the thought develops out of and as a counterpart to the natural setting' (p 66). On the importance of the greater Romantic lyric to twentieth-century poets, see George Bornstein *Transformations of Romanticism in Yeats, Eliot, and Stevens* (Chicago: Univ. of Chicago Press 1976).

16 Quoted in Peter Allen *The Cambridge Apostles: The Early Years* (Cambridge: Cambridge Univ. Press 1978) 143

17 Charles Tennyson p 117

18 In his *Tennyson's Style* (Ithaca, N.Y.: Cornell Univ. Press 1976), W. David Shaw writes that 'The spectacle of the fusing lights is not, in Yeats's phrase, "out of nature" … The midsummer lights are not, as I once thought [see Shaw's review of *The Major Victorian Poets* ed Isobel Armstrong, in *Victorian Studies* 13, 4 (1970) 459], a vivid piece of Arctic surrealism; at Lincoln's latitude of 53 degrees, 15 minutes, north, Tennyson could have seen them in an actual English garden' (p 48n). That is to say, the mixing of East and West is a natural, not a Natural phenomenon.

19 My use of the terms 'sacred' and 'profane' is derived from Mircea Eliade. See his *The Sacred and the Profane* trans Willard B. Trask (New York: Harcourt, Brace 1959).

20 *Memoir* I, 321n

21 In chapters 2 and 3 of his *Mysticism Sacred and Profane* (Oxford: Clarendon Press 1957), R.C. Zaehner distinguishes among three main kinds of mystical experience. First, there is 'natural mystical experience,' a kind often experienced by those who are not otherwise known as mystics, in which the self attains a sense of unity with the visible world, and in which the boundaries of space and time seem to have been transcended. This experience, says Zaehner, has nothing to do with union with the Absolute or with the Deity. Second, there is Hindu mysticism, which is characterized by complete absorption of the individual soul into the Absolute. Third, 'there is the normal type of Christian mystical experience in which the soul feels itself to be united with God by love' (p 29). Only the last two kinds of mystical experience may be properly described as religious. They are to be sharply distinguished from natural mystical experience, since the sine qua non of religious mysticism is 'the exclusion of all that we normally call Nature' (p 33). The word 'Nature' here includes not only the physical world but also such things as personality and memory. By these criteria, it is not possible to describe section xcv as a religious mystical experience. It is not necessary to decide here whether xcv may be said to describe a natural mystical experience. According to Zaehner, this title may be given to a wide variety of experiences, which include the mescaline experiments of Aldous Huxley, the infinite moments Proust describes in *A la recherche du temps perdu*, the *dérèglement de tous les sens* of Rimbaud's *Une Saison en enfer*, and Tennyson's own description of 'a kind of waking trance,' in which 'individuality itself seemed to dissolve and fade away into boundless being' (*Memoir* I, 320).

22 Jerome H. Buckley says of xcv: 'This section, the climax of the poem, describes ... a solitary mystical experience, which brings reassurance of the infinite life' (*Poems of Tennyson* ed Buckley [Boston: Houghton Mifflin 1958] 531). In a detailed examination of xcv, Alan Sinfield says '*In Memoriam* turns upon the poet's mystical experience in section xcv' ('Matter-Moulded Forms of Speech: Tennyson's Use of Language in *In Memoriam*,' in *The Major Victorian Poets: Reconsiderations* ed Isobel Armstrong [London: Routledge & Kegan Paul 1969] 51). W. David Shaw, in his '*In Memoriam* and the Rhetoric of Confession '*ELH* 38 (1971) 89, states: 'The moment in section xcv ... when Tennyson achieves his closest communion with Hallam is also the moment when he receives his clearest intuition of immortality.' F.E.L. Priestley calls xcv 'the climax of the whole poem,' in which the poet 'receives his most complete assurance in the form of something like a mystic experience, an immediate sense of his friend's presence, which brings with it also a powerful intimation of cosmic purpose and harmony' (*Language and Structure in Tennyson's Poetry* 156). The fullest discussion of xcv from a religious and mystical point of view is Carlisle Moore's 'Faith, Doubt and Mystical Experience in *In Memoriam*' *Victorian Studies* 7 (1963) 155–69. Moore says of xcv: 'It was the record of a genuine

mystical experience, a clear sign from a beloved spirit in the next world which, because it effected, or seemed to effect, the dispelling of all religious doubts, had all the earmarks of a conversion comparable in its way with Saint Paul's' (p 165).

23 Quoted by Hallam Tennyson in his edition of 'Author's Notes' to *In Memoriam* (New York: Macmillan 1906) 256. A similar statement was made by Tennyson to James Knowles. See Knowles' 'Aspects of Tennyson' *Nineteenth Century* 33 (1893) 186: '*The* living soul – perchance the Deity. The first reading was "His living soul was flash'd on mine" – but my conscience was troubled by "his." I've often had a strange feeling of being wound and wrapped in the Great Soul.'

24 Rosenberg p 234n. Paull F. Baum, in his *Tennyson Sixty Years After* (Chapel Hill: Univ. of North Carolina Press 1948), also feels 'The living soul' must be Hallam's: 'In the poem no other interpretation is possible' (p 307). Baum goes on to assert that Tennyson 'sacrificed the integrity of his poem for the sake of the record' (p 309).

25 It is true that in the following section, cxvi, Tennyson does attempt to posit a more than natural meaning for cxv. 'The life re-orient out of dust' is there said to be so affecting because it heartens trust 'In that which made the world so fair,' the 'that which' presumably being God. This seems a belated attempt to attach to cxv a meaning it does not contain, and which, if accepted, would greatly diminish the poem's effectiveness. Compare Tennyson's changes in the text of xcv.

26 10 September 1864 letter to A.W.M. Baillie; in *Further Letters of Gerard Manley Hopkins* ed Claude Colleer Abbott (London: Oxford Univ. Press 1956) 219

CHAPTER 4: SEXUALITY AND VISION IN *IDYLLS OF THE KING*

1 The five studies are: Clyde de L. Ryals *From the Great Deep: Essays on 'Idylls of the King'* (Athens, Ohio: Ohio Univ. Press 1967); John R. Reed *Perception and Design in Tennyson's 'Idylls of the King'*; J. Philip Eggers *King Arthur's Laureate: A Study of Tennyson's 'Idylls of the King'*; John D. Rosenberg *The Fall of Camelot: A Study of Tennyson's 'Idylls of the King'*; J.M. Gray *Thro' the Vision of the Night: A Study of Source, Evolution and Structure in Tennyson's 'Idylls of the King'* (Montreal: McGill-Queen's Univ. Press 1980). Ryals is concerned 'to demonstrate some of the complexity of Tennyson's thought' (p vii); Reed's focus is on the 'moral design' of the *Idylls* (p 3), and Eggers' on 'the social meaning of the poem' (p xii). Rosenberg's study, the best of the five, argues that the *Idylls* is 'the culminating achievement of [Tennyson's] career' (p 5) and 'one of the four or five indisputably great long poems in our language' (p 1). Rosenberg also speaks of the poem's 'remarkable unity' (p 13) and 'subtle architectonics' (p 33), while Eggers says that 'The *Idylls* became an organic whole when Tennyson added *Balin and Balan* in 1885' (p 185).

2 In her 'Tennyson's Serial Poem' (in Geoffrey and Kathleen Tillotson *Mid-Victorian Studies* [London: Athlone Press 1965] 80–109) Kathleen Tillotson asserts the unity

and cohesiveness of the *Idylls*. She says that 'By 1855 Tennyson had planned the final shape of his long poem' (p 90) and offers the 'true and the false' and 'Order and Disorder' as two of 'the large simple antitheses that are among the "vertebrae" of the whole poem' (pp 90–1). But little more than these vague statements is forthcoming. We are told that 'His latest additions make it clear how closely related in his mind were the formal, the narrative, and the moral shape of his poem' (p 108), but we are then told little about what the formal and moral shape of the finished poem actually is. One's final impression is that Kathleen Tillotson has not distinguished between intention and execution.

3 *The Uses of Division: Unity and Disharmony in Literature* (London: Chatto & Windus 1976) 11

4 My terminology here is derived from Martin Price 'The Fictional Contract' in *Literary Theory and Structure* eds Frank Brady, John Palmer, and Martin Price (New Haven: Yale Univ. Press 1973) 151–78. Price writes: 'We tend, for good reason, to concentrate upon the cognitive functions of the work [of art], to extract from it a structure of meanings. We tend at times to be foolishly rigorous in our search for meaning, and the result is the kind of bathetic rhetoric of overinterpretation, of forced profundities and of evangelical platitudes (each church, including those that favor the inner light, having its own)' (p 177).

5 Rosenberg p 11

6 Hunt 'The Poetry of Distance: Tennyson's *Idylls of the King*'

7 This paragraph is indebted to Northrop Frye, 'The Romantic Myth,' the opening chapter of his *A Study of English Romanticism* (New York: Random House 1968) 3–49.

8 F.W.H. Myers 'George Eliot,' *Essays: Classical and Modern* (London: Macmillan 1921) 495

9 'Tennyson's *Idylls*' *UTQ* 19, 1 (1949) 40

10 See Frederick C. Crews *The Sins of the Fathers: Hawthorne's Psychological Themes* (New York: Oxford Univ. Press 1966). My terminology here is indebted to chapter 1 ('Psychological Romance') of Crews' excellent study.

11 Two discussions of *Balin and Balan* from which I have learned are John D. Rosenberg's in *The Fall of Camelot* (pp 77–83) and J.M. Gray's *Tennyson's Doppelgänger: Balin and Balan*, Tennyson Society Monographs 3 (Lincoln: Tennyson Research Centre 1971). Gray remarks: 'The shift of emphasis in the final idyll [*Balin and Balan*] may be the price the poet's creative unconscious exacted for so much epistemology previously. Here within Balin's seemingly irrational conduct there is psychological exploration, perhaps in compensation for the failure of so many conventional quests for morality, although it is noticeable that in all the later-composed idylls the promptings of dream, fantasy and the inward life become more apparent' (p 23).

12 Reed pp 131–2

13 Rosenberg p 79
14 Lionel Trilling and Harold Bloom, eds *Victorian Prose and Poetry* (New York: Oxford Univ. Press 1973) 472n
15 Gray p 19
16 For example, Robert W. Hill, Jr writes: '*Gareth and Lynette*, which Tennyson started almost immediately after finishing *Pelleas and Ettarre*, seems deliberately designed to contrast the fortunes of two young knights. Whereas Gareth's idealism prevails and wins him Lynette, Pelleas' similar qualities cannot possibly sustain him when faced with Ettarre's lascivious conduct.' *Tennyson's Poetry* ed Robert W. Hill, Jr, Norton Critical Editions (New York: Norton 1971), 374–5n. In the fourth chapter of his *Sexual Repression in Victorian Literature* (Lewisburg: Bucknell Univ. Press 1970) 82–102, Russell M. Goldfarb has an interesting discussion of sexuality in *Pelleas and Ettarre*, but he does not relate the idyll to *Balin and Balan* or *The Last Tournament*.
17 Hill p 391n; Eggers p 86; Reed p 117; Priestley p 41
18 Eggers p 174
19 Florence Emily Hardy *The Life of Thomas Hardy, 1840–1928* (London: Macmillan 1962) 377–8
20 *Per Amica Silentia Lunae* (London: Macmillan 1918) 21
21 Ryals pp 109–10
22 *Tennyson's Major Poems: The Comic and Ironic Patterns* (New Haven: Yale Univ. Press 1975) 210, 157
23 *Moby-Dick* ed Charles Feidelson (Indianapolis: Bobbs-Merrill 1964) 26
24 *Wuthering Heights* ed Hilda Marsden and Ian Jack (Oxford: Clarendon Press 1976) 414
25 'The Course of a Particular,' *The Palm at the End of the Mind: Selected Poems* ed Holly Stevens (New York: Vintage Books 1972) 367. In the printing of the poem in Stevens' *Opus Posthumous* ed Samuel French Morse (New York: Knopf 1957) 97, the reading 'final finding of the air' is incorrect.
26 Kincaid p 213
27 Culler p 225
28 *Memoir* II, 90
29 *Sartor Resartus* ed C.F. Harrold (New York: Odyssey 1937) 227
30 'Nature,' *Complete Works of Ralph Waldo Emerson* I, 10. For a general discussion of Romantic moments of vision see Abrams *Natural Supernaturalism* 385ff.

CHAPTER 5: SWINBURNE'S INTERNAL CENTRE

1 Cecil Y. Lang's six-volume edition of the poet's letters (1959–62) is the single contemporary work of Swinburne scholarship of fundamental importance, though Lang's *New Writings by Swinburne* and Francis Jacques Sypher's edition of *A Year's*

Letters (New York: New York Univ. Press 1974) were certainly welcome. As late as 1971, Lang could state in his introduction to a 256-page compendium of articles on Swinburne (*Victorian Poetry*, special Swinburne double number, 9/1–2 [1971] [ix]) that 'It is hardly too much to say that serious evaluation of Swinburne's poetry begins here.' Since then the only important full-length item has been Jerome J. McGann's brilliant *Swinburne: An Experiment in Criticism* (Chicago: Univ. of Chicago Press 1972). There have been only a few important articles, particularly John D. Rosenberg's overview of the poetry, which was reprinted as the introduction to his edition of *Swinburne: Selected Poetry and Prose* (New York: Modern Library 1968).

2 *Swinburne* (London: Macmillan 1926) 3

3 Rosenberg (*Swinburne: Selected Poetry and Prose* xxxiv) uses the same analogy.

4 *Collected Letters of D.H. Lawrence* ed Harry T. Moore (London: Heinemann 1962) I, 474

5 *Works* XXVIII, 55

6 Quoted in J.W. Mackail *The Life of William Morris* (London: Longmans, Green 1899) II, 74–5

7 29 April 1889 letter to Robert Bridges; in *The Letters of Gerard Manley Hopkins to Robert Bridges* ed Claude Colleer Abbott (London: Oxford Univ. Press 1955) 304

8 *Selected Essays* 282–5

9 Lafourcade *La Jeunesse de Swinburne* I, 26n

10 Quoted in Robert Gittings *Young Thomas Hardy* (Boston: Little Brown 1975) 81. The 'garland of red roses' lines, and the 'quick glad surprise,' are from 'A Singer Asleep,' Hardy's elegy on Swinburne.

11 'Charles Baudelaire,' *Bonchurch* XIII, 419

12 *Letters* IV, 124

13 These lines, reminiscent in both statement and language of some of the choruses of *Atalanta in Calydon*, are not in the original manuscript of the poem and appear to be a later interpolation by a Swinburne caught up in the concerns of his Greek drama. Consequently, there is good reason for viewing this section as a post factum addition to the text, not as an integral part of the poem. For a full discussion of the matter see Edmund Gosse 'The First Draft of Swinburne's "Anactoria"' *Modern Language Review* 14 (1919) 271–7. I have followed Gosse's reasoning.

14 *The Life of Thomas Hardy* 287

15 Fragment 71 *Lyra Graeca* trans J.M. Edmonds (London: Heinemann 1922) I, 233

16 Barbara Charlesworth *Dark Passages* (Madison: Wisconsin Univ. Press 1965) 26

17 *Bonchurch* XVI, 365

18 In a letter to W.M. Rossetti, Swinburne said that in his work he had 'proved Dolores to be little less than a second Sermon on the Mount, an Anactoria than an archdeacon's charge' (*Letters* I, 186). In a letter to F.G. Waugh (*Letters* I, 202) he

described his pamphlet as both 'sarcastic and elucidative.' The phrase 'tongue-in-cheek' is Robert L. Peters' in his *Victorians on Literature and Art* (New York: Appleton-Century-Crofts 1962) 221. Hyder (*Swinburne's Literary Career and Fame* 57–60) unconvincingly defends the seriousness of the 'Notes.' In a subsequent discussion ('Introduction' to *Swinburne Replies* [Syracuse: Syracuse Univ. Press 1966] 1–5) Hyder, surprisingly, did not address himself to the question.

19 'Swinburne' *The Cornhill* no 1061 (Autumn 1969) 384

20 *A Year's Letters* ed Sypher, pp 99–104 (also printed in *Bonchurch* XVII, 179–84)

21 These quotations are from 'In the Bay,' 'Inferiae,' 'In Memory of John William Inchbold,' 'After Sunset,' and 'A Study from Memory.'

22 *Letters* IV, 267. In a letter to his mother concerning the death of Hugo, Swinburne makes a similar, though fainter, assertion: 'When I think of his intense earnestness of faith in a future life and a better world than this, and remember how fervently Mazzini always urged upon all who loved him the necessity of that belief and the certainty of its actual truth, I feel very deeply that they must have been right – or at least that they should have been – however deep and difficult the mystery which was so clear and transparent to their inspired and exalted minds may seem to such as mine. They ought to have known, if any man ever did: and if they were right, I, whose love and devotion they requited with such kindness as I could never really have deserved, shall (somehow) see them again' (*Letters* V, 110).

23 'Introduction,' *Letters* I, xxv

24 *Letters* III, 152

25 *Letters* III, 137

26 'Two or Three Ideas,' *Opus Posthumous* 211

27 'Adagia,' *Opus Posthumous* 165

28 In his excellent analysis of the poem (*Swinburne: An Experiment in Criticism* 310), Jerome McGann has accurately described 'Ave atque Vale' as 'one of Swinburne's most characteristic poems, and not only because it deals with themes of death and transience. In it is clearly defined his theory of the artist's ideal life as well as his insistence upon accepting the natural cycle of birth, life, and death as the norm of all human action. Though there is no question but that man is subject to fate, the clear-sighted understanding of this fact can create in his life heroic dimensions.'

29 Cited in Ricks, ed *The Poetry of Tennyson* 913n

30 'The Poems of Dante Gabriel Rossetti,' *Bonchurch* xv, 23. Swinburne would not have agreed with the twentieth-century attempts of T.S. Eliot and W.H. Auden to Christianize Baudelaire. Yet he anticipates some of Eliot's points in his observation that 'The intermittent Christian reaction apparently perceptible in Baudelaire was more than half of it mere repulsion from the philanthropic optimism of sciolists in whose eyes the whole aim or mission of things is to make the human spirit finally comfortable' (*Bonchurch* xv, 23).

31 *Selected Critical Writings* ed Norman Henfrey (Cambridge: Cambridge Univ. Press 1968) II, 229. The questions of Swinburne and Santayana both anticipate those of Wallace Stevens in 'Sunday Morning' (*Collected Poems* [New York: Knopf 1954] 69), his great poem of naturalistic acceptance:

> Is there no change of death in paradise?
> Does ripe fruit never fall? Or do the boughs
> Hang always heavy in that perfect sky,
> Unchanging, yet so like our perishing earth,
> With rivers like our own that seek for seas
> They never find, the same receding shores
> That never touch with inarticulate pang?
> Why set the pear upon those river-banks
> Or spice the shores with odors of the plum?
> Alas, that they should wear our colors there,
> The silken weavings of our afternoons,
> And pick the strings of our insipid lutes!

CHAPTER 6: SWINBURNE AFTER 1878: FOUR READINGS

1 F.L. Lucas *Ten Victorian Poets* (Cambridge: Cambridge Univ. Press 1948) 163; Edmund Wilson, introduction to *The Novels of A.C. Swinburne* (New York: Farrar, Straus 1962) 3. Two recent (but by no means unprecedented) examples of the neglect of Swinburne's later poetry are: Ian Fletcher's *Swinburne*, Writers and their Work (London: Longman 1973) which devotes one and a half of its fifty-one pages to the second series of *Poems and Ballads* and all of the subsequently published verse; and Robert Nye's *A Choice of Swinburne's Verse* (London: Faber & Faber 1973). Nye's choice consists of the choruses of *Atalanta in Calydon*, twenty-five poems from the first series of *Poems and Ballads*, and three from the remaining forty-three years of Swinburne's life.

2 *Letters ... to Robert Bridges* 304

3 The poem, which Swinburne had finished by July of 1880, was published later that same year in *Studies in Song*. The poem has received virtually no critical attention. Even two such sympathetic commentators as Georges Lafourcade and Samuel Chew mentioned it only in passing, contenting themselves with the suggestion that it illustrated some of the less happy features of Swinburne's later poetry. The former found a 'fatal discrepancy between matter and form' (*Swinburne: A Literary Biography* [London: Bell 1932] 270). The latter made an equally damning judgment when he said that 'By the North Sea' was the finest of those pieces in which 'Swinburne elected to sing the praises of the sea,' 'relinquished gladly the unnecessary function

of thought, and yielded himself to the rhythmic undulations and eddies of the verse that seems to take color and motion from its theme' (*Swinburne* 158–9).

4 Rosenberg *Swinburne: Selected Poetry and Prose* xxxi

5 'An Ordinary Evening in New Haven,' *Collected Poems* 469

6 Poems in which the seashore setting is used with one or more of these ranges of meaning include 'The Triumph of Time,' 'In the Bay,' 'Thalassius,' 'On the Cliffs,' 'Evening on the Broads,' 'Neap-Tide,' and 'On the Verge,' where the title has a double meaning. Although its setting is a lake-shore, 'The Lake of Gaube' could be added to this list, as could several parts of *Tristram of Lyonesse*.

7 *Letters* IV, 176

8 The second stanza of section 1 describes the 'weft of the grass' as

> Thick woven as the weft of a witch is
> > Round the heart of a thrall that hath sinned,
> Whose youth and the wrecks of its riches
> > Are waifs on the wind.

The witch is Venus: her thrall Tannhäuser. The description in the ninth stanza of section 1 of the sleep of those buried in the seaside cemetery is very close to the description of the numbed peace of the dead in 'The Garden of Proserpine.'

9 Matthew Arnold *Letters* ed George W.E. Russell (London: Macmillan 1904) III, 105. Chew's summation of the poem's main defects is not unfair: 'an impression of strain, of constant effort after large effects, of attempting to sustain the whole at a consistently lofty level, in meter, diction, imagery and idea. At times success crowns this display of effort and energy; more often the faults of redundancy, flamboyance and incontinence which had been growing upon him mar the work' (p 170).

10 'Find Meat on Bones,' *Collected Poems* (London: Dent 1952) 66. Another of Thomas' poems, 'The Force that through the Green Fuse Drives the Flower,' is equally apposite to Swinburne's point.

11 *English Poetry and its Contribution to the Knowledge of a Creative Principle* (Carbondale: Southern Illinois Univ. Press 1963) 280

12 This is how Chew views the matter: 'Dramatic "relief" is sought but not very well obtained by introducing one or two unrelated episodes such as the story of King Arthur's incestuous love. In itself the passage is interesting as an indirect attack upon the Tennysonian conception of the "blameless King" but in the context it forms an irritating interruption of the narrative' (p 171n).

13 *The Dark Sun: A Study of D.H. Lawrence* (New York: Macmillan 1957) 216

14 Wallace Stevens 'Adagia,' *Opus Posthumous* 165: 'In the presence of extraordinary actuality, consciousness takes the place of imagination.'

15 'Swinburne's "A Nympholept"' *South Atlantic Quarterly* 57 (1958) 64

16 *Collected Poems* 372–3

17 Although 'A Nympholept' makes use of the mythological figure of Pan, Swinburne is not a pantheist in any meaningful sense of the word. The poem can perhaps be described as a poetic re-creation of a 'natural mystical experience,' to use the phrase of R.C. Zaehner in his *Mysticism Sacred and Profane*. Zaehner distinguishes this type of experience – when man feels that he has become one with external reality, and is experiencing something which makes everyday reality seem 'pathetically unreal' (p xiii) – from religious mysticism. Baum says of 'A Nympholept' that it is 'an attempt to put into words the combined vagueness and reality of a mystical experience' (p 59). If this comment is to be helpful, it is surely necessary to say that Swinburne is describing 'natural mystical experience.' I am inclined to think, however, that it is not particularly useful to speak of the poem in this way. Zaehner names two major characteristics of 'natural mystical experience': (a) there is a merging of self and other; and (b) death becomes an 'almost laughable impossibility' (p 41). By these criteria 'A Nympholept' should not be described as a mystical experience, since nothing in the poem suggests that the speaker's selfhood becomes dissolved in the otherness of nature (or vice versa), or that the awareness of mortality is put aside. One aspect of 'A Nympholept,' however, is undoubtedly similar to 'natural mystical experience.' Zaehner makes clear that to apply the term pantheism ('all-god-ism') to this experience is a 'misnomer' (pp 28, 50). 'A Nympholept' perhaps describes a 'panphysistic' or 'pan-en-henic' experience ('of Nature in all things or of all things as being one'). But the poem does not identify God with Nature.
18 This is Swinburne's own description of the poem in *Letters* v, 209.
19 Chew (p 285) makes the same point.
20 'Esthétique du Mal,' *Collected Poems* 325
21 *Bonchurch* XIII, 320–1

CHAPTER 7: TENNYSON AND SWINBURNE

1 See Jerome C. Hixson 'Cauteretz Revisited,' *Tennyson Research Bulletin* 2, 4 (1975) 145–9.
2 See Culler p 247.
3 Culler p 246
4 *Letters* VI, 98
5 Chew p 181n; Staines 'Swinburne's Arthurian World: Swinburne's Arthurian Poetry and its Medieval Sources' *Studia Neophilologica* 50,1 (1978) 68. Swinburne did allow himself some additions, principally the nature descriptions, the seasonal pattern and the references to Fate (which serve to de-emphasize Balen's rashness as the cause of his troubles). His only deletions were Malory's references to future events unconnected with the story of Balen, retention of which would have made his poem seem incomplete.
6 Paul F. Mattheisen 'Gosse's Candid "Snapshots"' *Victorian Studies* VIII, (1965) 341

Index

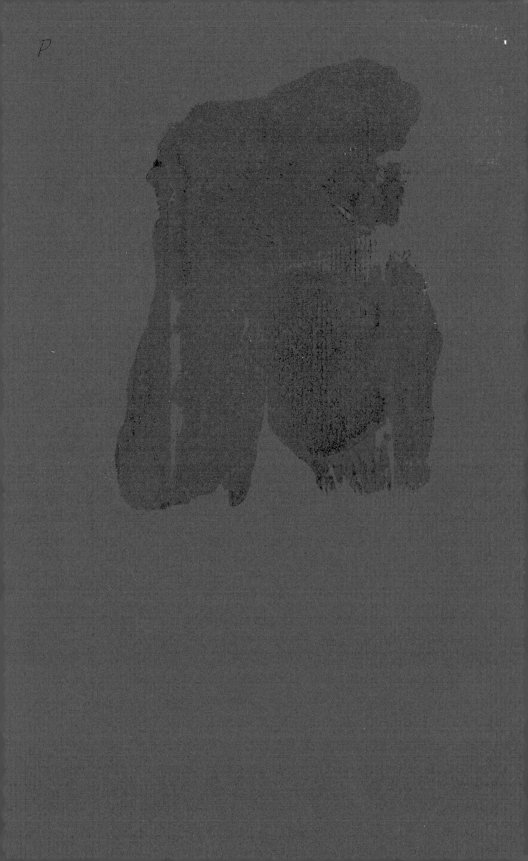